GET MORE PLEASURE AND SATISFACTION FROM EVERYTHING YOU DO!

- Do you sometimes feel oppressed by routine?

- Often feel tense?

- Hide your anger?

- Rarely have time for those you love?

- Harbor regrets about the past?

You probably suffer from what Dr. Bloomfield would diagnose as anhedonia — the inability to experience pleasure.

Providing detailed case histories, helpful suggestions and practical exercises, this world-renowned psychiatrist teaches you how to shake the daily doldrums and unlock your

INNER JOY

INNER JOY

HAROLD H. BLOOMFIELD, M.D.
& Robert B. Kory

A JOVE BOOK

INNER JOY

A Jove Book / published by arrangement with
the author

PRINTING HISTORY
Playboy Press Paperbacks edition / April 1982
Jove edition / April 1984
Fourth printing / March 1986

ISBN: 0-515-08589-8

Jove Books are published by The Berkley Publishing Group,
200 Madison Avenue, New York, N.Y. 10016.
The words "A JOVE BOOK" and the "J" with sunburst
are trademarks belonging to Jove Publications, Inc.

PRINTED IN THE UNITED STATES OF AMERICA

For Robin

with our love

and appreciation

CONTENTS

CONTENTS

I

Choosing Inner Joy

The real voyage of discovery consists not in
seeking new landscapes but in having new
eyes.
— MARCEL PROUST

THIS BOOK will help you begin using your full potential
for inner joy. It will convince you that developing and
sharing inner joy are among the most important things you
can do to get more pleasure and fulfillment from everything
you do and from all your relationships.

Inner joy is a power source. The better you feel, the more
you can draw on your natural energy and ability. Your mind
is sharper, your thoughts more creative, your insights more
to the point. You feel at ease with yourself and can take
life's ups and downs with more equanimity. This insulates
you from helplessness and self-defeating behavior, while
expanding your horizons of personal freedom and fulfilling
experiences. The greater your inner joy, the greater your
confidence in your own ability, the greater your enthusiasm
for living.

Inner joy is also the foundation for declaring your uniqueness and for expressing those qualities that allow you to
use your very own special talents most effectively. Nothing
is more destructive to the human spirit and to personal happiness than never quite knowing who you really are, what
you really want, and what you were put here on earth to
accomplish. Although our culture pays lip service to the ideals
of individuality, most of us are still afraid to stand up and

3

say: "This is me, this is what I want, this is what I stand for." Instead, many of us spend too much time attempting to be like someone else, maybe a media image, maybe the person our parents wanted us to be, or a friend we admire. We exhaust ourselves trying to live up to other people's expectations because we don't know how to live up to our own. Inner joy puts you in touch with your deepest self, and with an inner voice that knows what you must do to get the most out of your life. In doing so, it allows you to make a greater contribution to others and the world around you.

Inner joy enhances the ability to love and the pleasure of loving. You need only look around at the divorce courts, the singles' bars, and the hip resorts to see that many people are having difficulty fulfilling the basic need to love and be loved. Even with the old sexual restraints broken down, there is little reason to believe that there is any more intimacy or any more sexual satisfaction. The reverse may be true. No matter how much we talk about openness, many of us still fear reaching out. We're embarrassed to share our feelings, afraid of being hurt. Inner joy nurtures the capacity to love from within by giving you confidence that allows you to risk your feelings and to give freely of yourself. You learn that there is no greater gift than sharing yourself without restriction. The greater your inner joy, the more you have to give—physically, emotionally, and spiritually—and the more able you become to sustain loving relationships.

Finally, inner joy is a key to more pleasure and fun in everything you do. Most of us are unable to enjoy ourselves fully because we are *anhedonic*; we inhibit our basic capacity for pleasure. We burden ourselves with unnecessary guilt, we worry about things we can do nothing about, we are programmed to find pleasure only in a restricted few favorite activities and therefore close ourselves to so many other opportunities for enjoyment in each and every moment. Inner joy takes you out of this anhedonic programmed way of routine living and brings you fully into contact with your here-and-now. The greater your inner joy, the more fresh and alive each moment becomes, the more often you can reach states of peak enjoyment. Inner joy is reawakening to the ever-present gift of life.

Why the Word *Inner?*

There is a crucial difference between the pleasure of getting something you want and the *inner joy* that empowers you to go after it in the first place. The first is an effect, the second is the cause. When you get a long-sought promotion, of course you feel joyful. When you make love, you naturally experience pleasure. When you receive good news, you can't help but feel delight. Inner joy, as we use the term throughout this book, is something different from these passing experiences of pleasure. We're talking about your internal state *before* you act, what is called your *baseline experience of living*. This is the emotional ground on which you stand to face the world, day in and day out. It's your basic level of energy, self-confidence, and moment-to-moment pleasure.

What has been too long overlooked is the degree to which this baseline level of satisfaction can be raised, and the empowering effect that this inner transformation can have on our lives.

Most of us live, as William James once wrote, "in a very restricted circle of our potential being." We routinely ignore our strengths and follow our weaknesses. The instinct to do nothing, to stay put, to choose security over challenge, to follow the herd, and to accept the second-rate is often stronger than the drive to get the most out of life; it's been built into the personality so solidly that it is usually difficult to overcome. People routinely put up with feelings of dissatisfaction, problems in their relationships, and regrets about what might have been because they feel powerless to do something concrete that will change their lives and help them begin getting everything they really want out of living. The primary cause of these feelings of powerlessness, this willingness to go on playing life small, is a scarcity of inner joy.

Why not begin playing your life for all it's worth? That's what this book is about.

If there is one tragedy of the human condition it's to go through life using only a small fraction of your potential energy and intelligence, to experience only a fraction of the pleasure and satisfaction you are capable of. "People don't lack strength," wrote Victor Hugo, "they lack will."

Most of us use but 5 or 10 percent of our intellectual and emotional capacity, so obviously we all have enormous reserves of strength that we rarely use. By awakening your dormant capacity for inner joy, you begin drawing on those untapped reserves that lie within. The more you learn to cultivate your natural inner joy, the more energy, enthusiasm, creativity, confidence, and courage you'll find available to you, and the more able you'll become to create the life you really want.

The process of increasing inner joy is an *inner shift* that opens new dimensions of personal ability and significantly heightens your moment-to-moment enjoyment of living. This shift is not superficial. It isn't primarily a matter of changing your attitudes or adopting a new way of thinking, though that may help. It's really a growth, a development of consciousness. You move from one level of functioning where energy, self-confidence, and joy may be in short supply to a higher level where these qualities are abundant.

Creating this inner shift is an adventure in self-discovery and personal transformation, and we'll see you through this shift in these pages. We will ask you to examine what you may be doing to sabotage your enjoyment of life, and to work at changing any self-defeating attitudes and behaviors. We will also explain in detail many specific techniques for contacting and using the untapped resources of your inner self. Our program will help you shift your whole personality to a higher level of integration where you truly function at your best and get maximum satisfaction from what you do.

You can produce this shift through specific steps and insights. Above all, you will discover that at every moment *you are the creator* of your experience, and that you have the power to create it joyfully even when things may not work out as planned. You'll also:

- discover a new sense of mastery over your life by transforming your "I'll be happy when . . ."s into "I can create my own joy now"
- learn to conquer all your fears by changing your "What if"s into "So what if"s
- start feeling more than just pretty good about yourself, and go on to love yourself (and that also means others) fully
- end depression by eliminating the regrets, resentments, and the anger which you hide
- enhance your success profile and your satisfaction at work, by learning to "do less, but accomplish more"
- end needless guilts by cleaning up troublesome "should"s, and learn to live according to your own values rather than other people's expectations
- learn how to make your way through the three stages of healing that follow loss and disappointment to discover a wiser and greater you
- learn how to create and sustain terrific relationships by mastering the eleven principles of loving communication
- learn how to start listening to your inner voice, and take advantage of those intuitive messages that often lead to maximum success at work and to the most rewarding relationships
- learn how to create more ecstasy in and out of bed by choosing to open up to all the pleasure available each moment

"Living is the process of continuous rebirth," wrote Erich Fromm. "The tragedy is that we die before we are fully born."

It's true: most of us routinely tend to underestimate ourselves. We sell short our ability and shy away from the challenges that prompt self-discovery and rebirth. Your capacity for inner joy is almost certainly far, far greater than you would give yourself credit for at the moment. Only by accepting the challenge of self-discovery and rebirth can you ever tap your full measure of energy, intelligence, vitality, and all the satisfactions that go with becoming fully born.

How to Get the Most out of This Book

You probably won't agree with everything in these pages, and that's OK. Given your own values, beliefs, prejudices, and personal history, you will have a tendency to read into the cases exactly what you want to hear. Taking a look at yourself with the idea of wanting to change might be something you *say* you want to do, but your *behavior* often speaks otherwise. If you're like most people, every fiber of your being is likely to resist the challenge of eliminating the thoughts and attitudes that sustain your self-denying feelings and behavior.

So now what? A sense of humor will help you. So will a willingness at least to experiment with some of the strategies that you resist at first. You have your pessimism to lose and joy to gain. None of the techniques is difficult. All you need is the desire and commitment to grow, the willingness to discover your ability to make inner joy a given daily part of your life.

The remaining chapters in this book are like counseling sessions, written to give you maximum opportunity for self-training and self-transformation. Each chapter asks you to make two steps. The first is to gain insight into a major category of self-nullifying attitudes and behaviors. We discuss where these attitudes came from, and why they persist even though they're destructive and undermine your maximum enjoyment. (Sometimes you may think that a particular behavior is so common that it's harmless. A closer examination will prove otherwise.)

The second step, the heart of every chapter, is behavior change. We detail uncomplicated strategies for eliminating self-destructive feelings and behaviors, and show you how to cultivate inner joy. Detailed case histories in each chapter will show the problems that arise and how to overcome them.

Each chapter also goes into the payoffs you get from self-negating behavior. Yes, payoffs.

Almost invariably, your primary reward is avoiding risk,

especially the risk of sharing your real self and putting your deepest feelings on the line. Let's face it here and now: Inner joy is exciting because it allows you full self-expression and maximum power, but it is also frightening because *it separates you from the crowd!*

All the heady talk about individuality aside, it's easier and safer to conform, even to behaviors that are injurious, than to stand up and say, "This is me, I'm different; this is what I have to offer and that makes me special." Psychological studies have shown over and over again that most people will conform, follow the herd, rather than face possible rejection for expressing their real feelings. You'll see as you examine many self-nullifying behaviors that the fear of affirming your individuality is a common denominator that explains why most of us resist change. Once you genuinely recognize this resistance in yourself, you have taken the first step toward overcoming it.

At times, the format of the chapters may seem repetitious. That's good! It's a positive sign. It means the message is sinking in. I know from thousands of hours with patients that an insight doesn't take hold when it's said just once. It must be repeated again and again before change begins in earnest. The payoffs of this book come only if it's read and understood as a total program, as a whole. Only by examining self-nullifying behaviors in many areas of your life can the principal message come through. And only then can you really fully benefit from the shift toward inner joy.

If you're determined to get the most out of this book, you will soon succeed in making positive changes in your life that will surprise you. You'll begin asking yourself questions you've never asked before, seizing opportunities for joy that you formerly passed by. Instead of letting your happiness depend on what happens to you, you will create your enjoyment by expressing your unique qualities and talents.

"*Why am I choosing to inhibit my enjoyment right now?*" and "*What can I do to get more out of what I'm doing?*" These are the questions you'll ask yourself when you move away from self-suppression toward inner joy.

Here are some questions to give you an overview of what to expect in the remaining chapters. A yes response indicates a high measure of inner joy.

1. Is your life full of pleasure and satisfaction?
2. Are you free from tension and anxiety?
3. Do you fully appreciate what you have?
4. Are you aware of your unique talents and abilities?
5. Can you love yourself and others fully and freely?
6. Are you comfortable with anger and can you express it effectively?
7. Is ecstasy a frequent part of your life?
8. Do you feel your life has meaning and purpose?
9. Are you free from regrets and resentments?
10. Have you learned to face disappointments without bitterness or feeling cheated?
11. Do you have all the energy you want?
12. Do you laugh often?
13. Are you able to stand up for yourself without hesitation?
14. Have you put approval seeking behind you?
15. Do you take full responsibility for your happiness instead of blaming others?
16. Can you choose to create joy even when things may not be working out?
17. Is your sex life ecstatic?
18. Do you know how to nurture joy in your love relationships?
19. Do you enjoy your job?
20. Do you bounce back effectively and fully from loss and frustration?
21. Are you free from incessant striving that makes you a slave to your work?
22. Have you eliminated needless guilt from your life?
23. Do you welcome opportunities for new experiences?
24. Do you feel you are in control of your life?
25. Are you in touch with your inner voice?
26. Do you enjoy contributing to the lives of others?

The key to saying yes to all these questions is discovering

and using the power of inner joy. Once the inner shift begins to take place, you'll experience a very special joy: you'll look back at these questions and you'll see how much you have gained.

Which Motivation Is Yours?

People assume two basic attitudes toward their own growth. Most of us start with the negative and wind up treating ourselves not as a friend but as a roommate we don't like. We spend most of our time examining weaknesses and pointing out shortcomings. A critical self-inventory reads like an interrogator's report from an inquisition: "I'm too fat," "I'm too shy," "I'm not smart enough," and so on. This is *deficiency motivation* because it stems from a desire to repair alleged flaws in the personality.

The other approach begins with the positive. It encourages the identification of personal strengths and the transcendence of limitations on the expression of those strengths. Operating from this perspective you might say: "I'm friendly, but I'm not giving myself a chance to express my feelings," or "I've got talent as a writer, but I keep staying with a job that doesn't give me a chance to write," or "My best feature is my eyes, but I haven't learned how to give them a flair to make me look as attractive as I'd like." This is called *growth motivation*. It reflects your desire to extend your personal reach, to become everything you choose to be.

I raise this issue here to make sure you don't fall into the trap of keeping your eyes riveted on your weaknesses. The key to inner joy is affirming yourself, discovering qualities that make you special, and overcoming any limitations in the expression of those qualities. If you focus on your weaknesses, forget it; you'll just keep on and on racing after an unreachable rabbit, measuring yourself against some ideal you carry in your head. Whatever this ideal is and wherever it comes from, you'd better cancel your subscription. You'll never measure up to it, because an ideal is just that: an ideal, not a reality.

Deficiency motivation squeezes your personality into a mold; it is destructive to begin with and keeps on reinforcing destructive behavior. Growth motivation entails the risk of getting excited about discovering new dimensions of your personality, doing things you've never been able to do before. This takes courage. As long as you focus on your deficiencies, everything will remain predictable but you won't achieve new levels of satisfaction; you will be able to go on complaining about your weaknesses, but repeating the same old rationale of your beefs won't do anything to expand your happiness.

Growth motivation means stepping out into unfamiliar territory and discovering new parts of yourself. It means accepting yourself as you are and working from there rather than merely lamenting your fate, wishing you were somehow different. Growth motivation means self-discovery of the highest order for the rest of your life.

In his autobiography *Out of My Life and Thought*, Albert Schweitzer summed up his commitment to a lifetime of personal growth:

> Affirmation of life is the spiritual act by which a person ceases to live unreflectively and begins to devote himself to his life with reverence in order to raise it to its true value. To affirm life is to deepen, to make more inward, and to exalt the will to live.

To devote yourself to your life with reverence so you can raise it to its true value. What a wonderful idea! This is no call to narcissism or hedonism, but to break the bonds of self-inflicted, needless limitation. The rewards are worth every ounce of the effort required. That's been my personal experience and the experience of my clients.

II

Anhedonia

INNER JOY is a simple experience. It's the natural inward glow of self-confidence when we are in full command of ourselves. It is the pleasure of internal harmony when we are at ease. It is the swelling of vitality when we are attuned to our physical, emotional, and spiritual needs. The more sensitive we are to our inner selves, the more inner joy we feel, and the more power we have. At bottom, inner joy is a state of *being*, not a result of *doing*. Why then is inner joy so rare?

For most of us, inner joy is usually in short supply because we are locked in a prison that keeps us trapped on the *surface* of our lives. The psychological term for this prison is *anhedonia*. Derived from the Greek *an-*, "not," and *hedone*, "pleasure," it literally means the inability to experience pleasure.

Anhedonia is a state of inhibition with multiple causes. Fear of pleasure, worry, guilt, unbridled success striving, fatigue, approval seeking, and sexual anxiety are among the principal ways we make ourselves anhedonic. Invariably anhedonia involves the censure of desire, the confusion of values,

13

and the lack of understanding about the dynamics of internal growth and personal fulfillment. Anhedonia is not one-dimensional; it's a web of emotional traps and self-nullifying behaviors. It forms a veil between our everyday self-awareness and our inner selves, thereby diminishing access to our real power and inhibiting our basic capacity to enjoy our lives. It's a prison of adult life and it has many walls.

William James was the first psychologist to recognize the significance of anhedonia for normal, healthy people. "Everyone is familiar with the phenomenon of feeling more or less alive on different days," he wrote. "Everyone knows on any given day there are energies in him which the incitement of the day do not call forth. . . . Compared with what we ought to be, we are only half awake. Our fires are damped, our drafts are checked."

Why do we accept as normal this common state of diminished vitality when we have all experienced days when we're in full command of our inner resources and functioning at a peak of enjoyment? Because these days are infrequent? Because most of us lack knowledge of our inner selves? Or might it be that we are simply too willing to accept the mediocre for ourselves? Whatever the justification in the past, there is no reason to go putting up with anhedonia in the future. The understanding and the strategies for overcoming anhedonia and nurturing inner joy are available.

The more I have used this idea with thousands of people in therapy and seminars, the more rewarding it has become, because *most* of us do not know how to enjoy our lives; in fact, we're just as likely to make ourselves unhappy through self-defeating behavior as we are to generate self-fulfillment. The problem is not neurosis, much less some deep psychosis. I do not subscribe to the belief that most people need therapy to lead fulfilling lives. Nor can the problem be dismissed in terms of the human condition or original sin. I do not subscribe to the belief that the human condition is basically unhappy and that we ought to be grateful for a few moments of joy that come our way. The problem as I see it is a lack of understanding of our inner selves and our power to create our lives joyfully. Meekly, we have come to accept many ordinary behaviors and attitudes that undermine the basic capacity for pleasure and put a wall between our normal self-awareness and our inner selves. The net result is anhedonia, not the totally incapacitating state that inhibits all pleasure, but the universal inhibition that shuts us off from our full measure of vitality and diminishes our enjoyment of everything we do.

Anhedonia may also be a useful tool for understanding what is happening to our society. For some years now, we've been in the paradoxical position of producing more wealth than any culture that ever existed, while simultaneously suffering a steadily rising level of tension and frustration. Consumption on an unprecedented scale seems to be doing little to promote confidence in our collective future, much less real joy and satisfaction. Popular culture has become a series of fads as the entertainment business strives to create ever greater spectacles and excitement to elicit anything more than a ho-hum from mass audiences. Values are confused as hedonism and narcissism become foremost in a society where everyone is concerned with getting theirs and looking out for number one. While the symptoms of social decay may have many complex causes, anhedonia provides a window into the ways individual psychology may be at work.

The less able we are to experience inner pleasure, the more material symbols we need to satisfy our thirst for it. We need more cars, more stereos, more drugs, bigger houses, more spectacular movies, and louder music because we are shut off —numb to inner joy and the pleasure of everyday living. Surrounded by unprecedented wealth, we feel frustrated by our own lack of fulfillment; so we strip ourselves of the traditional values of moderation and give ourselves license to the unrestricted pursuit of material satisfactions, all in the name of personal growth. Cut off from ourselves, we affirm the right to look out for our personal self-interest above all else in hopes of grasping the power that we have buried within. We're like a hungry person who can't digest his food. The more we eat, the more frustrated we feel, because the hunger persists, and we only get tired and bored.

Of course, anhedonia is not the whole answer. It is one of

many factors at work in our society. Nevertheless, overcoming anhedonia does far more than increase personal inner joy. If it changes our values, it may also help change the world we have created.

The Origins of Anhedonia

Anhedonia is usually overlooked because its primary causes are often taken for granted. Indeed, the causes of anhedonia are quite ordinary; each one alone may not seem very significant. Only when you consider several causes together does the full picture of anhedonia come into focus. It's the faces of anhedonia that make it so tenacious.

Here are the principal causes:

Fear of pleasure. Most of us bring a mixed attitude toward pleasure because we have been told all our lives that it's often selfish, usually unproductive, and sometimes wrong. So we rarely give ourselves the permission to let go, to function at full power, to admit our strongest desires, and to be true to ourselves. We accept the habit of anhedonic self-suppression as a necessary part of responsible behavior.

Success striving. The unbridled drive to "make it" can lead to feeling so pressured that you put aside family, health, and your own personal needs. This is usually justified with the belief that "making it" will compensate for all the prior struggle. All too often one crucial fact gets overlooked: When you are working so hard that you become anhedonic, productivity, creativity, and your chances of "making it" plummet.

Fatigue. If you have difficulty falling asleep or awakening refreshed, or if you need caffeine to wake up or keep going, or if you feel your energy sinking during the day, then you are well aware of the relationship between fatigue and anhedonia. Chronic fatigue makes us irritable, uneasy, and emotionally brittle. Joy becomes almost impossible.

Stress. Elevated blood pressure, rapid heart rate, accelerated breathing, and increased adrenaline production are among the primary components of the stress responses. Unless you are skilled at allowing your body to return to a state of balance following a stressful day, you gradually accumulate a backlog of tension. In a very real sense, you physiologically diminish your sensitivity to pleasure. The longer the stress persists, the less open you become to joy.

Getting stuck. The need for security often leads many of us into jobs, relationships, marriages, and responsibilities that stifle creativity and individuality. The result is boredom or worse, a sense of personal suffocation and powerlessness. It's easy to justify the feeling that you can't change because so much seems beyond individual control—inflation, oil prices, and all the other problems you read about in the newspapers. To fasten on to this rationale is to give up your power, make yourself a victim, and accept your anhedonia.

Guilt. No matter how often most people may tell themselves not to feel guilty, many seem to be addicted to this form of self-punishment. You may feel guilty about not spending enough time with your family, about how you treat your parents, about not reaching your goals, about your secret desires, about almost anything. The result is something like driving with the brakes on; you put a drag on your basic capacity for joy.

Worry. Almost everyone knows that worry rarely changes anything, but few people are entirely free from this cause of anhedonia. What sustains the worry habit is the hidden payoff. Worry can be used as proof that you care, that you're trying to do your best, that you're working hard, or that at least you're doing something. By inhibiting inner joy and the sensitivity to pleasure, worry can make you feel that you are doing what you ought to be doing. It's like pinching yourself to make sure you're awake. It hurts, but it serves its purpose.

Sexual anxiety. The relationship between sex and pleasure is no secret. The greater your sexual confidence and enjoyment, the greater your vitality and ability to feel pleasure. Despite all the talk about liberation, few people are fully comfortable with their sexuality. Anxiety abounds: How often? How long? How good? How many? To whatever degree sexual anxiety persists, to that same degree vitality, pleasure, and joy are inhibited.

Approval seeking. Society pays lip service to individuality, but encourages approval seeking on a massive scale. You're told to trust the experts, never yourself. Advertisers spend billions to convince you to buy their products so other people will think you're terrific. Fads and celebrity worship appeal to the desire to be like someone else—and deny yourself. When someone else's opinion of you becomes more important than your own, you lose touch with your inner voice and your deepest sources of creativity and power. Inevitably your capacity for joy suffers.

Self-rejection. Obviously, when you reject even a small part of yourself, you invest some of your energy in holding yourself back. You put brakes on your feelings and drain energy that could be available for fulfilling your desires. Many people feel pretty good about themselves, but few are completely free from self-rejection and able to appreciate themselves fully.

Anger. If you're short-tempered, if your anger lasts a long time, if your anger makes you uncomfortable, or if you have difficulty getting angry, then you have a problem with anger that may inhibit your basic capacity for pleasure. Anger is a powerful emotional tool that can be used constructively. When it becomes destructive, it also becomes anhedonic. The key is learning to be comfortable with anger whether you're on the giving or receiving end.

Loss and disappointment. There is no way to escape the downside of life; some losses and disappointments are inevitable. The problem is: Few of us know how to grow from them. Most people wind up with repressed bitterness, hidden regrets, lingering self-doubt—and a diminished capacity for joy.

Loss of values. Human beings need ideals to direct their lives. Simplistic declarations like "If it feels good, do it" don't hold up. We need ideals, goals, and principles that we're willing to live by and die for. Commitment to a set of personal values is crucial to tapping spiritual energy, and the special joy that it affords.

Sure, anhedonia is complex. The causes intertwine to form a mesh that blocks inner joy. Trying to overcome anhedonia can be like trying to punch your way out of a plastic bag. When you move in one direction, you feel closed in on another. But a breakthrough is attainable if you work on several causes at once, while keeping your eye on the goal: the shift to a baseline level of joy. Overcoming anhedonia is not sequential surgery. You don't do away with one cause after another. The process is more like a refining of the total personality. To stimulate the growth of inner joy is to encourage the gradual disappearance of self-defeating behaviors.

A Brief Self-Inventory

The first step in overcoming anhedonia is to understand its presence in your own life. You may be one of those unusual people who, in the words of Thomas Mann, "gives each moment its true and due fulfillment." If so, congratulations! You are a rare person indeed. On the other hand, you may be like most of us: sufficiently anhedonic to deny ourselves a significant amount of inner joy. It is not easy to see ourselves honestly. If we see the truth, we have to accept responsibility for our feelings and summon courage to change. The safe harbor of habit exerts a strong pull, especially when you measure it against the apparent risks in an adventure of personal growth. Nevertheless, the road to a deeper understanding of anhedonia starts with an honest look at your own life.

Here, then, are the sixty-four most common signs of anhedonia (the code numbers are explained at the end of the list):

- boredom (VI)
- fatigue, midafternoon slumps (III)
- oppressed by rigid "should"s and "should not"s (VII)
- bodily aches and pains, headaches, indigestion, constipation (III)
- feeling constantly under pressure and short of time (IV)
- insomnia, difficulty falling asleep or awakening refreshed (VII)
- irritability (VIII)
- mild depression, feeling blue or down in the dumps (IX)
- lack of satisfaction with your accomplishments (IV)
- frequent angry outbursts (VIII)
- many regrets and resentments (IX)
- frequent fights with your spouse or lover (VIII)
- difficulty enjoying quiet pleasures like reading or taking a walk (III)
- diminished sense of self (X)
- a need for approval, always asking others for their opinion (V)
- indecision, difficulty making up your mind (VII)
- muscular tension, especially in the neck or back (III)
- excessive eating, overweight (V)
- clenched teeth, bruxism (VIII)
- difficulty enjoying the pleasure of others (X)
- difficulty sustaining intimate relationships (V)
- performance anxiety (X)
- feeling insecure, unsafe (VII)
- feelings of loneliness or isolation (V)
- poor muscle tone or posture (III)
- easily hurt, fear of rejection (IX)
- lack of spontaneity, feeling inhibited (V)
- lack of vigor or zest (III)
- blaming others for how you feel (V)
- mental cloudiness, lack of alertness (IV)
- inability to relax, mind keeps racing (VII)
- few close friends (V)
- lack of humor, infrequent smiles and laughter, taking yourself too seriously (III)
- feeling like a victim: things work out for everyone else but not for you (VI)
- overly critical attitude toward yourself, feeling you can't measure up (V)
- lack of sexual energy or vitality (X)
- feelings of frustration or defeat (IX)
- habitually putting off fun, wishing for happiness but missing the opportunities (VI)

- compulsive overachievement at work or school, constant inner striving (IV)
- obsessed with the past and/or fearful of the future (VII)
- feeling guilty (VII)
- obsessed with sex, overly concerned about it (X)
- dependence on others for your happiness, difficulty enjoying yourself alone (V)
- feelings of shame or embarrassment, especially about your body (V)
- inability to break out of a routine, feeling stuck in a rut (VI)
- difficulty unwinding, letting go (IV)
- spiritual malaise, lack of meaning (X)
- fear and/or unwillingness to try something new (VI)
- difficulty expressing love, tenderness, and caring (V)
- anxiety about sex (X)
- compulsively saying yes when you want to say no (V)
- knot in the stomach, tightly drawn shoulders (VIII)
- feeling uncommitted, without purpose (X)
- feeling unattractive, wishing you looked different (V)
- remorse, ruminations about what might have been (IX)
- feelings of missing out (VI)
- frequent use of drugs or alcohol to relax or have a good time (III)
- difficulty standing up for your beliefs (V)
- conning yourself into believing you're enjoying something (for example, a party) when you don't (III)
- complaining but refusing to work on improvement (VI)
- disappointing orgasm, boring sex (X)
- loss of interest in sex (X)
- fulfilling your obligations without much satisfaction (IV)
- jealousy of others, envy of their good times (V)

The symptoms of anhedonia in our culture are so abundant that we could fill pages just listing them all. This inventory, however, should be enough for you to begin assessing the role of anhedonia in your life.

In reviewing the items you checked pay special attention to those that seem to overlap. Notice that difficulty expressing love, feeling unattractive, and lack of spontaneity are each followed by the roman numeral V in parenthesis, while mental cloudiness and feeling constantly under pressure are followed by the numeral IV. Each numeral refers to the chapter in which the sign of anhedonia is discussed. By looking back over the items you checked and comparing the numbers, you can discover a pattern to your personal manifestations of anhedonia. Now you know where you need the most work and the chapters which deserve your special attention.

Some people who read this list feel that none of the items applies to them directly. You may be one of them. Or you may feel that the items you checked form little more than a list of dirty laundry and aren't particularly helpful. "I already knew these things," you may say. In that case, you may want to try another means of assessing anhedonia. This one takes a little more time and effort. You'll need pencil and paper, a watch, a comfortable place to sit, and ten minutes of uninterrupted time alone.

The test is simple. Begin by sitting down comfortably, closing your eyes, and letting your mind go. Don't try to do anything, just relax. This is a time to take a break for five minutes of idle enjoyment. Try to keep your eyes closed for the full period. If you open your eyes and see by the watch that you haven't been sitting for five minutes, close your eyes again and continue the test. At the end of the five-minute period, open your eyes and write down what crossed your mind, how you felt, whether the time passed quickly or slowly, whether you felt anxious, bored, annoyed, worried, calm, joyful, or whatever.

Now do this exercise before reading any further!

Done? OK, what happened? Surprised to find how long five minutes really is? The experience of time is highly variable. Pardon the cliché, but time does seem to fly when you're having a good time; it crawls when you have to do something unpleasant. If you were completely free from anhedonia, your experience of this five minutes would be one of settling down into a quiet state of inner joy. This is the baseline experience of the person who is fully open and alive. If you're like most people, the time passed slowly. So what? So everything, because that's the first indication of anhedonia.

What else did you experience? Some people fall asleep. That means you have been overloading your body and mind, denying yourself the rest you need. Many people feel bored and restless. This indicates emotional tension that won't let you enjoy the present moment. If you tune in to all the sensations of being alive, if you let your consciousness expand with this opportunity for inner stillness, then you won't be bored at all. On the contrary, you'll enjoy a modestly ecstatic state.

Perhaps your mind was filled with thoughts, all the things you have to do or plans you're in the process of making. This is the anhedonia of constant striving. You're so absorbed in what you're doing or plan to do that you block your ability to enjoy where you are. Perhaps you noticed some tension in your neck or felt some anxiety in your chest. Another common experience is to dwell on the past, feeling guilt about something you did or regret about something you didn't do. Some people report generalized worrying or headaches or indigestion. Perhaps you started feeling angry about having to sit through what appeared to be a waste of time. Whatever your experience, this test is a reliable means of gaining insight into your personal anhedonic tendencies.

Too Much: The Hedonistic Trap

Our culture has been racked by rising expectations of personal happiness. Awareness of human potentialities is growing; but there is a decline in important values and new anhedonic traps have opened up. Frustrated with the inability to experience pleasure and tired of feeling inhibited, millions of people have discarded traditional restraints in the pursuit of self-gratification. Old sexual and social barriers are down. The new credo is "If it feels good, do it!"

Hedonism and narcissism reign. If you understand anhedonia, this is not surprising. The frantic pursuit of pleasure is a natural reaction to the inability to experience it.

The problem with hedonism is, of course, that it leads not to self-fulfillment but more often to self-frustration, and occasionally to self-destruction. If your capacity for pleasure is inhibited, you can never expect fulfillment in pursuit of one new pleasure after another. You wind up like a child eating candy bars; each one provides less satisfaction than the last, and the final result is a bellyache. Or you live like the person who can't digest food, remember? You starve, no matter how much you eat. The solution to anhedonic inhibition is not to redouble the pursuit of pleasure, but to discover inner joy.

The hedonistic trap is most prevalent among young adults who are enjoying some of the best America has to offer.

Cynthia is one of these people. She has just turned thirty-one. It's her birthday and she is spending the evening alone, not because she's sick or unattractive, or because she lacks friends, or because they all forgot. She's alone because she wants to sort out the gnawing feelings that her life isn't any fun anymore. An attractive woman, with large blue eyes and long blond hair, she wears clothes like a model and is the envy of many of her friends. If you believe the media fantasies, you'd think she could be a prime candidate for a Pepsi commercial. Ask her, and the real picture is quite different.

"For a long time I didn't want to face my real feelings," she said. "I was caught up in living out my dream, the wonder woman of the advertising world, on my way to the president's suite by age forty. Then last year everything started to go flat. Now I'm confused, I'm bored, I'm disappointed. There's the awful feeling that living isn't any fun anymore. When I try to have fun, I usually wind up with a letdown.

"At parties, I have to convince myself that I'm enjoying it so I don't walk out ten minutes after I arrive. Weekends on Fire Island leave me cold. It's the same crowd, talking about the same things, looking for a quick fix in bed with a new partner. Work, my last refuge, has become the biggest source of anxiety. My future is finally beginning to dawn on me, and I don't like what I see: year after year, striving for bigger accounts and more money. The worst time is in the morning when I look at myself in the mirror. I ask myself the same question every day, 'Is this all there is?' "

Cynthia can't pinpoint exactly when this malaise began, but one incident marks a turning point. Twelve months ago she was given a major assignment at work and it failed.

"The firm was in the running for a two-million-dollar account. That's not major by the firm's standards, but it was the biggest I'd ever worked on. I got the assignment to put together the proposal. We were competing with three other firms. I knew it from my boss's signals; if we landed this one, I was on my way to a vice-presidency. I worked twelve hours a day for seven weeks, put everything else aside, did what I thought was my best work. A week before I had to present it, my boss told me it was terrific. We were a shoo-in. I remember him saying that.

"The proposal bombed. Two days later, I got the client's real reaction. Amateurish, they said. 'Too simple, lacks class.' I was furious. Our president took me aside to say he thought the proposal was good and the client was too dumb to see a brilliant idea served on a silver platter. He also said it wasn't a black mark against me. But I'm still not a vice-president and I'm still shaken."

Cynthia had a long history as a superachiever, graduating with honors from her midwestern high school, winning a national yearbook award as editor, dating as much as she liked. She went to college at a prestigious girls' school in New York. It was a time of rebellion, the late sixties. Many students sacrificed education to activism, drugs, new lifestyles. Through sheer energy, Cynthia managed to sustain a high level of academic achievement even though she immersed herself in protests and social experiments, too.

"I arrived in New York a real innocent. My roommate during freshman year was a girl who grew up on the East Side. She was one of those rare girls, so friendly that you liked her immediately. Within our first hours together, we'd become friends. The evening after classes began, I walked in on her in the bathroom. She was fiddling with a small rubber disk, apparently washing it."

" 'What's that?' I asked. I was so naive.

" 'What do you think?' she responded with a grin.

" 'Am I supposed to know?'

" 'Oh, God, Cindy,' she answered, amused but sympathetic. 'It's my diaphragm. I'm seeing an old friend tonight, and I'll probably stay over at his house. Parents are in Paris for the week. Get the picture?'

"I couldn't believe it. The first thing that flashed through my mind was: 'She goes all the way, wow!' Where I came from, a girl never went all the way, at least not until she was engaged. The sexual revolution hadn't yet reached the Midwest.

"That moment was the first shot in a personal revolution for me. Here was a girl I admired and she not only went all the way, but talked about it, told me everything, was sympathetic, understanding, and encouraging. Not long after, I had a diaphragm of my own."

Since her college days in New York, Cynthia has done everything or close to it. Her first eighteen months out of college she used a small inheritance from her grandmother to travel around the United States and later spent several months in India. "I wanted to immerse myself in life; throw off all the restraints; get intoxicated with the vitality all around me."

For three months she stayed on a commune outside Santa Fe. The commune was devoted to establishing "New Age relationships," which meant sex without any restrictions. "The only taboo was to have sex when you didn't honestly want to or to force yourself on someone else." Everything else including group sex, incest, homosexuality, adultery was permitted, as long as "no one got hurt."

Cynthia describes her feelings: "It was an awakening for me. I worked through a lot of sexual issues. . . . Last I heard, the commune broke up, which didn't surprise me because the place was a sexual pressure cooker."

She went from Santa Fe to India with Chuck, a thirty-two-year-old seeker of enlightenment. They traveled around India for a short while, then headed north into the Himalayas to stay at Chuck's guru's ashram. There Cynthia got into tantric yoga and didn't take anything stronger than a glass of mineral water. When her money began running low, she faced the crucial decision about what to do to support herself, decided she wasn't cut out for life in the ashram and didn't want to stay with Chuck. She returned to New York, found herself an apartment and soon a position in a management training program with an advertising company. Just as she had thrown herself completely into everything that had gone before, she devoted herself to mastering the requisite skills to advance in the company.

The single life in New York meant parties, weekends on Fire Island, bars, and, most of all, men. She learned the hustle and took cocaine, the one drug that had up to that point eluded her. She worked long hours, but still had enough energy to partake of all New York's dazzle in the evening. All the while she was making steady progress at work. One of the executive vice-presidents took a liking to her, and took her under his wing. She had a mentor, the crucial element for a fast rise to the top.

On the way she met Ron, a recent graduate of Harvard Law School and now a junior associate of a prestigious firm. They had so much in common—education, family background, sixties protests and seventies self-development seminars. A whirlwind romance was inevitable. When Cynthia brought Ron home to meet her parents, her mother and father welcomed him. A big wedding was planned, an announcement appeared in the *New York Times*. They honeymooned in Europe and returned to New York to set up housekeeping in a new East Side apartment. For a long while after their return they were the envy of their friends, the perfect couple living an exciting life in New York. But appearances are often deceiving, especially when you're looking at a couple. Three years after their wedding, they were divorced.

"The divorce was the right move," Cynthia tells herself today with a mixture of relief and regret in her eyes. "Lots of things began to go wrong. We were basically too independent, and didn't know what we were getting into. Ron wanted a traditional wife, kids, the whole bit: a support system so he could have the best of both worlds, a fantastic home life and all the satisfaction he craved at work. He thought I would work for a few years and then give up my career to have kids, be a mother for the next twenty, then go back to work. That's not how I saw it at all. My career is just as important to me as his is to him. We couldn't resolve it."

Cynthia's mother attributes her current unhappiness to this decision. "When I told mom that we were separating and would probably get divorced, she was angry," Cynthia recalls. "She loved Ron and wanted grandchildren desperately to fill her empty life. I think she feels I owe them to her. With no children at home, and no grandchildren to dote over, what does she have to look forward to for the next twenty years?"

Cynthia doesn't want to be tied down to children. "I ask myself: Would I really be any happier stuck with a houseful of kids? The answer is always the same. There are too many unhappy mothers."

Cynthia is now at an emotional crossroad and doesn't understand her confusion. Look at her objectively and you see a beautiful woman with a promising career, but she feels she's suffocating with emptiness. If she were to come to you for help, what would you tell her? "Stop being so self-involved." "Look for a new job." "Have children." "Be thankful for what you've got." Perhaps you'd just tell her she's an overindulgent member of the "me" generation and should "grow up." Cynthia tends to take this hard line with herself, but this stock advice doesn't seem to help.

What Cynthia has been searching for is inner joy. All her adult life, she has blamed her lack of fulfillment on external constraints; the real problem is her inability to experience pleasure and her diminished capacity for joy. She hasn't learned that she has the power to create her life joyfully, or that fulfillment ultimately lies in the joy she can achieve in *being*, not a succession of pleasures from *doing*. Only the increase in her baseline level of satisfaction can slake her thirst for pleasure and empower her to create the life she dreams for herself.

Part of discovering inner joy, however, is learning to accept limitations. Cynthia wants to "have it all," but like King Midas, she is learning that greed (whether for gold or experience) inevitably leads to frustration and loss. Cynthia expects ever-growing fulfillment from achievements at work, from parties, from sex, from buying things she wants. What she is finally learning is that greed leads to a dead end. The last road sign reads EMPTY.

Cynthia has also never learned to accept failure and grow from it. Her crisis was precipitated by her failure at work. Suddenly her self-image crumbled; she saw that the world isn't fair, good work is not always rewarded. Success and failure are unpredictable and depend on many factors beyond any one person's control. From the vantage point of her own narcissism, this was unacceptable. Cynthia's reaction to failure was to make herself miserable, much like a child throwing a tantrum. Cynthia's tantrum is more sophisticated.

Cynthia is like many frustrated people whose problems aren't easy to define. In some ways, what she needs to do is more difficult than eradicating a group of self-defeating behaviors. The solution to Cynthia's anhedonia lies in cultivating a new attitude toward pleasure. She needs to stop dividing her world into work and play, stop looking for pleasure outside of herself, and start recognizing that the source of her fulfillment ultimately lies within. Cynthia has to learn that in the final analysis *joy is not something that happens to you. It's something each person creates.*

After several months of work on her own self-transformation with many of the strategies described in this book, Cynthia began to get the message. The key to maximum enjoyment and personal fulfillment is discovering inner joy, that quiet nondemand state of awareness where energy and pleasure overflow. From that state of integration, it is possible to have a new perspective on pleasure. No longer must pleasure be confined to entertainment, vacations, or sex. It becomes possible to choose enjoyment and, indeed, have peak experiences at will under any circumstances, even while doing the dishes or waiting in line.

Cynthia has made a major step. Most people go through

their whole lives unaware of their capacity for inner joy. Now Cynthia has put her self-nullifying doubt behind her, and she recognizes how much richer, deeper, and more satisfying her life can become. She is now committed to her own growth.

Awakening from the American Dream

Marty tells us about another side of anhedonia. He's older, fifty-two and no longer troubled by the struggle for success. He has made it. An executive vice-president with a six-figure income and many bonuses, Marty has achieved the so-called American dream. Due to his shrewd investments over the last ten years, he could retire today with a guaranteed income that would maintain his elaborate life-style. But for Marty that's out of the question. He's driven. The word *enough* does not exist in his vocabulary. It's a lack he pays for dearly.

Born to a blue-collar Polish family on the south side of Milwaukee, Marty remembers his childhood and adolescence as a long struggle to escape. "I was the second youngest of six children. We lived in a small house, only two real bedrooms. Three of us slept in the living room, everyone shared the one bath. My father barely brought home enough to feed the family. The only work my mother could find until World War II was taking in wash. Thank God for that war. It meant work, money, and my chance to get out. All my older brothers had quit high school because they had to go to work doing anything they could find for ten cents an hour, but with the war, my mother got a full-time job on the night shift. She insisted I finish school and try to go on to college."

Marty tells about a shop teacher in eighth grade who implanted an idea that has driven him ever since. "The war came and suddenly everyone had work. My brothers started bringing home thirty-five dollars a week before they went into the service. That was a lot of money to me, and I wanted to get a skill so I could drop out and go to work as soon as possible. When my shop teacher heard me boasting about my plans, he took me aside and told me I was a fool for taking wood-shop, that if I had any sense I'd be hauling my tail to get into college. 'Try to own the shop, not work in it,' he said. Those words have stuck with me ever since."

In high school and college Marty learned the habits that would sustain his drive to "own the shop." Though he had a scholarship and didn't have to work in college, he didn't want to wait to begin building his fortune, so he worked throughout his years in college and business school. To make his grades and work a thirty-hour week he had to cultivate a reduced need for sleep. He trained himself to get by on four and sometimes two hours per night. Constantly short of time, he learned to hurry everything he did. He spoke quickly, ate quickly, and moved quickly. You never saw him taking a leisurely walk. He was always on the run to some-where. Vacations and weekends were out of the question. Whenever he had time off from classes, he filled it with unfinished projects from work or school. Coffee and ciga-rettes became essential crutches to keep his energy level high. He was not a brilliant student, so what he lacked in acumen, he made up with relentless drive. College also helped him develop a keen sense for competition. He had some good friends, but in the back of his mind he viewed all his rela-tionships competitively. Who would get there first? Who would be number one?

Marty graduated with honors and went on to business school where he met the daughter of a prominent lawyer. She fell in love with his dynamism and he with her refine-ment and position. They had their first child right away and two more within the next four years. Marty thinks his wife was content in her role as mother and homemaker. In any case, he never had time to ask her. His rise in the corporate world was not sensational but steady. "I learned the laws of the jungle the hard way, but I never got stabbed in the back twice," he says. Ask one of Marty's peers and you will hear about the trail of friends he stepped on in his march from assistant manager to plant manager, corporate vice-president, and executive vice-president.

In the sixties, Marty got into the stock market and made a small fortune. He got out just in time to miss the downturn at the decade's end. He bought a huge house and two expensive foreign cars, joined the finest country club, but rarely took time to enjoy the accoutrements of his wealth. He put all his energy into making more. Foreseeing the real estate boom of the seventies, he invested in condos and shopping centers that multiplied his holdings manyfold. But he still didn't have enough.

At age forty Marty seemed to have his world running like clockwork, but you would have seen otherwise had you looked inside his family. In retrospect, his wife is bitter about what happened to their two older children and to their marriage. "Marty was never home, never took an interest in the children other than to push them to perform up to his standards," she mourns. "There was so little warmth, so much conflict. My oldest son was having trouble in college. We knew he wasn't motivated. This was the time of all the protests and drugs. During his junior year he said he wanted to quit for a while. His father said no, but he quit anyway. Took off to California and has never gone back to school. He married a girl out there and they live on a small farm. We never see them. Two years later, my daughter was arrested for attempting to sell marijuana. She had all the money she wanted, but she got in with a group to sell drugs. Why do you think she did that if it wasn't to strike back at us? I can count on both hands the number of times Marty took off just to be with the kids. A mother alone can't provide all the warmth and support children need."

His wife's bitterness is not just for the children, but for herself as well. "Marty and I didn't get closer as we grew older, just busier. Even our vacations, when Marty would take them, were in a rush. He could never put his business totally out of his mind. He was always under pressure and everyone around him could feel it. Our sex life deteriorated over the years but for appearances we still share the same bedroom. I tried to stay attractive for him, to keep my weight down, but I don't think he really cared one way or another.

Only because I love him has the loneliness and feeling of rejection hurt so much."

What finally prompted Marty's search for help was a head-on collision with himself. At age fifty-one he began suffering from intermittent impotence. He couldn't "get it up" with his wife, or with a willing secretary who had an apartment a few blocks away from his office. Shaken, he sought help from his family doctor, who discovered no organic cause of his sexual trouble but did diagnose high blood pressure and chronic bronchitis. When the doctor insisted that he take antihypertensive medication and give up smoking, he was doubly upset. All at once he felt his world was falling apart. He was vulnerable; his body was unreliable. When he confided his troubles and fears to his wife, she suggested they get help.

There is an old English proverb, "To the wise man, enough is as good as a feast." Marty's despair is testimony to the wholesale lack of this wisdom in our culture. The ordinary person today has material comforts and personal freedom that by the standards of any other century would rank as the luxuries of royalty. We take for granted automobiles, television, dish and clothes washers, radios, the telephone, the stereo, to say nothing of air conditioning, central heat, and hot water from the tap and the flood of other conveniences basic to any modern household.

The luxuries of modern life don't stop with material comforts. The airplane and the economics of volume travel put the exotic corners of the world within reach of millions. Abundant opportunities for personal entertainment exist in every community: color TV, movies, discotheques, restaurants, theaters. Yet, because our culture feeds on the constant striving for more, this feast of wealth and opportunity does little to lessen discontent. (Look at the national statistics: divorce, crime, family conflict, child abuse, depression, sexual complaints, pornography, drug abuse, alcoholism, runaways are edging upward.)

"What's the point?" Marty asks himself. "The money, the house, the cars, everything I've been trying to achieve. I've lost my children, my marriage is breaking up, my health is slipping. It's like I've awakened from the American dream and discovered it's a nightmare. I've been a fool."

Marty is a tragic example of an old lesson. "Joy is not in things; it is in us," wrote Richard Wagner. For fifty-two years Marty ignored his inner self because he believed that the key to happiness was acquiring as much as fast as he could. The result is an anhedonic person who has sacrificed the primary joys of marriage and children. Of course, it's men like Marty who are responsible for the enormous industrial growth of this country. Nevertheless, the question is: "What's the point?"

Marty has learned the hard way that anything he owns provides only as much pleasure as he is capable of experiencing and that sacrificing his inner life leads to deterioration of everything that he holds most dear—his health, his relationships, even his marriage. Human beings need the nourishment of joy from within. Without it, we become emotionally withered, like plants that do not get enough water. This lesson is so simple that it's hard to believe our culture could have ignored it for so long.

There is some hope in Marty's story. A man of tremendous drive, Marty has not foreclosed on the possibility of his own growth. In fact, he is now excited about the possibility of cultivating inner joy. He is committed to making his inner life a new priority, not to the exclusion of his work, but complementary to it. He is also committed to reviving his marriage and trying to reestablish a relationship with his children. None of this will happen overnight, but with Marty's commitment, it can happen, through the strategies that we describe throughout this book.

It's Hard to Lie in Bed

Nowhere has the reaction to anhedonia been stronger than in sexual relationships. The sexual revolution is a wholesale cultural effort to tear down anhedonic inhibitions. Yet it's a fact: Despite all the public unveilings, sex remains filled with white lies, fake feelings, anxiety, dissatisfaction. There may have been a revolution, but gains in satisfaction have been small indeed. In fact, the most significant result of the sexual revolution may be the new freedom to admit the extent of sexual dissatisfaction. Dr. William H. Masters, the most famous sex researcher, estimates that nearly half of all marriages are threatened by sexual dysfunction. In a study of 42,000 men, only 20 percent reported real satisfaction; over 30 percent said that sex was often a burden. The Hite Report gives some indication of the extent of dissatisfaction that women feel about sex. Taken together, these studies reflect not only widespread sexual discontent, but the extent of anhedonia.

There is an irony about the new attitudes toward sex. In keeping with the mechanistic and anhedonic tendencies in our culture, the new emphasis in therapy and popular sex manuals is on technique. If you can do it standing on your head eating a banana, or something equally outrageous, so the story goes, you're headed for the greatest orgasms of your life. The fact is, as many therapists are now learning, technique is not the key. Satisfying sex isn't primarily a matter of athletic prowess but of feeling. If you are fully open to pleasure and can exuberantly share it with your love, then the plain old missionary position may be enough to send you both into orbit. If you want to improve your sex life rather than spend hours experimenting with exotic techniques, you'd be better served by coming to terms with your anhedonia.

Anhedonia doesn't always show up in a sexual relationship as a specific problem like premature ejaculation or inability to climax. It also appears in feelings of boredom, disappointment, or diminished interest. Though less specific than the major sexual problems, these complaints are far more widespread and just as damaging to a relationship. Sex is a barometer of the fire in a relationship. When sex goes flat, the relationship is often on its way to trouble.

Ted and Vicky tell a familiar story. Ted is a thirty-one-year-old engineer and Vicky is a twenty-eight-year-old schoolteacher. They married seven years ago and have two children. Now that the children are in nursery school and kindergarten, Vicky has gone back to work part-time. From the outside it appears that they have an ideal relationship, jobs they enjoy, children they love, a bright future. They don't talk about their problems with friends. In the bedroom, the problems become clear. "When I come on to her at night, she isn't interested anymore," Ted complains. "I don't know what the problem is or what she expects, but holding back isn't going to solve anything. I'm getting to the point where it's not worth it anymore. I'd just as soon forget the whole thing."

Vicky says: "If only Ted could see himself! It's always the same routine. He kisses me and caresses my breasts. Then he kisses my nipples awhile. We have a little oral sex. Before he gets too excited he enters me. He usually comes in five minutes or so; sometimes I climax, mostly I don't. It's boring, the passion is gone. It's like watching the same movie over and over."

Ted and Vicky seem to be prime candidates for a sex manual that would add some variety to their sex lives. That may be a fine theory, but it doesn't mean much in practice. "We have *The Joy of Sex*, big deal," Vicky says. "So we do it in a different position or add a little more oral sex. It's not really new. New techniques are great when you're just getting to know someone sexually, but Ted and I have been together a long time. We've tried all that stuff, and once you've done it, you've done it."

Vicky's honest appraisal is far more astute than that offered by many therapists. Boredom is the principal problem in long-term sexual relationships, and its solution is not usually found in new sexual games. Sexual boredom is often symptomatic of other aspects of the relationship going stale.

"There's no more adventure in our lives," Ted laments. "Every evening is the same. I come home from work exhausted. While Vicky puts the dinner on the table I have a few minutes with the kids. We eat, I help clean up, the kids are put to bed. Vicky and I may watch the tube for an hour or so, then I may have one or two hours of work to do. When I come to bed, Vicky is frequently asleep. If she wakes up, she's irritated with me, and only very rarely responds to sexual overtures. We're in a rut, but I don't know how to get out of it."

Vicky has her own complaints. "Ted comes to bed at 1:00 A.M. and expects me to be ready and waiting for him. He hasn't paid any attention to me all day, isn't sensitive to the fact that I have to get up before he does to get breakfast before we all leave the house. He doesn't spend time with me on weekends, either. If he doesn't have work around the house, he has work he's brought home or there's some damn sports event he has to watch. Tell me why I'm supposed to be waiting for him, all steamy and wet like some whore in a movie? That's what it's like. Sex with hardly a word between us."

Ted and Vicky are not alone. Millions of young couples are faced with similar problems. Sociologists have cataloged ad infinitum the cultural forces (such as the corporation, the growth of suburbia, the isolation of the nuclear family) that exacerbate the anhedonic attitudes crippling marriage. The solution to Ted and Vicky's problem lies in discovering how they are asphyxiating the magic in their relationship. The real issue is not whether they can revitalize their sex lives, but whether they can eliminate the anhedonic patterns in their lives. The answer lies not so much in changing their relationship, but increasing their individual inner joy so they have more to share. In the final analysis, the secret of ecstatic sex is two joyful people.

Developing Your Program for Change

How, then, is anhedonia to be overcome? We live in a culture that is fundamentally anhedonic and we have had anhedonic thinking and behavior drilled into us all our lives. Clearly, overcoming anhedonia and discovering inner joy isn't something that gets accomplished overnight. Nor is it a matter of finding the "right technique" and adjusting the personality to run smoothly. Human beings aren't sports cars in need of a good tune-up. Something more is required: a new vision of the fully functioning person, a new model of individual fulfillment, a new philosophy of growth through the adult life cycle.

The creation of this new vision for the human condition is an enormous task that has been going on in many universities and institutions all over the country for the last twenty years or more. A new psychology based on the concept of the human drive for self-actualization has been born, even though the full vision of human potential is incomplete. The basic precepts for a psychology of growth are discernible. For your personal practical purposes, enormous progress in the discovery and creation of practical techniques for overcoming anhedonia has been made.

For these techniques (and therefore this book) to be most useful, you need more than techniques. Some ground rules for personal growth are fundamental to every chapter and technique in this book. These principles may differ from your usual conception of yourself and perhaps your relationship to your world. They aren't a dogma, and we don't ask you to accept their validity on faith. We present them to challenge the dominant anhedonic view of human potential and encourage you to consider their implications for your own life and your view of your potential for inner joy.

Here are the basic principles:

Human beings are endowed with the ability to experience joy as a baseline reality of living.

This is a revolutionary idea. For the past several thousand years, the dominant view of human potential for happiness has been bleak. Freud wrote toward the end of his life that he doubted anything more than brief happiness was a real human possibility. The more you understand anhedonia, the more clearly you will see all the ways you have been brainwashed into accepting this atrophied view of your own potential for joy.

From religion you have learned that pleasure is suspect and suffering inevitable, while happiness awaits you in heaven if you can endure with faith. From psychology you've been told that suffering is indispensable to the creative process, as if the greatest human achievements come from the agony of pain rather than the joy of inspiration. From history you've been inundated with records of the long series of wars, famines, and cruelty that devastated humanity century after century. From the evening news you get the tension and strife from around the globe delivered into your living room in brilliant color. From the advertisers you're told that you never have enough; you've got to keep striving for more gusto. Since childhood you've been told that you can't expect to be happy all the time. All this suggests that a search for inner joy is a futile undertaking. Fortunately, science is based on evidence, not philosophy or faith, and the evidence suggests a much brighter picture of human potential than has so far been accepted.

You have the capability to sustain inner joy even in the face of major problems and personal challenges.

Again, this idea is revolutionary because it directly contradicts the long-standing belief that problems must inevitably make you miserable. When a husband came in to join his wife in a personal growth seminar, one of his first statements was aimed at undercutting the possibility of overcoming anhedonia. "Life is too full of problems," he said. "There's no way to avoid it."

"Does that mean the problems have to make you unhappy?" he was asked. There ensued a discussion of typical rationales people use to justify putting up with their discontent. Do you use any of these?

- "I'm not so happy, but who is?"
- "Life is full of problems."
- "Look at what's happening in the world."
- "Everyone is getting divorced these days."
- "You can't feel safe with all the crime."
- "Expect the worst, then you won't be disappointed."
- "You can't get ahead in this world."
- "This country is for the rich; the little guy doesn't have a chance."
- "It's a dog-eat-dog world."

I had a patient once who pulled out a veritable grab bag full of these rationales to explain why he was persistently unhappy. Week after week he came into my office full of excuses about why he hadn't tried to put into practice any of the self-affirming behaviors we had discussed in the previous session. Every time it was the same; somehow, the world was always standing in his way.

Finally we broke through this cultural brainwashing. He claimed he couldn't go out because of crime. I asked him whether he had ever in his forty-six years been a victim of crime. He said he hadn't. "If your only experience with crime is what you read in the newspapers," I said, "what you're afraid of is the idea of crime, not something you've personally experienced." Finally the message got through.

Of course, crime is a real problem, but millions of people go about their lives every day, year after year without becoming crime victims. Even more millions complain about crime to justify their discontent. Whenever you find yourself dragging up some worn-out generality about the miserable condition of the world, ask yourself how that idea applies to your life *right now*. If you look at it squarely, you'll see it's just another tired complaint that has no real bearing on your present-moment happiness. The real issue is whether you have the courage and the determination to take charge of your feelings and choose to get everything you want out of life.

We live in a world of abundance, but fail to appreciate it, due to anhedonic thinking.

Look at the millions of years human beings have survived

on this planet, and it is obvious that nature has been very generous in providing everything needed for us to survive and prosper. Nevertheless, the struggle to survive creates a psychology of scarcity; there is always a fear of not having enough. This psychology of scarcity is basically anhedonic because it fosters the belief that joy and happiness lie in things rather than in ourselves. Despite the enormous wealth of modern society, the psychology of scarcity still reigns. No doubt the basic needs for food, clothing, affection, education, and work must be met for inner joy to become a real possibility. If we could reappraise our values in light of the potential for inner joy, we might see that the basic needs of the world's population can be fulfilled, and the psychology of scarcity can be set aside as a relic of the past.

Fundamental to discovering inner joy is to be who you are.

This means breaking down the barrier between your inner and outer selves, creating your life according to your unique talents and desires rather than trying to mold it according to other people's values and expectations. Our consumer culture depends on people who believe that they can't be themselves, and have to buy whatever they are told will make them enviable in the eyes of others. The poet e.e. cummings summed up the tremendous power of the cultural forces allayed against you when he wrote, "To be nobody but yourself in a world that is doing its best, night and day to make you like everybody else, means to fight the hardest battle which any human being can fight, and never stop fighting." Nevertheless, it's only when you're yourself that you can become the very best you and discover your capacity for inner joy.

Part of learning to be yourself is achieving an integration of opposite values and opposing forces within the psyche.

Anhedonic perception is either/or thinking; the world and the self appear fragmented, dichotomized, polarized. The shift to inner joy is also a shift away from this dichotomized perception toward a unified frame. You'll find it possible to accept yourself and others as selfish *and* unselfish, compassionate *and* indifferent, individual *and* social, rational *and* irrational. From the either/or vantage point, the polarities in the world and in the self appear to struggle toward release of tension and finally death. From the vantage point of inner joy, the tension between opposing forces produces energy for growth, a new form (and higher level) of functioning.

Anhedonic perception often leads to the denial of parts of the self (for example, desires, wishes, fantasies), to minimize tension and maintain the personality. With the discovery of inner joy, it becomes natural to accept all the conflicting parts of the self—the big and small, the good and bad, the noble and base—and to appreciate the grandeur as well as the limitations of being human.

Cultivating inner joy requires that you recognize your power to create your experience.

With the premise that happiness lies outside you our culture reinforces the mistaken idea that feelings are largely beyond your power. You have probably grown up with the idea that emotions are difficult to control. You've been taught that fear, anger, jealousy, sorrow, as well as love and joy are events that happen to you, not experiences you create.

To make it easy for you to avoid taking responsibility for your emotional life, our culture provides you with a wealth of expressions for defending against the real cause of your feelings. Here are some of these sayings. What messages do you deliver when you say them?

- "You turn me on."
- "You hurt my feelings."
- "Stop making me feel bad!"
- "My boss makes me angry."
- "Apologize for embarrassing me in public!"
- "Crowds make me feel uncomfortable."
- "I'm lonely without him."
- "I get frightened by heights."
- "I can't help the way I feel."

These are not innocent expressions that signify a simple feeling. Each phrase also says implicitly, "I can't control my feelings; someone or something else is responsible for the way I feel."

Anhedonia

If you don't control your feelings, how can you ever control your happiness? Next time you catch yourself blaming someone or something else for how you feel, stop and ask yourself whether it makes sense to put control over your happiness in someone else's hands. Instead of relying on one of the old standby phrases mentioned above, state the situation accurately. Like this:

- "I'm choosing to get angry because of something my boss does."
- "I am letting myself feel bad because of something you said to me."
- "I am arousing myself sexually by looking at you and enjoying your beauty."
- "I let myself be lonely when you are away."
- "I make myself feel uptight when I'm in a crowd."
- "I frighten myself when I'm up high and look down."
- "I let myself feel powerless because I don't believe I can control my feelings."

Finally, the growth of inner joy is not merely a matter of changing attitudes, but also of refining the physiology.

Mind and body are not separate. They're polarities on the continuum of the self. Emotional tension shows up in changes of bodily functioning such as muscular rigidity and stress. Anhedonia can be diminished through approaches that aim at changing attitudes as well as through strategies that work directly on the body. The mastery of stress and a healthy, dynamic body are two of the keys to inner joy.

III

Overcoming the Fear
of Pleasure

Hold every moment sacred. . . . Give each
its true and due fulfillment.
—THOMAS MANN

CAN YOU ENJOY YOURSELF without inhibition?
Or do you tend to hold yourself back?

If you're like most people, you may well be suffering from
a fear of pleasure that plays an important role in all your
anhedonic thinking and behavior. The fear of pleasure is
primary in chronic feelings of boredom, tension, fatigue,
and frustration. It contributes to dissatisfaction at work and
the sense of missing out on life. It is almost always an element in sexual problems. The concept of a fear of pleasure
may seem paradoxical. Nevertheless, the facts exist and can
be examined. Fear of pleasure is so common that few people
are entirely free from it.

It's most apparent in the lack of permission most people
give themselves to enjoy their lives. For most of us, pleasure
is a highly regulated reward we believe we must earn. Our
lives are carefully divided into activities for which we allow
ourselves pleasure and activities for which we don't. Most
of us expect to enjoy making love, but few know how to
find pleasure in putting fresh linen on the bed. We enjoy
sports, but we're hard pressed to find much pleasure in

writing a paper or doing work at home. Parties are great, but we dread cleaning up. Everyone loves to eat, but few are able to get much pleasure out of doing the dishes. All this may seem quite natural. The question remains: Why must so much of life be a chore and so little of it wonderfully pleasurable?

The place to look for an answer is not in what you do, nor in dogma about living, but in your basic attitude about pleasure and your own potential for abundant enjoyment of living.

The consensus is that pleasure must be strictly controlled. Consider a typical office. Have you ever noticed how people get suspicious when someone comes in smiling and happy? If you seem bored or tired, no one takes notice. But come in with a cheerful grin, and everyone becomes curious and you hear, "What's got into you?" The message is clear. You're not *supposed* to walk around in a state of pleasure unless you have good reason for it. If you come in every day with a big smile and never have a particular explanation, many people will begin to think you're peculiar. It's the same wherever you may be in public. If you're waiting on line, shopping, driving on the freeway, or buying groceries, you're less likely to make others uncomfortable if you maintain a dour expression than if you radiate energy and enthusiasm. Most of us fear pleasure not only in ourselves, but in others.

Most people are unaware of their fear of pleasure because they take its symptoms for granted. Muscular tension and restricted breathing are primary physical signs. In the body, fear means contraction and suppression of energy; so many of us walk around in a constant state of isometric tension, pushing against ourselves to restrict the natural flow of energy. Emotionally, the fear of pleasure shows up as doubt, insecurity, lack of enthusiasm, difficulty letting go. Pleasure increases emotional vitality and the feeling of personal freedom. Most of us are uncomfortable with personal freedom, so we block the pleasure that feeds it. The spiritual effect of fearing pleasure is a depressed outlook on life. The less moment-to-moment enjoyment you experience, the more confirmed you're likely to become in the belief that life is a game that few people can win.

In my seminars I often stress how important it is to cultivate the capacity for pleasure in order to become fully human and alive. The effect is something like pushing an alarm button or waving a red flag in front of a bull. I'm told that cultivating pleasure is selfish, sinful, and weakening; that it will lead to laziness and disregard for others; that it's unrealistic and hedonistic. Behind each of these responses is the unspoken belief that pleasure is somehow dangerous and the desire for pleasure often destructive.

The issue in this chapter is: How much permission are you willing to give yourself to savor your life? The irresponsible pursuit of pleasure, hedonism, is obviously destructive. The trouble is that to meet this potential danger most people accept the regulation and restriction of enjoyment without even considering other possibilities. So indoctrinated are most of us with the fear of pleasure that we go through life unaware that we're naturally capable of experiencing abundant pleasure in just being alive. Most people are like fish who complain of thirst but are afraid to drink. Pleasure is all around at every moment! You need only give yourself the opportunity to appreciate the pleasure of your own existence.

The exercises and cases in this chapter show that you can function at a higher level of personal maturity and enjoy abundant pleasure in just being alive. Not only will you increase your day to day enjoyment; you'll also experience more energy, better health, and more enthusiasm in everything that you do.

Reappraise What You've Been Taught

To overcome your inhibitions about pleasure, you have to challenge what you've been taught about the need to regulate it. Above all, you have to set aside the old idea that pleasure is a reward for something you do and discover that, more basically, it is the *primary* experience of being alive and the most fundamental energy of growth. Nothing, nothing at all, is more important! Your whole biological and spiritual self is organized to move toward pleasure and away from pain. Pleasure is the primary indicator that you are growing in the right direction and that you're getting what you need to develop fully as a human being.

The effects of pleasure are wholly positive. Physically, pleasure improves circulation and increases energy. The emotional effects include greater self-esteem, increased self-confidence, and a generally sharper mind. Spiritually, enjoyment enhances your appreciation of your blessings and contributes to a brighter outlook. Experiencing pleasure also allows you to have compassion for others when they are suffering. Pleasure is a source of strength to help others and contribute to the world.

If you're like most people, you've been bombarded since childhood with a barrage of culturally sanctioned messages to instill apprehension about your desire for pleasure. Your parents may have told you that having fun is wasting time. In a difficult and sometimes cruel world, success, you may have heard, depends on your ability to put your "nose to the grindstone" and put pleasure aside. In school you learned to control your enthusiasm. Teachers didn't like it if you were bubbling over with energy. They wanted you to sit quietly, speak only when spoken to, and raise your hand to answer questions. The lesson from the beginning to the end of each school day was that you aren't supposed to have fun learning or working. The clergy very likely told you that the pursuit of pleasure can lead to depravity and sin. Virtue was equated with the ability to set aside personal desires in favor of "the right thing," as if doing what was right could never be the most pleasurable course.

For children these lessons have some value. Children have voracious appetites for pleasure and limited understanding of how to achieve it and the full range of pleasures available. To gain a wider appreciation of their own potentials, children need to be taught about sharing, helping around the house, doing homework (even when it might be more fun to play), respecting rules, and obeying authority. These lessons help a child discover greater opportunities for fulfillment than he or she could otherwise perceive. The child discovers the pleasures of achievement, friendship, respect, and caring.

The issue is maturity. The careful regulation of pleasure during childhood ceases to be necessary as you grow older and the attitudes toward pleasure learned in childhood become counterproductive during adulthood, if they inhibit your ability to experience pleasure and enjoy your life fully.

Because you are no longer a child, you don't have to go on treating yourself like one. The belief that pleasure must be strictly controlled is based on an extremely narrow appreciation of human potential. The human body is the most complex and magnificent known being in creation. You can experience enormous pleasure in your day-to-day activity if you give yourself permission to appreciate your own magnificence. The greatest pleasures stem not from doing, but from being. The greater your inner joy, the more sensitive you become to the dynamics of pleasure and the more natural it becomes.

Pleasure itself is never harmful. It's nature's sign of well-being. *The belief that pleasure is harmful arises from a confusion between the experience of pleasure and excess in the pursuit of it.* Eating a small piece of cake is pleasurable and not harmful. Overeating can make you sick. Generally you can do almost anything you enjoy without negative effects as long as you do it in moderation. When you are able to derive abundant pleasure from the simple joys of being, then moderation in your activities in the pursuit of pleasure comes quite naturally. You don't have to regulate your pleasure; the flow of pleasure has become part of your baseline experience of living.

If there is one difficult obstacle in overcoming the fear of pleasure it may be accepting the personal power that pleasure provides. The more easily you can experience pleasure, the better you will feel about yourself. Your energy level, your self-confidence, and your enthusiasm for living all increase dramatically. These psychological changes bring about a significant increase in personal feelings of power. For some people this feeling of power can cause discomfort. If you are frightened of change or determined to live according to a dreary routine, then opening up to a whole new dimension of pleasure will take adjustment. Yet confronting your inhibitions and breaking free from the myths that inhibit you will make you much happier to be alive.

The Myth of Either/Or

Some people move through life as if they're running the gauntlet, pushing themselves for every last bit of performance. They get their satisfaction from knowing they have lived through one ordeal and moved on to the next. Taking time to savor life or indulge their fantasies is out of the question; they fear that slowing down means falling apart. For them, life is *either* hard work and achievement—*or* idle play and self-indulgent pleasure.

Beth, a twenty-three-year-old attractive, intelligent law student, is one of these people. She sits in my office, apparently calm and collected. Her clothes are neat, her hair is perfect, and she tries to wear a smile. The only sign of her anxiety is the way she sits on the edge of her chair. As she speaks, she grips the arms of the chair as if she must hold on tightly or risk losing control. "I'm slipping into the second half of my class," she says between clenched teeth. "I can't seem to study. Work is piling up, and I can't get to it. I read a case and it doesn't sink in. My mind wanders all over the place. If this goes on, I'll never make it through exams. I need help!"

Underneath Beth's cool exterior is a young woman in a panic about what she sees as the disintegration of her abilities. She does indeed feel she is losing control over herself, and says she feels queasy periodically throughout the day. All her life she has been drilled to divide her time very carefully between work and play, with work getting the lion's share of her attention. She comes from a well-educated family (father a doctor, mother an anthropologist), and ever since grade school has been at the top of her class. Now that she is in law school, she feels as if she is on the final stretch of a horse race. She desperately wants to graduate with honors so "all my efforts will finally pay off." Her problem is, the harder she pushes herself, the less she gets accomplished. Beth is terrified.

People like Beth expect a quick fix for their problems. She has treated herself like a machine all of her life, so she views her visit to me much like taking her car into the shop for a tune-up. She didn't come to learn anything about herself. She wants a prescription for a tranquilizer that will transform her back into her old self, or barring that, some technique that will help her cope. She is very clear about her goal. "I'm here to get back my ability to study," she says.

When I point out that she may have to take a look at a little more than her study habits, she reacts negatively. I finally convince her to wait on the medication by agreeing to give her a prescription if she makes no progress after three weeks. In the meantime she agrees to give some other things a try.

Beth's problem isn't hard to understand. Ever since grade school, she recalls believing that life is a constant trade-off between achievement and pleasure. She was told throughout her childhood that she was highly gifted and shouldn't waste time chasing after fun. "There's more to life than happiness," she recalls her mother saying. So Beth carefully cultivated her ability to push herself up to (and beyond) her limits.

In law school, she pushed herself too far. No one seems to have mentioned that you can whip a horse only so long before it finally breaks down. Since she first began law school she has been allowing herself almost no pleasure or recreation. Her stress level is enormous. She has become so anhedonic that she is making herself miserable enough to impair her ability to study.

When I first suggested that her problem might be that she was starving herself of pleasure, she was highly resistant. "My problem is that I've got to study more, not less," she insisted. "I'm already having trouble with my courses; I don't need you to tell me to start goofing off." I assured Beth that I understood her reasoning, but I asked her to consider the possibility that she might be caught in a self-sustaining and self-destructive stress cycle. I pointed out that by working so hard she might be creating so much stress that she was impairing her concentration, her recall, and her health significantly enough to account for her difficulties. (The cycle is self-sustaining because the more trouble she has with her work, the worse she feels about herself, and the more stress she creates.) Beth finally accepted the possibility that she might be caught in such a cycle.

She had two choices. She could take medication to cope with stress. That road led to a lifetime of anxiety and the lingering fear that she could at any time slip back into a stress cycle and suffer similar crises. Or she could decide to change her anhedonic life-style and develop better balance in her life. Once the choices were clearly presented, Beth didn't have much difficulty making up her mind. We joked that she would have to learn how to treat herself at least as well as she would treat a fine sports car.

Beth went on a specific growth program with two primary goals: first, to create more pleasure in her life; second, to restore her previous high level of performance. Beth had been so indoctrinated with the belief that pleasure undermines performance that it was necessary at every step to take pains to overcome her resistances. For example, one major step involved changing her sleep patterns. She was trying to get by on three or four hours per night. I insisted she get at least six, preferably seven hours. She said it was impossible. Eventually she was willing to test the idea that if she were really well rested, she might understand in one reading what otherwise might take ten. When it worked, she thought it was a revelation.

Though Beth was really convinced that she had no time for herself, her program called for her to take at least one hour per day specifically for her own self-development. I suggested she learn the Transcendental Meditation (TM) program and practice the technique twice a day for its value in reducing stress and anxiety. I also suggested she start running at least four mornings per week to improve her physical fitness. Again she resisted terribly and had to be strongly encouraged to get into these activities. After about six weeks, behold, she began to see the payoff. Her feelings about herself had improved and she had experienced a radical turnaround in her work.

One of the most significant parts of Beth's program was her assignment to find *something* to enjoy in each of her classes and her papers. Work and enjoyment were so segregated in her mind that it took her several weeks before she began making any progress. When she complained of feeling stuck because there was too much work and too much pressure for any of it to be enjoyable, I suggested that she forget about grades and concentrate exclusively on finding something to get *excited* about in each class. The breakthrough came with a term paper assignment. It had never occurred to her to choose a subject solely because it interested her. This time she let her interest in the rights of American Indians sway her decision, even though she knew the paper would have no practical benefit for her future career. She wound up having a terrific time doing the paper, and got an A besides.

Over the three months that Beth was involved in our program, she changed dramatically. Perhaps the most obvious change was her newfound ability to laugh. No longer was she the tight-lipped girl forever serious about her work and her responsibilities. Now she was able to laugh at herself and laugh with others. Her anxiety diminished markedly. Her symptoms of tension disappeared. Her transformation was like that of a plant when you take it from a dark place indoors and put it out in the sun. From a tired and unhappy girl Beth blossomed into a vibrant and confident young woman. No longer did law school feel like a burden, because she no longer felt she absolutely *had* to be there. For the first time she could really tell that law was what she wanted and enjoyed.

Perhaps this integration of pleasure and work was her most significant change. She began to understand what Oliver Wendell Holmes meant when he wrote: "The rule of joy and the law of duty seem to be all one." Throughout her previous school years Beth had labored under the belief that struggle and tension were signs that she was doing her best. She finally discovered that the real indicator of optimum functioning is joy. She learned that the more she is able to enjoy what she does (studying, writing, doing library research, taking care of her apartment), the more she accomplishes and the better she does it. Beth discovered the power of inner joy.

Fear of Losing Control

Some people run their lives like a military dictator afraid of revolution. They have sexual fantasies that they would like to explore, but they dare not for fear of losing control and being overrun by their desires. They dream of taking extra time off from work for an adventure vacation, but they don't because they fear becoming a beach bum and never coming back. At a wild party, they want to let go and get into the uninhibited spirit, but they can't because they fear making fools of themselves. They may see an attractive person whom they'd like to meet, but they don't introduce themselves because they fear being forward or improper. Every day of their lives they dream of dropping the reins and letting themselves come out and run free, but years of self-control keep them caught in an emotional pen of boredom and routine.

Listen to some of the common reasons I hear for maintaining this self-suffocation:

· "I can't act out my sexual fantasies. I'll become a nymphomaniac."
· "I can't ask my boss for a two-week leave of absence. He'd think I had gone off the deep end."
· "If I let myself go at a party, I'd go wild. I have to keep the lid on."
· "If I really went to Tahiti, I might never come back. It's better for me to take my vacations close to home."
· "I can't introduce myself to her. I might make a fool of myself."
· "I want to buy that outfit, but I don't dare. It's too expensive."

This list of "I want to but I can't" could go on for pages because this fear of living out dreams and fantasies is one of the most common self-nullifying behaviors in our culture. If you're holding yourself back in this way, you've got some work to do and much to gain.

Tracy used to be unhappy with her sex life. "I can't come with David," she complained. "He's kind and considerate, takes plenty of time, but I don't come. I know I'm orgasmic because I can have great climaxes on my own as long as I do it just the right way." Talking to Tracy, you see a blond, dark-eyed woman of twenty-eight, independent, liberated, a feminist. "I was hesitant about coming here," she admitted. "I thought maybe I should forget men altogether."

When Tracy relaxes enough to open up, she reveals her fears of her own passion. She has a recurring dream of making love with two men. The dream begins when she meets them on the street and invites them to her apartment. There she makes the first move by unbuttoning her blouse and encouraging them to get out of their clothes. The two men caress and kiss her until she finally pulls one inside her. With each thrust she cries out for more, she becomes wildly excited with pleasure, but the dream always ends before she comes.

Tracy also had a fantasy of masturbating in front of David. I suggested she talk to him about it and if he agreed, they try it together. "Why didn't you tell me this before?" David said, surprising her. They chose a quiet afternoon for their experiment. David put on some sexy music, they shared some wine, and he sat back in a terry-cloth robe while she indulged her fantasy. She undressed seductively, caressing her breasts, teasing herself and David into high sexual excitement. "When I saw he was getting aroused," she says, "I felt a release inside. I got very excited and lay down on the floor. My fingers traced the outline of my body. With one hand I probed my vagina. With the other, I massaged my clitoris, until my body began to writhe with pleasure. David started fondling himself too and that got me doubly excited. He finally yelled 'Come!' and that pushed me over. I screamed, "Yes! Yes! I'm coming!" And I had the wildest orgasm of my life."

This simple experience had a profoundly liberating effect on Tracy. For the first time, she discovered that it was OK to use her fantasies in her real life in order to express herself, get closer to people, discover new parts of herself, and just have a lot of fun. She began exploring other fantasies with David, one where she was the innocent virgin, another where she was his master. Soon she was enjoying her sex life so much that she entirely forgot about her initial complaint.

Yes, she started climaxing during intercourse, but that was a relatively inconsequential gain. "The most important change," she says, "is the new sense of freedom, not only in my sex life, but in everything I do. I am more able to express myself with other people. I have more confidence, don't take everything so seriously. The other big change is the new intensity I feel for living. I'm no longer so bottled up inside. When I'm happy or enthusiastic or feel friendly toward someone, I don't feel I have to control or hide it. I let it shine and I'm finding that it helps other people shine back."

The key to overcoming fears of losing control is learning to trust yourself. The great poet and philosopher Goethe once wrote: "As soon as you trust yourself, you know how to live." Why not try giving yourself more credit than you ordinarily do? Self-control and discipline are admirable qualities, but so are imagination, fantasy, spontaneity, and enthusiasm. The key is maturity. If you start letting your dreams and fantasies play a bigger role in your life, you'll discover that you needn't fear losing control, because the lessons of personal discipline have become second nature. When you go far enough, the brakes will come on quite naturally. You won't even have to think about it.

"I'll Be Happy When . . ."

There's a strange paradox in our culture. On the one hand you hear all kinds of talk about the pernicious desire for instant gratification. Hedonism is said to be so rampant that everyone wants undelayed pleasure, overnight success, quick sex, and immediate fulfillment along with their instant coffee, fast food, and fifteen-second cold relief. Yet look around, sit in any psychotherapist's office, and you find something very different. The promises of instant gratification may be everywhere, but the number of people who get any real satisfaction from all this is small indeed. On the contrary, many people are caught on a treadmill that runs on the belief "I'll be happy when . . ." You can fill in the last words any way you choose. Here are a few that I hear quite often.

- ". . . I make my first million."
- ". . . I get the pool finished."
- ". . . we go to Europe."
- ". . . the kids are out of school."
- ". . . I make my second million."
- ". . . we move to the country."
- ". . . we move to the city."
- ". . . I get the promotion."
- ". . . I start my own business."
- ". . . I retire."

- ". . . I get married."
- ". . . I get divorced."
- ". . . I got to heaven."

For some people fulfillment is always just around the corner or over the next hill. This might not be so bad if, once they got over the next hill, they could finally enjoy themselves, but that's rarely the case. Instead, another hill looms on their personal horizon and the promise of future happiness makes it impossible for them to enjoy what they have. This idealization of the future is a cultural disease that affects millions. One of the most celebrated victims is William Randolph Hearst, whose life story was the basis of the movie *Citizen Kane*. He created an enormous publishing empire, acquired a huge fortune, built a vast estate, filled it with art treasures from all over the world, but he died an unhappy man, one for whom fulfillment always remained elusive.

Frank, another self-made millionaire born with little means, is also a victim, but he knows he needs help. "If only Gail would make breakfast for me," Frank says, "I'd be happy. I really think I would." He is a forty-four-year-old real estate magnate who built his fortune over the last ten years of the real estate boom. He has three children, four cars, homes in California and southern France, two dogs, three thoroughbred horses, live-in servants, and an aquarium. He vacations all over the world and his children are doing well in fine private schools. Despite all this, he is troubled, and doesn't really know why.

He has finally reached the point where his old defense against facing his own fear of self-fulfillment no longer works. What can he add at the end of "I'll be happy when . . ." now that he's got everything? But old defenses die hard, so he has rummaged around and managed to dredge up a new one. He truly believes that his wife preparing breakfast every morning might just be the key to the happiness he has yet to find.

It took a good deal of time with Frank before he began

to understand the game he was playing with himself. Ever since high school he had adopted the habit of idealizing the future. Like millions unable to cope with their lack of happiness in the present, he began projecting an unrealistically great satisfaction arriving with the achievement of some future goal. At first it was getting his own car. Next it was getting accepted to the college of his choice. Then graduation and marriage were supposed to bring the fulfillment he longed for. Of course each achievement brought some enjoyment, but his basic unhappiness was still there. A gnawing feeling of being trapped, never being able to do what he really wanted, kept haunting him. The reality could never live up to his expectation once he achieved it.

How does Gail see the situation? Six years younger than Frank, Gail is a lovely articulate woman who got a degree in journalism, but quit work to raise a family. "From the outside I know it looks like we have an ideal marriage. Beautiful children doing well in school, financial security, travel, almost anything we want. But it all hides the emptiness between Frank and me. He works hard and comes home late; I spend my time caring for the house and chauffeuring the children. When we're alone together, the silences are all too conspicuous. We haven't got much."

Look into Gail's personal history and you find that she faces the same crisis of discovering that "I'll be happy when . . ." can't go on forever. In high school she dreamed about college. When she got there, finding a husband seemed to be the key to a future. She got excited about a career in journalism, but put that aside not long after she got married. She expected marriage to fulfill all her dreams. When it didn't, having children seemed to promise a way to something more. "I wasn't ever unhappy," she says looking back now, "but I've got the feeling that it has all been a letdown, futile, missing real joy. I'm back to questions that I'd thought I left in high school and college. Like 'What's life all about? It can't be just this.' "

Caught in the "I'll be happy when . . ." syndrome, Frank and Gail reinforced each other's self-nullifying attitudes and behavior. They grew apart because it became increasingly difficult to share simple joys. They drew their emotional sustenance from the excitement of each new car, house, vacation, antique, or business success. But shared excitement can nourish a relationship for just so long; eventually the emotional vacuum between excitement peaks casts its pall. Frank and Gail might have become another statistic in the divorce column if they hadn't made a commitment to avoid blaming each other for their mutual unhappiness. They sought help.

What Frank and Gail had to learn was *how to begin living in the present*. Think about it: there is in fact no other moment you can live. The future is just fiction until it becomes another now. This simple logic, however, isn't enough to break the "I'll be happy when . . ." syndrome which is so much a part of our consumer culture.

To end their chronic over-anticipation of the future, Frank and Gail had to make a conscious effort to focus on getting their fulfillment from the present. This required a fundamental change in their attitudes. Instead of spending time on redecorating their exterior lives with new cars, new furniture, and new travel plans, they began discovering how to deepen their interior lives. Each set aside one hour a day for such quiet pleasure as reading, meditation, and prayer. They also made a point of spending more time together enjoying nature. At least once each week they went for a two-hour walk together in a local park or forest. Instead of putting up with their perfunctory sex lives, they made an effort to discover new pleasures, especially how they might act out each other's fantasies. They stopped going to cocktail parties that they both found boring, and began inviting friends over more often for casual dinners that allowed more intimate sharing of friendship. They joined a great-books group at the library to provide a shared base for examining some of the basic issues of human existence.

All these changes did not come suddenly and did not supply a magic answer to their discontent. Frank and Gail still attend a couples group and neither is sure that their marriage will last. On the other hand, both are less frightened of the prospect of major change, and that alone is an important step. Both admit their lives are undergoing profound transformation, more significant than anything they can remember. They are learning an important lesson: A life well lived is not just doing arithmetic for tomorrow but painting a picture for today.

Fear of Self-Discovery

Some people treat themselves like criminals. They keep a tight lid on how much joy they allow into their lives for fear of discovering something terrible about themselves. Supporting this belief are years of religious and cultural indoctrination about selfishness, greed, and lust, supposedly the bedrock of human nature. The tragedy is that this belief keeps millions chained to an inner struggle for happiness. Instead of welcoming opportunities to expand their self-understanding and express their creative potential, they hold on to the status quo because that promises safety from themselves.

Listen to a few of the objections people offer when encouraged to expand their capacity for joy:

- "I can't open up. If I do, I know I won't stay in my marriage."
- "I don't have time for all this. People need me."
- "Too much pleasure isn't good for you. You lose your perspective on the suffering of others."
- "If I make happiness a priority, I'd quit this job right now. Then where would I be?"
- "If I don't control myself, the greedy person inside me would take over."
- "It's a sin to be happy all the time."
- "If you're going to be a good person, you've got to expect to suffer in this world."
- "If you're happy, you stop striving to be better; too much happiness is dangerous."

The logic: by denying yourself pleasure, you become a better person. Look at this logic closely, and you find the hidden message: "I'm afraid to change because I might discover something terrible inside me."

If you confront your fear of self-discovery and take steps to explore your innermost self, you'll discover that your inner nature is far from threatening. As they reappraise Freud's original description of the unconscious as a caldron of seething desires and aggressive forces, psychologists are finding that the core of the human psyche is an incubator of what we recognize as the best human qualities and highest ideals. Each of us is endowed with an inner nature that contains in seed form energy, love, trust, compassion, humor, kindness, concern, affection, joy, curiosity, strength, confidence, and joy. The more we bring this inner self to awareness, the more able we become to express those qualities.

When we fear self-discovery we really fear the emotional wounds and unfulfilled needs we never confronted and resolved. To the extent that we all have these inner scars, we all harbor a share of the greed, jealousy, envy, anger, malice, and deceit that these scars produce. The existence of negative feelings does not change the fact that the core of the psyche is essentially positive, just as the essential strength of the inner self does not preclude the presence of many negative feelings. This basic fact explains how Freudians and the new self-actualization psychologists can describe two radically different pictures of the inner self. Having studied unhealthy people with many unfulfilled needs, the Freudians saw the emotional results of deprivation and lack of contact with the inner self. Having studied healthy people with few repressed needs, the self-actualization psychologists saw the results of growth and the blossoming of the inner self.

The point is that you are endowed with the power to refine your personality, heal the old wounds, fulfill repressed needs, and bring to awareness all the grandeur and vitality of your inner nature. The only thing to be feared in this process is fear itself. Personal change, especially when it involves long-term relationships, employment, or attitudes, is difficult. Because the results are uncertain, the whole endeavor is frightening. Rather than face the fear directly, human beings have a penchant for concocting rationalizations to explain why they must hold on to the status quo.

If you're among those who harbor a fear of self-discovery, here's the question you have to ask yourself: Is it really worth putting up with a future of self-forfeiting attitudes and marginally satisfying relationships to avoid the risks of growth?

The desire for the expansion of happiness is the most powerful drive in the human psyche. To resist this impelling drive toward personal growth requires enormous energy; you must continually erect barricades against your real feelings and innermost thoughts. Are you prepared to continue in the role of construction worker, building defenses against expressing your dreams? The alternative does involve risk. If you set out to start allowing your real feelings to play an important role in your life, you may find yourself faced with some difficult questions. Should you stay in your marriage? Should you change your career? Should you go back to school? Do you really want to have children? These questions rarely have easy answers, but I have yet to meet a person who was not better off for having struggled with them openly instead of foreclosing on the possibility of change.

The Psychological Payoff Behind the Fear of Pleasure

Examined objectively, fears of pleasure are plainly irrational. They lead to the forfeit of opportunities for present-moment happiness and long-term fulfillment. Why then would anyone keep on behaving this way? Shouldn't insight into one's futility be enough to motivate change?

Insight isn't sufficient because self-forfeiting behaviors

aren't all that irrational. All behavior has causes; even self-nullifying behavior has its rewards. These psychological benefits, no matter how unhealthy and limited, explain both the persistence of self-defeating behavior and the difficulty of changing it.

To change behavior on your own, you need insight not only into the behavior but also into the rewards you derive from it. Understanding the *why* behind your behavior can be a tricky process, because self-deception is a seductive road to avoiding the task of change. If you understand the rewards of self-defeating behaviors, you can develop strategies for change. Here are a few of the many potential rewards for ignoring opportunities for self-fulfillment and hanging on to the fears of pleasure:

You can complain about how difficult life is and what a rotten world we live in.

This allows you to shift responsibility for your happiness off your own shoulders and onto "the world." For many people, shunning responsibility for their happiness seems far easier than undertaking the challenges of self-affirmation. The opportunities for complaint are an added bonus.

You can call on others for sympathy and commiseration about your troubles.

With so many people sharing your feelings, it's not difficult to find friends to offer consolation, especially if you're willing to reciprocate. This leads to a mutual complaint and consolation society. Everyone gets a turn to berate "the world" and bask in approval when everyone else in the group nods agreement. Group approval is a powerful psychological tranquilizer; many people prefer it to the alternative of declaring their independence and affirming their unique abilities.

You can maintain grandiose expectations of the future.

If you keep putting off appreciating what you have and rely on "I'll be happy when . . ." you never have to risk a letdown, nor do you have to assess your real talents and abilities. You're saved from a confrontation with your real feelings and your capacity to deepen your experience, and can keep on redecorating the exterior of your life. The false hope derived from the "I'll be happy when . . ." is your reward.

You can avoid the hard work of taking an honest look at how happy you are with your job, your relationships, and your life-style.

Being honest with yourself is very difficult, and taking steps to change is harder still. Rather than face this challenge, many people choose to hang on to the belief that they don't have the right to more happiness. It's easier to foreclose on the possibility of changes right from the outset rather than risk a major upheaval in your life.

You can avoid the risks involved in expressing your unique talents and abilities.

Rather than plunge ahead and write your novel, start your own business, go on an adventure vacation alone, you can sit back, dream, and do nothing. You may not be very happy but at least you won't have risked failure. For some people, this reward is enough to hang on to the status quo.

You can suppress parts of yourself that you haven't yet learned to accept.

It's said that nothing great can be accomplished without passion. Yet passion is difficult to control and often arouses anxiety. It's far easier to shut off your passions than to work on integrating them into your life.

You can make endless excuses for your feelings of discontent.

Parents and teachers make excellent scapegoats for personal unhappiness. If they won't do, there is always your boss, a onetime friend, or the IRS. Some people prefer to fill up their present moments with excuses rather than accept the challenge of growth.

You can tell yourself how good and noble you are for continuing to follow all the "should"s you learned in childhood.

Examining your list of "should"s is likely to shake your whole belief system. It's much easier to let others think for you than to think for yourself. When your "should"s lead to unhappiness, you get to play the role of martyr. This can be a great reward for putting up with self-made discontent.

You can take solace in the fact that your life may not be what you want it to be, but at least it's safe and familiar.

"Taking a new step, uttering a new word," wrote Dostoevsky, "is what people fear most." If you hold on to the fear of pleasure, you don't have to face the fear of taking a new step.

In the face of a few hurdles or hardships forfeiting your potential for self-fullment may be easier and less anxiety-producing than exercising your power for happiness. It boils down to what you want out of life. You can remain the way you are and gradually grow bitter about your life not measuring up to your expectations, or you can decide to make some changes, difficult though they may be, and extend your reach for joy.

Strategies for Expanding
Your Satisfactions and Pleasure

To be fully vibrant and alive is to be wide open to the pleasures of each and every moment. Pleasure is nature's indicator of well-being. It's a sign of optimum functioning and maximum growth. You can no more have too much pleasure than you can have too much well-being or live life too fully.

It's fundamental for expanding pleasure that you discover you can exist almost all the time in a natural state of effortless enjoyment. It doesn't matter whether you're doing the dishes, rushing to meet a deadline, or waiting in a traffic jam; you have the innate biological and psychological ability to enjoy a state of ease that provides a continuous flow of pleasurable energy from within. This means a high degree of restfulness along with alertness and vitality. It is a state of attunement and balance, maximum self-awareness and minimum self-inhibition; it is giving yourself the permission to enjoy all the pleasure and power of your own being.

The following exercises will help you create and sustain this state of restful alertness. At first you will notice increased pleasure, primarily during the exercises themselves. In time you will find that the pleasure carries over and you can sustain this state of joy no matter what you may be doing.

Here are the basic strategies for expanding your capacity for pleasure:

Begin by recognizing that you are bigger than your mind.
While your mind engages in thoughts, you control them. You are bigger than any localized thought, feeling, or sensation. At the core of your being you are awareness itself, a source of pure energy and intelligence capable of moving your life in any direction you wish. We all have "smallness" —our narrow interests, our conditioning, our childish wishes, our pettiness, our emotional red buttons—but you don't have to let the small dimensions of your personality determine how much enjoyment you are going to experience. The point is not to deny your conditioning and your small self but to learn that you can deal with all your thoughts and feelings from that place where you feel in control of your life. To do this, you must take full responsibility for creating your experience rather than lazily sit back and react to the world as you always have. You have the power to expand your horizons of pleasure; it's up to you to use it.

Realize that you can control anhedonic thinking rather than let it control you.
Anhedonic thoughts arise from (and contribute to) distress and disequilibrium. Feeling anxious, upset, off center, worried, depressed, exhausted, confused, tense, nervous, and helpless are all anhedonic emotional states. When these feelings arise, you only make them worse by taking seriously the thoughts that accompany them. They are products of stress, not your real self, so they deserve no more attention than you pay to static on the radio. Any sign of anhedonic

thinking should be a signal to step back from your problems of the moment and get back to a state of greater balance and enjoyment. Anhedonic thoughts tend to be weak, narrow in focus, irrational, uncreative. The more anhedonic you feel, the less powerful and effective is your thinking. Rather than waste time pushing yourself when you're feeling anhedonic, take a break. Go running, meditate, listen to music, do anything that restores your feeling of being centered and in control of your thoughts and feeling. It's impossible to keep anhedonic thinking from ever returning, since, as a biological being, you can always get tired or frustrated. But once you learn you can control anhedonic thinking, you'll never choose to let it persist for long again.

Enliven your imagination.

Daydreaming about something you would like to do (or a goal you want to achieve) is perfectly natural and helpful to the creative process. Through your imagination you get to taste the pleasure of your goal, and that helps motivate you to achieve it. Many people seem to have the idea, perhaps learned in school, that daydreaming is a destructive form of escape, to be avoided. Over the years they have systematically inhibited their daydreaming and squelched their imagination. This is highly anhedonic. You short-change yourself of innumerable pleasures and a considerable degree of personal power if you allow your imagination to atrophy. When was the last time you made up a story? Drew a picture? Arranged some flowers? Did anything creative to stimulate your imagination? If it's been some time, you can enrich your life significantly by giving imagination a greater priority.

The simplest and one of the most useful ways to reawaken your imagination is to give yourself permission to start daydreaming again. Don't feel embarrassed about it. Above all, don't feel you're escaping from your responsibilities. You may find it helpful to set aside a specific time to relax and let your mind go. A playful attitude is best. Try getting very relaxed and picking out a goal—spending a weekend in the mountains, getting a promotion, moving into a new house, anything you might desire. Then imagine fully and completely what it feels like to achieve your desire. Let yourself believe you're living your daydream so you'll fully enjoy its pleasures. When you come back from this excursion, notice the energy and alacrity you feel. Enjoy the additional vitality and take it with you into the rest of your day.

Give yourself permission to feel good even when you have problems.

Many people tell me that anxiety, worry, and tension are unavoidable as long as they're struggling with an unsolved problem. Taking time off for relaxation seems to them like an escape. This misguided belief is a nasty little anhedonic trap that only undermines your ability to solve your problem and prolongs your distress in the process. We can't emphasize strongly enough the principle that *you think best when you feel best.* The way to maximize your creativity is to cultivate as much inner joy as possible and give yourself all the permission you need to enjoy yourself fully. Taking time to feel good in the face of a problem is a very wise— even economical—step.

Experiment with your power to create ecstatic moments under many different circumstances.

For example, there is no reason why you can't choose to create ecstasy while doing the dishes. You've read correctly. The key to ecstasy in whatever you are doing is to allow yourself to be fully engaged in doing it. That means: *not* complaining to yourself about it, *not* worrying about how long it'll take, *not* planning what you'll do when it is over, *not* watching yourself to see how well you're doing. Engaging fully in what you're doing is just that, letting your feelings, thoughts, and movements blend in one graceful flow of activity, while you passively attend to what's going on. When you get the hang of it, you'll find that the dishes seem to be washing themselves while you stand there appreciating the timelessness of the moment and enjoying a quiet state of inner joy. It takes practice, but you have the ability right now. Eventually you'll find it happening quite naturally under many circumstances. Then you'll know you've achieved a major shift of consciousness toward inner joy.

Overcoming the Fear of Pleasure

Favor the positive.

Whatever you direct your attention to increases its role in your thinking and action. This is an obvious basic psychological principle that few people seem to appreciate. Instead of choosing to put their minds on constructive thoughts and useful actions, they exhaust themselves complaining about how they feel or why they can't be happy. Every time you indulge in complaining, caviling, or pointless criticizing, you give who (or whatever) upsets you greater control over your life. It's like flypaper: the harder you try to shake it off, the more it sticks to you. The point is: You don't have to waste your time being negative. At every moment you can choose to focus your attention on plans, creative projects, friendly conversation, helping others, or any number of positive activities that enhance emotional freedom and fan your inner joy.

Let yourself be enthusiastic and loving.

Many people seem to believe that decorum demands that all enthusiasm and open affection be kept to a minimum. They hold themselves back, dampen their energies, and restrict the outward flow of loving feelings. This self-inhibition usually stems from early childhood training at home and in school. Now that you are an adult, emotional discipline is second nature, and it's time to get back some of that open childhood exuberance. Enthusiasm is contagious and almost always well received. You needn't fear a negative reaction. On the contrary, there is every reason to believe that by getting your energy flowing, you'll be valued as a more dynamic and exciting person. The energy of enthusiasm creates charisma.

Accept all your desires.

The ability to desire is basic to the energy of life. Without desire there would be no growth. The stronger your desires and the more clearly you understand them, the more effective your actions. Desire is the excitatory link between your inner self and your biological being.

From time to time everyone has desires that are inappropriate, destructive, and unacceptable. While these desires need not be acted upon, why punish yourself for having them? Destructive desire arises from the narrow and petty small self that is a part of our limited biological existence. Denying negative desires is an effort to deny the small self and make yourself anhedonic. Punishing yourself for having destructive desires inhibits the excitatory impulse toward growth and your basic sensitivity to pleasure. If you have a destructive desire, let it be. You don't have to act on it. It'll pass on its own.

Take time every day for some quiet solitude.

In the hectic push of modern life the rejuvenating rest of a quiet period every day is more important than ever. During this interlude you may choose to meditate, go for a walk, or read something uplifting. The point is to give yourself an opportunity to release some of the tension you've picked up, set aside your anhedonic feelings, and get recentered. Here's what one client enjoys:

When I come home from work, my husband won't get home for another hour and a half. That's when I can be alone and enjoy revitalizing my body, mind, and spirit. I tell the children that I don't want to be disturbed and retreat to my bedroom where I disrobe and climb into a lushly warm bubble bath. At first I didn't know what to do but soak. Shows you how inhibited I was! Now I soak awhile, then begin giving myself a slow gentle massage all over my body. With real love and attention, I soothe all the aches everywhere. I spend lots of time on my feet, calves, and thighs. Then I might massage my breasts very gently just to enjoy the pure relaxing pleasure of caring for myself. Depending on my mood, I might spend a long while massaging my clitoris and enjoying the warm, tingling pleasures I can give myself. I don't look to climax, but to prolong the enjoyment of sensual relaxation. After about a half hour in the tub, I get out. I'm usually not in a rush to dry myself; I prefer to appreciate my naked wetness for a few moments. After patting myself dry with a soft towel I put on perfume, some powder, but no clothes. Not even a robe. I go into my semi-darkened bedroom, pull back the sheets and sprawl out on the bed, nude and open. I relax for a while; let my mind wander, daydream, enjoy. About this time, energy begins pouring back into my body, so I cooperate. I might do some yoga breathing, or some gentle massage. Sometimes I pull my knees up to my chin and roll gently from side to side. Hugging myself, feeling my breasts against my knees, I sink into a deep feeling of security. I feel I can let go and just be me. Thoughts go through my mind, what went on at work, what I'm going to fix for dinner, fantasies, sometimes wonderful sexual ones, but I just let them drift by and let nature restore me. Often, toward the end of my hour, important insights may come about myself, my family, or my work. I have to emphasize that I don't spend any of this precious hour problem solving. *Insights come* simply as a by-product of tuning in to myself.

The purpose of this period of solitude is not just to take a bath or enjoy a walk. These activities are pleasurable in themselves, but if you make this break a regular practice, you'll also find that the inner joy of your solitude carries over into the rest of your day. Restful alertness becomes a more frequent part of your life. That's the real goal.

Unlock your breathing.

One of the most basic blocks to pleasure is restricted breathing. Most people learn when very young to control feelings by holding the breath. Restricting breathing becomes a habit in response to intense emotion. Anxiety is in large part a result of restricting breathing to control excitement. If you unlock your breathing, you find that situations that formerly made you anxious now produce only intense and pleasurable excitement.

Here's one exercise for unblocking your respiration. Sit comfortably and loosen your clothes so you can breathe easily with your abdomen. Now inhale through the left nostril and hold for a count of four, then exhale through the right nostril. Count four. Then inhale through the right nostril, count four, and exhale through the left. Continue this alternate nostril breathing for three minutes and let yourself enjoy it. The point is to breathe deeply, easily and pleasurably. Notice the streaming energy with each inhalation as oxygen fills your lungs. You'll soon become very relaxed. If at some point during the day you feel tense, this exercise will bring relaxation in a matter of three to five minutes.

Unlock your body.

Muscular rigidity is another obvious component of anhedonia. When you learned to block your breathing to inhibit strong feelings, you also learned to tense your other muscles. Many old emotional wounds get lodged in the psyche partly because of chronic muscle contraction. If you have a tense neck, a sore back, tight jaw, slumped or raised shoulders, you are a good candidate for stretching exercises to break up your muscular tension.

Here are some simple exercises. Do them slowly and mindfully so you feel the full benefit of each exercise and minimize the possibility of injury. Above all, enjoy yourself and don't strain. The goal is to feel the tingling streaming sensations of a good stretch, not to win a contest. Remember that breath is energy, so breathe freely and enjoy energizing yourself.

1. *Pelvic and back stretch.* Lie down on the floor and get comfortable on your back. Now sit up, extending your hands above your head. Reach toward the ceiling and breathe easily through your abdomen. Feel the energy streaming up from the base of your spine toward your head and into your arms. Now continue to bend forward, stretching toward your toes until you feel a warm tingling sensation in your lower back. Breathe easily and feel the warmth of the stretch. Hold this position for a count of ten. Then lie back down and rest.

2. *Pelvic rotation.* Stand up and set your feet shoulder width apart. Relax and place your hands on your hips. Breathe deeply, and slowly move your hips around in a wide circular motion. Try not to lead with your shoulders or head, but instead allow your pelvis to initiate all the motion. You may feel awkward at first, but continue the rotation in one direction five to seven times; you'll start to feel the release of energy. Rest a moment, then do the same movement in the opposite direction another five to seven times. You may feel streaming energy in your legs, buttocks, pelvis, groin, and back. Enjoy it.

3. *Neck rotation.* Sit upright in a firm chair. Relax and breathe deeply, then let your chin drop slowly toward your chest. Continue to breathe normally while you slowly roll

your head to the right so that your right ear moves toward your shoulder. Feel the pleasant stretching in your neck, and keep rolling your head back until your chin is pointing toward the ceiling. Then continue further until you have returned to the original position with your chin forward toward your chest. Try five rotations to the right, then five to the left. You will unlock your neck, upper back, and shoulders. This exercise is great for avoiding tension headaches.

4. *Pelvic rock.* Lie on your back and relax. Then slowly bend your knees until your feet are flat on the floor. Breathe normally and relax. Next, press your tailbone against the floor to create a small arch in your back. Then slowly rock your pelvis back so that your back is pressing against the floor. Now repeat this playful rocking motion five to ten times. Enjoy the energy in your legs, hips, and back.

5. *Spinal roll.* Lie comfortably on your back and extend your arms out from your shoulders with your palms down. Relax, breathe deeply, and pull your knees up toward your chest in a comfortable position. Now roll your head to the right while you roll your hips to the left until your legs are resting on the floor. Rest, breathe, then turn your head to the left while you roll your legs to the right until they rest together on the floor. Repeat this five times, and feel the tension flowing out of your back.

6. *Forward bend.* Stand erect, breathe deeply and raise your hands above your head. Continue breathing easily while you slowly bend forward until your hands are dangling toward the floor. Don't bounce or strain to touch the floor. Let your attention go to the stretching in your legs and lower back. Feel the tingly warmth, relax, and breathe. Now slowly return to the upright position.

Finish off a set of these exercises with two or three minutes of relaxation. Lie on the floor, on your back, close your eyes, breathe deeply, and enjoy your rejuvenating rush of energy.

Create optimum health.

Radiant health is an obvious source of inner joy and clearly fundamental to maximum enjoyment. A state of peak health creates the physiological conditions for pleasure in just feeling fully alive. The most recent scientific evidence suggests strongly that health today is largely a matter of choice. You decide whether you're going to be fit and slender or sedentary and flabby. You determine whether your diet includes wholesome foods low in fats, sugar, salt, caffeine, and alcohol or whether you eat without restraint. You decide whether to smoke or not. Enough has been written about these matters for us to make just three suggestions you might like:

1. Take one day off per week just to enjoy yourself.
2. Do something to perk up your environment at work or at home.
3. Give yourself permission to do something silly just for the fun of it. If you let yourself do something silly once in a while, you'll develop a sense of freedom that you'll cherish always.

Share a sexual fantasy with a lover and explore the possibilities of acting it out.

Go slowly and don't force yourself or your lover to do anything you don't want to do. Exploring sexual fantasies with a tender and sensitive partner provides many opportunities for discovering new parts of yourself and expanding your emotional freedom. It's a delightful way to root out any hidden fears of self-discovery and to build basic self-trust.

Choose to be satisfied in the present.

Whenever you find yourself thinking "I'll be happy when . . ." stop yourself and say, "*I will choose to be happy now.*" You can—if you stop idealizing the future and give yourself permission to enjoy your present. When you find yourself wasting time or becoming overly caught up in some romantic past or hoped-for future, a buzzer should go off in your mind. Look for something to do immediately to increase your present-moment satisfaction. You could read a book or go to a movie. If you feel like working, go ahead. Anything is preferable to fooling yourself with dreams that begin "I'll be happy when . . ." This doesn't mean there's anything wrong with dreams. It just means that healthy dreams begin with "I can be happy now and, by deepening my appreciation, even happier in the future."

Make a list of what you appreciate most about your life.

You'll find that most of the items are available to you all the time. You might list friends, family, your job, a pet, an upcoming vacation, a hobby—anything at all that makes you happy. This may sound like grandmotherly advice to "count your blessings." That's OK. Since when was grandmother wrong about counting blessings? It's a sound practice for uplifting your spirits and deepening your appreciation of your present moments.

These are basic strategies for overcoming the fear of pleasure and the self-forfeiting actions that flow from it. Naturally, this list isn't exhaustive. But if you'll make several of the suggestions part of your life you'll soon discover many other ways to increase your daily satisfactions. When you stop thinking that pleasure is something that must be pursued and discover that it is available all over the place and right now and in great abundance, you'll have mastered a primary principle of inner joy.

IV

Your Success Profile

You're not a man. You're a machine.
—GEORGE BERNARD SHAW

Being, not doing, is my first joy.
—THEODORE ROETHKE

THERE IS AN EPIDEMIC in our culture, a social disease that won't go away with a pill or vaccination. It's the belief that ultimate satisfaction is yours when you have finally amassed all the money, power, and glamour you covet. You see the effect of this delusion all around you: a wholesale cultural striving after the material attributes of success at the expense of the inner joy and primary life experiences that make success truly worthwhile. You find millions engaged in the anhedonic struggle for the external trappings of success—money, power, possessions, sex—while family life, health, personal integrity, and the ability to enjoy life suffer steady decline.

What have you already paid, physically and emotionally, for your success? What will the human costs be in the future? Are the satisfactions you have achieved worth the price?

These are difficult questions. No matter where you stand on the ladder of the American dream, your money and power are rarely enough if along the way your marriage falls apart, you begin chewing Maalox like candy, you become so tense that you hardly enjoy a day off, you compromise your values so often that protecting your self-interest becomes the mainstay of your personal ethics, or you often wonder if life has any real meaning beyond your ability to earn a bigger paycheck.

Much has been written in condemnation of what William James called "the American worship of the bitch-goddess Success." We do not subscribe to this view. The problem, as we see it, is not success, but what people do to themselves in their quest to achieve it. The solution to anhedonic success striving is not to retreat from the challenge of success, but to develop the basic knowledge that enables you to relish every moment of life. This is what we call the *200 percent success profile*—full inner development to complement maximum external achievement.

Having witnessed the mixed rewards their parents reaped from one-sided success, a new generation of young men and women is struggling to define a new vision. As one young lawyer put it, "The sixties didn't just die. They're still part of my life, just as the Depression is still part of my parents' lives." Among the new upwardly mobile generation now in their twenties, ambition, according to one survey, is regarded as the least important trait necessary for personal happiness. At the top of the list are noncompetitive values such as being loved, personal growth, and leisure for self-exploration. Money remains a confusing issue. Buried just beneath those aspirations for personal development is fear, on the one hand of not having enough money to live a comfortable life, and on the other hand of getting locked into a suffocating job in pursuit of economic security.

Lacking an easy solution to this conflict, many young pacesetters are opting for a delay of game. They are putting off marriage and children, and in some cases career choices, in the hopes of running into the right solution to their personal dreams. Never before has a whole generation had the wealth and privilege to postpone accepting the responsibilities and commitments of adulthood. The outcome of this experiment is yet to be determined. For some it may be a useful interlude that leads to a life congruent with their ideals. For others, it may lead to the deterioration of their lives into the exclusive pursuit of self-gratification, and a new anhedonic trap. To miss the opportunity for commitment to family, to raising children, to making a contribution to the world, is to miss life's greatest joys.

The issue in this chapter is how your personal vision of success (and your efforts to get there) are affecting your inner life. Human beings are created with a nearly unlimited capacity for growth. We can always extend ourselves to greater heights. No doubt this is basic to the American dream that given an opportunity, perseverance, and hard work, anyone can achieve the better things in life. What has been sadly overlooked is the one-sided application of this effort toward the acquisition of things worth *having* at the expense of the things worth *being*. Now the pendulum is swinging in the opposite direction. The culture is awakening to the need to reach not just for wealth but also for depth; not just for quantity but also for quality of experience; not just for exciting pleasures but also for lasting satisfactions. The challenge is integration, and the issues involved are vital.

Defining Success in Your Own Terms

The first thing to understand in assessing your own success profile is that there is no one to compare yourself with but you. Since childhood, parents and society have bombarded you with expectations about what you ought to become and what you ought to achieve. These expectations are not easily set aside. Nevertheless, do remember that you are unique; only you can know what you truly want out of life. The final measure of your personal success as a human being is whether you manage to create a life of abundant satisfactions that you reap from living life on your own terms.

But what about money? The American definition of success hasn't changed much over the last hundred years. What you own (not what you are) is still the primary criterion.

Given this heritage, most people are reluctant to consider the folly of this one-sided view until they begin to discover its consequences for themselves.

George Bernard Shaw once wrote: "There are two tragedies in life. One is not to get your heart's desire. The other is to get it." Here is the hidden pitfall and primary challenge in shaping your personal vision of success. No matter what your dream, achieving it will rarely live up to all your expectations. There will always be personal costs that you did not expect and parts of yourself that remain unfulfilled. The practical implication of this hard fact of life is that genuine success cannot be defined as the achievement of any particular goal.

Success is not static. It isn't the final reward for a single achievement—becoming president of the company, getting married, making a million dollars, writing a best-seller, having children, or buying a huge house. Real success is dynamic. It is growth. It is discovering opportunities each day to express your talents and abilities to the fullest. It is learning to create your life joyfully even when things may not be working out as planned. It is knowing each day that your work has meaning. It is making your life an adventure and living not just for yourself, but also for a better world.

This definition of success makes some people uncomfortable because it doesn't include any absolute measures. There are no status symbols to prove you have made it or any lists of perquisites to prove how powerful you are. The issue of personal success is taken out of the arena where you judge yourself by what others think of you and is placed squarely on your shoulders, what you think of yourself. Once you begin to define success dynamically, the key issues are those of personal values and satisfactions. Are you enjoying your life fully? Enthusiastic about what you are doing? Able to live according to your own values?

Through the interviews with hundreds of men and women caught up in the struggle to succeed, we have identified typical signs of an anhedonic success profile. You may well be caught on a treadmill of self-destructive striving if you:

- feel chronically short of time
- doubt whether your work or life has meaning
- are reluctant to go on vacation for fear of falling behind
- often compromise your values and beliefs
- find it difficult to enjoy leisure because you can't stop thinking about problems at work
- feel vaguely guilty whenever you relax, especially when you're facing a deadline
- spend less and less time with your family as the years go by, even though you resolve to change
- move, walk, and eat rapidly because you don't want to waste even a minute
- tend to be impatient, become upset when you have to stand in line
- avoid delegating responsibility for fear of losing control over your sphere of power
- frequently take work home and work late into the night
- feel all your success is due to speed and hard work rather than insight and creativity
- have developed a hostile attitude toward others, especially those people with whom you may be competing for promotion
- view everything in terms of "how much" and "how many"
- feel you always have to be "on," whether you're at work or at a party
- regularly suffer heartburn, headaches, muscle spasms, and/or anxiety
- frequently feel tense
- worry about your ability to keep your job

A less common but equally destructive success profile also emerged from our survey. It comes not from self-destructive striving, but from the new philosophy of not striving at all. We found it primarily among young people determined not to get into a life-style that they view as akin to a prison sentence. Avoid too much responsibility, postpone commitments, take it easy, be laid back. These are the primary characteristics of the new anhedonic success profile. The run from ambition becomes the flight into purposelessness. Here are other characteristic attitudes and behaviors:

- a fear of traditional commitments, marriage and children appearing only as a potential burden offering little or no joy
- cynicism, the belief that the world is not about to change, so why bother

- lack of personal goals, only a vague vision of the future
- inability to sustain love relationships, difficulty accepting the responsibility of intimacy
- boredom
- the desire to live comfortably by extending the minimum possible effort
- the absence of any desire to make a contribution or make the world a better place
- obsessive concern with personal pleasure
- the absence of ambition

Strive to climb the ladder and win status or wealth—or eschew the clamor for upward mobility and settle into a laid-back life-style. These two choices are the Scylla and Charybdis of the new American dream that promises not only a comfortable life-style but also personal growth. Now that the pendulum of success expectations has swung in both directions the anhedonic consequences of a life at either extreme have become clear. The new challenge is to find your own middle ground where a 200 percent success profile becomes possible.

The Superachiever

The desire to win is so strong in some people that they have cultivated the ability to push themselves at a peak of their capacity for weeks and months at a time. These are the superachievers, who have learned how to gear up for high performance under constant pressure. They can work long into the night when necessary, get very little sleep, and be bright and cheerful the next day. Nothing makes them shine more than a difficult problem that stretches their creative abilities. Their most distinguishing trait is the evident relish they take in almost everything they do. They have an awesome ability to enjoy their lives fully.

Most people who function at this high level can't explain how they manage to push so hard without becoming anhedonic. On occasion they may break stride and slip back into a state where pressure begins to take its toll in fatigue or anxiety. What causes the rhythm to be lost and later regained is usually only vaguely understood. "I take off for the weekend," says one corporation president, explaining what he does to get back in sync when his gears begin to grind. "Sleep," says another superachiever, "I slow way down and catch up on my rest." The remedy for a third is to get up every morning at six thirty and play tennis until eight. "If I stick to that routine for a week, have a sauna, let the problems sit on the back burner for a while, I snap back into shape." Most of the time these personal methods of reattunement work. The anhedonic striving along with the tension and anxiety passes; the old energy and clarity reemerge on their own. In some cases, however, the anhedonic symptoms don't diminish. In fact, they may grow, steadily diminishing performance and exacerbating anxiety.

When a superachiever gets caught in an anhedonic trap and can't get out, panic may set in. The experience can be emotionally devastating enough to prompt the search for help. "I felt like I was cracking up," is how one executive racehorse described his panic when he began suffering tension headaches and losing his sharp concentration. "I was always at the top. I could push myself and love every minute of it; then the sand started shifting under my feet. I began having doubts. I couldn't count on myself anymore." We have worked with many of these superachievers who have lost the inner attunement necessary to sustain their high level of functioning. In the process, we have gained insights into the dynamics of balancing a high-performance life-style with the personal growth necessary for inner joy.

Evelyn Davis has been a superachiever since grade school. Her first taste of big success came when she won a statewide speech contest in eighth grade. Through high school and college she managed to rank at the top of her class despite her busy social life. Blond and brown-eyed, with a California tan, she has never had to worry about what to do on a Friday night. After college she went on to business school, then to a series of jobs that finally brought her, at thirty-four, to the position of executive vice-president with a nationally known department store. Five years ago she married Michael. Two years later she had her daughter.

"I've been pleased with my life," she says. "When I've set out to achieve a goal, I've usually succeeded. Hard work and a lot of drive have been my two most important assets. In a world still dominated by men, you have to do more than just keep pace; you've got to prove that you are twice as effective as any man who's also being considered for the job. I don't consider myself special. I've simply tried to give my work all I've got and play my life to the limit."

Despite her modesty, Evelyn is clearly a woman of exceptional energy and unusual ability. With a job that takes her to New York or Europe almost every month, and very demanding hours at her West Coast home office, she could very easily lose touch with her family. To make sure that didn't happen, she started indulging her long-standing desire to become a gourmet cook. She also runs every other morning with Michael. Several nights a week she is out to a party or an opening.

"I've always thrived on the hectic pace," she explains. "There's never been any problem before. The pressure didn't get me down, it always made everything else more exciting."

And yet shortly before her thirty-fifth birthday something began to go wrong. She started suffering from several uncomfortable symptoms that severely diminished her energy and performance. At first she noticed an unusual nasal congestion and dull pressure over the eyes. Later she began having vertigo and ringing in the ears. She tried to ignore the symptoms for a month and got extra rest. When her symptoms only got worse, she consulted her family doctor. His examination did not reveal any specific problem, so he recommended that she see an ear, nose, and throat specialist. After an elaborate set of tests, including a neurological examination, her doctor concluded that there was no underlying illness.

This report might have been comforting had the symptoms begun to abate in time, but they didn't. They got worse.

The more uncomfortable she felt, the more anxious she became about her difficulties at work. Evelyn was slipping from her smooth high-performance life-style and floundering in growing anhedonia. Finally she sought help at our holistic health center.

Our examination confirmed the previous findings. Her symptoms were not a result of organic illness. During her first session, however, a clue to her problem surfaced. "I took the TM course," she said. "I thought it might help me cope with stress and be a quick way to recharge my batteries, but I haven't gotten much out of it. I close my eyes and say my mantra, but nothing much happens. Sometimes it just gives me a headache." This inability to experience relaxation from a simple meditation says something important. Evelyn doesn't know how to let go.

Evelyn's history and our tests indicate that her symptoms result from excessive stress that she covered up for a long time but never really learned to manage. Using biofeedback equipment, we measured her ability to relax her forehead and her neck muscles. She had great difficulty. Even though she appeared calm, psychological examinations showed an elevated anxiety level simmering underneath her collected exterior. The slight dark rings under her eyes and the furrowed brow reflected chronic fatigue and inner tension. She said that her symptoms got worse whenever she was under pressure. After executive meetings her headaches and muscle tension were often most severe.

Evelyn was aware of stress and thought she was taking steps to cope with it. "I meditate, I run, I cook," she said. "What more can I do?" What she could not see was the *way* she did all these things. She tackled meditation and running with the same competitive zeal that she used in any business undertaking. For her every activity was a performance with measured outcome, and she was determined always to be at the top. Evelyn only knew how to function in high gear; inner serenity was not part of her baseline experience. As a result, her efforts to cope with stress only compounded her problem.

To solve her stress problem without losing her drive,

Evelyn had to make an inner shift to experience more ease. Her initial response to this idea was wholly negative. "I've made it because I *am* ambitious and know how to get what I want. I can't give that up," she insisted in a manner typical of superachievers afraid of losing their dynamism. She feared trying to develop a new personal style because she had spent twenty years developing one that had taken her very far. After much persuasion, she finally agreed to try a program designed to assist her in making her inner shift. The reason behind her decision was simple; she had no alternative. Stress was gradually destroying her. Here is a synopsis of what she did; the full program is explained at the end of this chapter.

For the first few weeks, Evelyn's progress was slow. She kept putting too much effort into her relaxation exercises because she couldn't shake the habit of always trying to do her best. After several weeks, she finally had the crucial insight. "I was sitting in a meeting where we were discussing the new line of cruise wear; I felt we were bogging down in trivia, and I started becoming anxious and impatient. I had stacks of work back at my desk, and I hated wasting time. A knot formed in my stomach, and I felt my neck getting tight. Then it struck me. 'Why am I doing this to myself?' All at once I realized that *I* was creating the tension and *I* could stop it, so I sat back in my chair, and began noticing my breathing. With one ear I followed the meeting, but basically I tuned it out for a few minutes. Very shortly, waves of relaxation began moving throughout my body. Stomach, neck, shoulders all let go. After about five minutes, I had discovered that quiet place, a calm inner meadow. When I tuned back into the meeting, I felt refreshed and the impatience was gone. I felt like the Chesire cat who had discovered a secret as I looked at all the other tense faces around the table.

"When I walked out of the meeting, I didn't feel drained, even though the meeting was mostly a waste of time. I went back to my office with plenty of energy and tackled a stack of work in just two hours."

Once Evelyn achieved this insight, the real work of transforming her success profile began. She stopped fighting herself. She saw that inner joy and personal drive can coexist, even complement each other. The key is personal integration and raising self-understanding and self-mastery to a higher level where it becomes possible to do less, expend less energy in wasteful tension, and therefore accomplish much more.

Achieving this inner shift did not require that Evelyn learn new growth techniques as much as develop new attitudes toward the ones she was already using. For example, she stopped timing her runs, and began focusing on enjoying herself. That meant not running to the point of exhaustion but at an easy pace that left her refreshed and energized. The result was a breakthrough. "I've been running about five miles a day for over two years now," she explains, "and I never had the transcendental experience so many runners talk about. Yesterday it happened: after about two miles I was in an easy stride when I noticed that I felt like I was standing still. My legs were moving, my breathing was deep and regular, but there was absolutely no sense of strain. The quiet joy of this experience was indescribable. I don't know how I could have missed it for so long." Gradually Evelyn realized that this experience of ease and inner joy need not be relegated to a few minutes while running but can become a baseline part of living.

This insight also helped Evelyn begin getting results from her daily twenty-minute Transcendental Meditation sessions. She stopped trying so hard to get something out of meditation. After four months of meditating correctly, she became enthusiastic about TM for the first time. "I couldn't see why so many high-powered people thought TM was so worthwhile. Now I try never to miss a meditation. It makes me feel great."

A third technique that proved helpful to Evelyn was differential relaxation. The core of this simple technique is learning to relax a specific muscle while remaining fully engaged in normal activity. For example, when Evelyn felt her neck getting tense in a meeting, she learned to sit back in her chair and notice what was going on in her body. She could usually find one or two areas of muscular tension. To relax them, all she needed to do was let her attention feel the tension in a specific muscle. This technique takes practice, but once you get the hang of it, you can use it anywhere, anytime. The key is learning through practice that letting your attention gently notice the tension, just be with it and feel it, is enough to relax it. Of course, if you do this in a meeting, you may miss a few words, but so what. When you shift your full attention back to the meeting after achieving greater ease, you will have doubled your potential effectiveness and power of concentration.

What happened to Evelyn one year later? On the surface, her life hasn't changed all that much. She is still working long hours, flying to New York and Paris, and relishing the challenges of her work and being a mother. The significant changes can't be measured in the language of "how many" and "how much." Her physical symptoms of stress are gone. Her energy level is high. More important, she has stabilized an inner shift that took her upward to a level of inner joy.

"It doesn't matter what I am doing now," she says. "I can be pushing to meet a deadline or taking a walk with my husband and daughter, or doing the dishes, for that matter, and the underlying joy is there. It's a matter of choice. I create my experience; I've learned how to create it joyfully."

Caution: Workaholic at Work

There he is in his office working late again. He called his wife to say he wouldn't be home for dinner; she's used to that. Now it's 9:00 P.M., time to pack up his briefcase. In a few minutes he has collected from his overloaded desk more paperwork than he can possibly do at home before he goes to bed. On the way out the door, the heavy briefcase is reassuring. He is a man of weight; he works hard; the company can't do without him, or at least that is what he would like to believe. Lurking just underneath that self-importance, however, is a desperate fear of failure. He is vaguely aware that he gets too bogged down in needless paperwork and that his thinking is going stale. He occasionally has the feeling of pedaling very hard and getting nowhere. So pervasive is his concern about his job that he only rarely takes time off and when he does, he usually doesn't enjoy it. He is a workaholic.

Some people work long hours because they love their jobs and feel they're making a genuine contribution. Others spend most of their waking hours at work because they have become addicted to their jobs as a means of self-protection from their real feelings. The former are hard workers; the latter are workaholics. The principal difference between the two lies in the ability to stand outside of the job. Both enjoy working hard, but the hard worker can separate himself from it. He doesn't take his problems home, so he is able to derive enormous enjoyment from family and nonwork activities. The workaholic, on the other hand, is truly enjoying himself only at work, so he unconsciously strives never to be far from his work responsibilities. When he tells his wife and children that he is too busy to take a vacation, he would like to think it's true. In truth, he doesn't take vacations because he finds them boring and feels at a loss whenever he is away from the preset routine and pressure of the office. The ability to stand outside the job is crucial to creativity. That's why the workaholic tends toward routines and is excessively preoccupied with the stuff of business (memos, letters, meetings) rather than its substance, creative thinking.

The emotional price of workaholism is usually paid in the home, where neglect often leads to resentment and divorce. "He's married to his work, not to me," said the wife of one workaholic. Children also suffer from this absentee father.

Not until Larry's wife threatened to leave him if he didn't join her in counseling did he begin to wake up to what his workaholic success profile was doing to his family and his wife.

A thirty-two-year-old lawyer, Larry married Barbara six years ago in his last year of law school. They now have two children. "For the first few years," Barbara explains, "I was lonely, but I knew Larry was under tremendous pressure. First it was grades, then Law Review. After graduation, it was becoming a partner. Now the excuses have run out. Larry is well established but nothing has changed. He still brings home work every night; we rarely go out, and we don't have many friends. The children ask why their daddy never spends any time with them. Our sex life is worse than terrible; it is nonexistent. He is too busy to see that our marriage is in trouble."

Larry's initial response was typical of the workaholic. He was deeply hurt by his wife's outburst. "I didn't know you felt things were so bad," he responded. "I'm trying so hard. Can't you see that I've been doing it all for you and the kids?" He broke off in an obvious effort to hold back tears. "I've been struggling so hard to make it and I thought I was doing OK. Now you tell me I am a failure." He began to sob quietly; a backlog of deep hurts was pushing its way to the surface.

The primary psychological characteristic of the workaholic is a well-disguised low self-esteem. Tell this to someone who is losing him or herself in work and you'll trigger a torrent of denials. "That's ridiculous. I'm a success. How could I have a low self-esteem?" Look behind the facade, and the real picture comes into focus. The workaholic's desperate desire to stay busy is in reality a desperate run from failure. Once Larry began to see that despite his success as a lawyer he was failing as a human being, the dam burst and the source of his low self-esteem opened up.

"Both of my parents were lawyers. My mother is still in practice with a small firm and my father was a law-school professor. All my life I heard about what a great man my father is. It started when I was very young. One of my earliest memories is my grandmother telling me I shouldn't go into my father's study because he was working. By the time I was in first grade, I knew all about how he had skipped so many grades in school, graduated from Harvard Law School at twenty-two, and was a goddamned genius. My life has been one long effort to measure up.

"Did my dad ever spend any time with me? Sure, to find out how I was doing in school, help me with a problem; but we never spent time having fun, he was always too busy for fun." Larry grew up with the unspoken belief that the way to earn his parents' love was to try as hard as he could to measure up to his father's achievements. Larry still labors under the same misconception: The way to earn Barbara's love and the love of his children is to work as long and as hard as he can. What he brings home at night is not his warmth and affection, but a heavy briefcase and his achievements. The unspoken message in Larry's head is: "I'm not worth very much, no one wants my love." Because he esteems himself so little, he can't see how wrong he is.

In most marriages that deteriorate as far as this one, divorce is the probable outcome. There is too much resentment to resolve and too many wounds to heal. In this case, the commitment to save the marriage and the underlying love were strong enough to beat the odds. Larry and Barbara were willing to give each other the energy, time, and attention necessary for healing and growth.

After the complaints, hurts, and resentments were brought out into the open, Larry and Barbara were able to agree on specific steps to change Larry's (and therefore his family's) success profile. The heart of their agreement was very simple. They would set aside specific times when Larry would devote himself to the children and plan outings that the whole family would enjoy together. They also agreed to make time each week to spend together as they had when they were first dating. This may sound artificial or mechanical, and at first it is. This plan only works if all concerned hold each other to their agreements without making exceptions. Gradually a new and natural rhythm takes over.

At the outset, breaking workaholic habits is very difficult. "My palms sweat and my stomach knotted the first time I declined an important case to be with my family," remembers Larry. This initial stress is actually helpful for breaking workaholic habits because it forces you to use time more judiciously.

To make time for his family and to continue to progress

at work, Larry had to eliminate wasteful activities that primarily reinforced his feeling of self-importance. This is the key to breaking the back of anhedonic workaholism. He stopped reading and writing so many memos. He stopped going to meetings that weren't really important to his work. No longer did he make himself accessible to so many phone callers. He made a point of keeping the length of his phone conversations to a minimum. At the end of the day, he didn't bother to take home any work that he knew he wouldn't be able to do. He made a point of leaving his work on his desk so he could leave his problems in the office. That allowed him to enjoy his evening at home and arrive refreshed the next day able to begin work at optimum efficiency.

"To break the habit of wasting time on unimportant tasks," says Larry, "I asked myself from time to time throughout the day whether what I was doing at the moment was the most important thing I could be doing." This is a simple technique that can dramatically improve your use of time from the first day you try it.

Once Larry began making enjoyment of his wife and family a priority in his personal vision of success, opportunities were created for the marriage to heal. Barbara no longer feared that Larry would back out of plans at the last moment, so she began creating family outings and arranging romantic evenings. They bought season symphony tickets and made sure that they never had to give the tickets away. They went on picnics in the summer and skiing weekends in the winter. They went to movies and plays together.

They also began rediscovering their sexual desire for one another and the joyful intimacy that only wonderful sex can provide. As with many typical workaholics, Larry's performance pressure and fear of failure inhibited his sexual freedom. "When she starts giving signals that she would like to make love, I immediately start feeling anxious about whether I can make her come. It's a reflex," said Larry early in therapy. Barbara interpreted Larry's response as rejection. "I can feel him freezing up," Barbara says. "He doesn't say anything, so what am I to think? I don't turn him on!"

This pact of mutual silence and misunderstanding gradually asphyxiates sexual desire. Your sex life can't be isolated from your life. Larry created his own sexual anxiety by expecting that he ought to be able to push himself at work for twelve hours and then come home and be ready for sex. It just doesn't work that way. Workaholics often like to think of themselves as machines; when the sexual apparatus doesn't cooperate, they are stuck with feelings of failure and self-loathing. The irony about this self-created sexual anxiety is that it can be solved easily by making sexual pleasure a priority and setting aside ample time for unpressured sexual pleasuring.

Changing a workaholic success profile requires compromises. You can't expect to succeed in making more time for your family and for personal growth without a new philosophy. Larry began to change when he could finally measure himself against his father without self-rejection. His father died of a heart attack at age fifty-nine. The question Larry faced was simple. Did he want to struggle all his life to make enough money so he could afford his first heart attack? Or did he want to take control of his life and create a future of inner joy and lasting satisfactions? Larry did become less competitive. His priorities did change. His desire to enjoy his family rose to rank equally with his desire for success at work. He started putting in fewer hours at the firm, and occasionally turned cases down. Does this mean that he accomplished less? That is a very difficult question. He may not be working so hard at the office, but he is a much better father at home. Is winning a big case a greater accomplishment than raising a child well? This is a question that most workaholics fail to ask until it is too late and they are already in the middle of a divorce.

Your Success Profile

The New Dreamers

What about the success profile of the new generation weaned from college on the slogans of the sixties and now about to cross that once distant age barrier, the thirty-year mark? No one talks about a generation gap anymore, because the majority of those who once decried the establishment are now well on their way as its inheritors with their three-piece suits, short-hair, and attaché cases—as if to say that the upheavals of the sixties have long since been forgotten. Or have they? The newest studies of young pacesetters of the new generation indicate that the generation gap may not be as wide as it once was, but it is still there.

Many men and women in their twenties or early thirties are aware of all that we have said so far about the pitfalls of a success profile built around the accumulation of wealth. They reject this vision of the American dream. Their view of success includes ample time for personal growth and leisure. They are not willing to become coronary candidates just to climb one more rung on the corporate ladder. Nor are they willing to rape the land and pollute the cities to make an extra dollar. They are trying to balance conflicting internal and external pressures to create lives rich in personal satisfactions.

They take a comfortable life as a given, but they don't want to work too hard. They want to see problems of poverty and injustice resolved, but they don't want to sacrifice time needed for personal growth. They would like to have a lot of money (a million dollars would do as a starter) but they're wary of getting locked into any job that makes them just another cog in the corporate machine. More than anything else, they want to be loving and enjoy loving relationships, but they are wary of commitments—marriage and children—that put sustaining love to the test. The new pacesetters mold their personal visions of success out of trade-offs between these conflicting desires. Is this balancing act leading to a new integrated vision of success or to a moral paralysis that hides an underlying selfishness with uplifting talk about personal growth?

On the threshold of thirty, Allen is typical of the new generation of pacesetting young men. Ten years ago he wore his long hair and jeans as defiant symbols that he would never become part of the establishment. He looks back on those Ivy League years with a mix of nostalgia and cynicism. "The Kent State—Cambodia bombing student strike of 1970 was the real watershed," he says. "We thought we were really on the verge of something great. How naive! Three months later, it was all forgotten. After one big bang, the student movement died of a sudden coronary."

Allen sees his generation's obsession with personal growth as a logical outgrowth of the demise of the early student movement. "Anyone who thought they could change the world eventually saw how foolish they were. The forces at work are too big; and no one was really ready to make personal sacrifices. Talk, as they say, is cheap, especially when it's about ideals. I think we all started to see we were just as messed up as our parents. The new imperative became: 'Change yourself before you spout off about changing society.'"

Allen took that imperative to heart. Over the past decade, he can measure his personal history as an odyssey through the land of personal growth movements. "I tried a lot of things," he explains. "Some were very beneficial, others not so, but I didn't become fanatical about anything. I'd learned my lesson." Among the techniques on Allen's personal growth résumé are TM, est, yoga, running, natural foods, the Alexander technique, polarity therapy, and communal living. He also adds with emphasis, "I spent a lot of energy working on liberating my sexuality and trying to become a truly loving human being," which is another way of saying that he has slept with more women than he can count.

Allen is fond of talking about his trade-offs. To secure a financial future without getting locked into a nine-to-five job, Allen pursued his interest in computers. He is now a programmer with an annual income of over $24,000, and his hours are his own as long as he produces results. "My work suits my needs well . . . I get paid for my talent, not for my time. It's the ideal trade-off between having to earn a living and not wanting to work at all." Allen also talks about trade-offs in his love relationships. To maintain his personal freedom, he feels it is necessary to avoid any long-term commitments, by which he means marriage and children.

"You can't have a family without economic pressure," he believes, "and that I don't want." The thought of marriage reminds him of his parents, whom he sees as not unhappy but stuck on a no-growth treadmill. The trade-off, says Allen, is between "being loving and getting stuck. I have one woman who I've been seeing for some time now. I love her and feel I will always be committed to her on some level. I just don't want the form to get rigid. Monogamy isn't for me."

Listen to Allen tell you about himself for fifty minutes, and you might be convinced that he has achieved a success profile perfectly congruent with his needs. Listen a little longer, however, and a little secret, his reason for seeking help, slips out. Allen is unhappy with his sex life. The embarrassing problem is that he has lost his sex drive, and he is worried about it. This is surprising until you examine recent studies of sexual satisfaction and find out that Allen is not in the minority. Despite the new sexual freedoms, fewer than half of the men and women under thirty are satisfied with their sex lives. Many complain of simply losing interest in sex. This can happen much later in life, but in the early twenties it is startling.

What's going on? No textbook answers explain this phenomenon. We are confronting a new psychological problem emerging in a new social context. For the first time in history, the ability to control the reproductive cycle and the new emphasis on personal gratification are allowing the complete separation of sex from its central role in sustaining the species. The deepest pleasure and intimacy have been stripped of personal commitment and responsibility. Initially you might think this would prove enormously liberating and open many opportunities for expanding sexual joy. The fact is, it hasn't.

Sex has been reduced to the same level of personal gratification as that of a fine meal (ergo, the new manuals that compare sex to cooking). The connection with the joy of children and marriage, where satisfactions stem from commitment to another human being's growth and well-being, has been lost. The new *fear* is that sex may lead to children or marriage, and the commitment to someone other than self. Abortion is the new weapon to cope with that contingency. Implicit within the new sexual attitudes is the perverse belief that there is little joy to be derived from a sexual relationship other than gratification of personal desires for pleasure and tenderness.

We have not yet seen the full implications of this radically new attitude toward sex, but it is clear that for many people, such as Allen, it contributes to an exclusive self-preoccupation and a new anhedonic trap. This observation is supported by an interesting new study of young men under thirty. The single event that they report brings them the most joy and happiness is, believe it or not, having children. More than work, more than love of a mate, more than money, success, or fame, young fathers report that children are the source of greatest happiness. Least happy of the young men and women surveyed are those who report that they plan to remain single and childless.

Today's young people don't see themselves as loners, nor do they lack friends, so it's hard to conclude that their unhappiness stems from loneliness. The more likely cause is the failure to achieve the personal growth that they seek. It just may be that having children is the ultimate growth experience, because it forces the young parent to transcend personal boundaries in complete devotion to another human being.

Allen was initially skeptical about the relation between his self-preoccupation and diminished sexual drive. Nevertheless, he agreed to try several recommendations. First, it was suggested that he stop worrying about his diminished sex drive and start listening to what his inner voice might be trying to tell him. Instead of fighting the internal messages with his cortical expectations, he might accept his inner directives and consider a period of temporary abstinence. With the time and energy he had been devoting to the pursuit of women, he might consider trying to find a useful outlet that would bring him satisfaction and make some kind of contribution. We talked about the vitality Allen felt in college when he was active in politics. Perhaps that effort was not as foolish as he had come to think.

Over five months, it gradually became apparent from his renewed self-confidence and absence of anxiety that he was achieving a major inner shift that not only resolved his initial complaints but opened a new dimension of inner joy. At first he worried about giving up sex for a while. "What if my sex drive never comes back?" was his fear. After about two weeks he began enjoying his new independence and decided he might actually like getting politically involved once again. Where to start? He supported the politics of a presidential candidate from California, so he finally decided to call the candidate's office in Los Angeles and find out what he could do. That led to the candidate's local campaign office. Allen had found a new outlet for his creative energies.

For two and a half months he didn't date. At one point he commented, "The sense of freedom I am feeling is really ecstatic." Some time later, he renewed his relationship with a woman he had been seeing intermittently for two years. With the shift toward inner joy, he stopped worrying about his sexual performance. His anxieties, inhibitions, and problems disappeared on their own. He is not yet ready for marriage, and doubtful that he will ever want to have children, but he is on his way to a new level of personal integration that will expand his opportunities for deep satisfactions and inner joys.

Obstacles to Transforming Your Success Profile

Perhaps you have decided that you want to make some changes in your success profile. Between your intention to take hold of your life and the changes you want to make lie the psychological rewards you are reaping for remaining exactly the way you are. These psychological dividends explain why change is often difficult. The rewards cause psychological inertia. Awareness of these resistances is the key to surmounting them. Here are several to consider.

Your current success profile may be providing feelings of self-importance that you're reluctant to challenge.

Nothing is more difficult than letting the hot air out of your own ego. Still, that may be what you must do to find out what really provides satisfaction and where your doors of opportunity actually lie. A false sense of self-importance based on confusion between image and actuality of success is the greatest obstacle to a dynamic success profile. It is so easy to get caught up in memos, heavy briefcases, long hours, and appearances because these are the signs we use to convince ourselves and others that even if we haven't made it yet, we're at least on the way. All too often, that leads to anhedonic striving and a tremendous waste of energy or, in the words of one executive friend, "doing more but accomplishing less."

The look of success is helpful to a point, but far more important are high levels of energy, creativity, and personal enthusiasm. You can't develop these qualities as long as you keep yourself caught on the treadmill of constant striving. Instead, you have to learn how to turn the process around so you can "do less but accomplish more." This requires changing your success profile. Too bad that some people would rather hold on to images than accept the challenge of growth.

Your success profile may be protecting you from a fear of failure that you have yet to conquer.

To avoid the fear, you may be among those who always

adopt a defensive posture, rarely speak your mind, never risk disapproval, rarely volunteer to take on difficult tasks, never stick your neck out. You leave risks, and the fast track up the ladder, to others. You may maintain your feeling of security, but only at the price of personal stagnation. Unless you understand the dynamics of success, this may seem preferable to the risk of failure.

The irony is that failure is an integral step to success. No one ever made it to the top without risk, and risk inevitably leads to some failures. The lives of most great men and women are punctuated by failure. Look at them! George Washington was an abysmal failure in the French and Indian wars. During the Revolution he lost battle after battle against the British before finally winning at Yorktown and later becoming the first president. Abraham Lincoln lost his bid to unseat Stephen Douglas as senator for Illinois. The duke of Wellington was so inept in his youth that his mother said he was "no better than food for powder." Packed off to the army in disgust, he eventually became a field marshal and victor at Waterloo. Winston Churchill failed at school, failed as a cavalry officer, and failed to win many early elections. As first lord of the admiralty he single-handedly engineered a monstrous failure in the British attempt to seize the Dardanelles, and later failed dismally as chancellor of the exchequer. Yet in 1940, with England almost on her knees, he rose to become a national hero and a legend. To fail is clearly to join distinguished company!

Avoiding risks, hesitating to make changes, holding on to what you are (at the expense of what you could be) are sure paths to boredom and regrets! If this is your carefully considered choice, fine. The tragedy is to hover in a very restricted circle of your potential being without even *considering* all that you have the power to become.

Some people use the success striving as a justification for avoiding problems in love and marriage.

If you and your spouse are having difficulties, it's so much easier to say you have to work late than to come home and deal with the hassles that may await. Work is the classic excuse for avoiding sexual anxieties. When you and your lover both accept the myth that you have no choice but to work late night after night, neither of you has to face what may be going on in your relationship. After all, you're doing it all for the family. This gambit usually leaves you and your lover losing at work *and* at home. The underlying tension in the relationship saps your effectiveness at work and you miss the opportunity to resolve the problem and discover new joys. The longer this goes on, the more difficult it becomes to correct. Eventually, a crisis is likely to erupt. None of this may seem very rewarding, but there's a payoff nonetheless. The couple avoids facing the problem in the relationship for months or years. To some people, avoidance is preferable to growth.

The incessant struggle to succeed can become a means of avoiding issues concerning your own personal satisfaction.

This is another form of the "I'll be happy when . . ." syndrome. As long as you can convince yourself that your efforts will eventually lead you to nirvana, you don't have to think about the real level of joy you get out of living now, today. The reward is a short-term conservation of your energy. To change your success profile you have to expend some effort. Some people feel they're better off putting all their energies into striving for the top rather than investing in internal changes that may not seem to have an immediate result.

If you study 200-percent successful people, you'll find that they thrive on change, especially change within themselves. They're always looking for opportunities to discover new abilities and untapped sources of creativity. They adapt to failures and learn from their mistakes. Avoiding the issues of personal growth may appear sensible when you're overloaded with work, but that's the shortsighted view of the anhedonic person. In the long term, an investment in your own growth is an investment in your power to succeed.

An anhedonic success profile may also be your insulation against doubts about your personal values.

Are you satisfied with your job? What do you really want out of life? What would you rather be doing? These are value questions, and few personal queries are more difficult.

The answers aren't usually clear-cut, and when they are, they often point to a need to make major personal changes. Many people find it easier (and therefore preferable) to avoid asking the big questions in the first place. That way the issue of change is neatly avoided. The price of avoidance is less joy and less vitality, but some people would rather pay that price than face the possibility that they may have been on the wrong track. Better to keep striving and hope that the American dream comes true.

There you have the dividends of holding on to an anhedonic success profile. They all represent the choice to live at a level lower than you could achieve. The alternative is to accept the challenge and the risk of going for 200 percent of life, full inner and outer development. The strategies for change are available. To create success on your own terms you need only your will, the determination to use them.

How to Create an Integrated Success Profile

The ultimate solution to the conflicting pressures of a dynamic life-style is what we've called learning to "do less but accomplish more." You don't have to let yourself get forced into anhedonic choices between work and family, personal ambition and personal growth, achievement and enjoyment. You can have both. The best proof is the lives of the most successful people in business. At the highest levels of the corporate world, you find many people with an integrated success profile. They get a terrific charge out of their work— and also have time to enjoy their family and personal interests. They work hard, but they also make time to relax. One striking characteristic is their ability to sustain an inner sense of ease and well-being even during their worst high-pressure days.

One highly successful executive described this possibility very lucidly:

Money was never my primary goal. Sure, I wanted to get rich, everyone does. But it wasn't my primary reason for working. The main goal was to do something I could be proud of and have fun in the process. I began by taking over a small bankrupt company, assembled a good team. We turned the business around and then started growing. At each stage we were having a terrific time. The challenge of beating companies ten times our size was exhilarating!

Now I'm at the top, corporate jet, corporate helicopter, limousine. We have our own building in New York. Some people think I work so hard now that I can't enjoy the money. Bull! My work is a source of great satisfaction, and I have plenty of time for my family and for vacations. Sure, I do a lot of work at home, but it doesn't drain me to sit beside my pool in California. It's a terrific thing. I don't work harder than other people who are less successful. I've learned to enjoy my work and my life a lot more, that's all. I'm sure that's been the main ingredient of my success.

Another chief executive put it this way:

Success is a game. At first, you work very hard. You're young and just getting a feel for the business world, you don't yet know the real secrets of success, so you strive too hard and make yourself miserable. If you're going to make it to the top, you have to learn somewhere along the line that struggle and striving *isn't the key!* The guys who get caught at that level never make it all the way.

You have to stand away from the whole thing and see how funny it is. When you do that, you begin to relax. You ease up inside, and that makes for a tremendous increase in your energy and your creative ability. You discover how to maintain detachment under intense pressure. It's a kind of grace. When you stop trying altogether, you finally reach your peak potential. That's when it becomes a pure game. When you hit that moment, you've made it and nothing can stand in your way.

Here are some techniques to help you reshape your success profile.

Begin by giving yourself full permission to succeed.

Most people are held back by the fear that they don't have what it takes. While they may pay lip service to believing in themselves, they turn right around and complain about all the obstacles that stand in the way: the boss, the company, too much work, to little work, too many "bad breaks." The fact is that many successful people do not have exceptional ability and many have limited education. They didn't score at the top in IQ tests, nor did they go to the best schools or get the best grades. Many come from humble backgrounds and have had bad breaks. The common denominator among all successful and happy people is desire, determination, and confidence. Your chance of success and fulfillment is just as good as anyone else's, and probably much better than you think. Only when you understand this key fact can you plunge ahead with enthusiasm and start functioning at your full potential.

Think of success as a process, not a final destination.

Highly successful people don't set out to achieve one grand goal and, on achieving it, pronounce themselves successful. They view their lives as an adventure and themselves as the heroic players. Perhaps this seems a little grandiose to you, but it's far better to think of yourself as a hero and play life to the fullest than to minimize your abilities and never give yourself a chance to exercise all your talents. You are the creator of your life; why not create it heroically? It doesn't matter how old you are or where you may be on the success ladder. You have the power to create a life that will exceed your highest expectations. All you have to do is learn how to use it.

Make enjoyment of your work and your life, rather than money, your highest priority.

Not that the desire to be rich is bad. Almost everyone would enjoy being wealthy, and the desire for luxuries is healthy and normal. However, time and time again, studies have shown that people who make satisfaction in their work a top priority are the ones who perform best, receive the fastest promotions, and wind up making the most money. Those who make money the primary goal rarely achieve their economic goals and often wind up chronically unhappy. If you are stuck in a job that you don't enjoy, then you are unlikely to go very far in it even if you are being paid well, because money is simply not a sufficient motivator. Maximum performance comes from maximum enjoyment. If you make enjoyment of your work and your life your top priority, you will do your best, and very often that will be better than you think you can do. The result will be success, and the money follows just as naturally as morning follows the dawn.

Beware of any lingering fears of success.

It may surprise you to hear that many people block their success by fear, but the facts are there to be examined. Success implies change—in responsibility, life-style, relationships, and many other aspects of life—and for most people change is frightening. They're reluctant to surrender the safety of the routine and the familiar. Except in rare individuals, the instinct to resist change, do nothing, and accept the mediocre is measurably stronger than the desire to succeed.

People undermine their success in subtle ways. They choose wrong jobs, submit to employers who use them, behave in ways that undermine their chances of promotion, rely on weakness out of habit, and ignore strengths out of ignorance. To create a success profile of maximum opportunity you have to put an end to any lingering fears of success. You must be determined to discover your strengths and cultivate your talents; you must also learn to relish your own growth.

Set attainable goals and learn to enjoy each small step of progress.

One of the most common ways people sabotage themselves is by trying to achieve too much too fast. There is a Wall Street saying that warns against this folly: "Bulls make money, bears make money, hogs never make money." While learning to take risks is important, foolish risks are nothing other than foolish.

Remember that rest is the basis of dynamic activity.

Several thousand years ago the Chinese sage Lao-tzu wrote: "All action begins in rest." In our hedonistic culture we seem to have forgotten this simple wisdom. If you are most people, you push yourself during the day and often at night as well without getting the rest you need. Look inside the typical office. Sagging shoulders, dark circles under the eyes, yawns, and fuzzy thinking are the norm. Without the coffee and cigarette machines, half the people might well fall asleep at their desks.

The importance of getting enough rest cannot be overrated. Consider your own experience. Remember how you feel on those days when you wake up fully refreshed and come to work bristling with energy and mental vitality. Not only do you work more efficiently and creatively, but you enjoy yourself more. If you're tired, even small problems can seem insurmountable. The point is: Feeling fully refreshed doesn't have to be left to chance! You can feel that way every day without cutting back on your busy life-style if you take the time to learn how to master a technique for getting very deep rest in a short period of time. The most dynamic people at the top of corporations often come upon these techniques by instinct. You may have to spend a few hours learning one.

We will discuss three methods. All these techniques are meditative in character. You practice them regularly, usually twice a day, but they can also be used for a quick energy boost. Common to all are the initial steps of sitting comfortably, loosening your clothing, and closing your eyes.

Here are the four steps for a technique that uses positive imagery:

1. Close your eyes and take three or four deep breaths, preferably through the nose. Notice the soothing effects of the air filling your lungs, then flowing out through the nostrils.

2. Gently direct your attention to your toes and feel them relax. Let your attention glide slowly up your body—feet, ankles, calves, knees, thighs, hips, abdomen, back, chest, neck, hands, arms, face—and stop at each part to feel relaxation taking place. Let the warm heaviness of relaxation spread through your body.

3. Now imagine that you are floating in space, or lying in a warm meadow. Create any mental image that you find peaceful and deliciously enjoyable. Let the world slip away and drift naturally in your reveries.

4. After ten minutes, slowly make your way back to aware-

ness of your body and surroundings. Take a few minutes to get oriented before opening your eyes. When you're finally back to reality, you will feel terrific. It's as if you've taken a vacation.

Dr. Herbert Benson at Harvard Medical School developed a technique he calls the relaxation response. Some people find it effective. It too has four steps:

1. Sit comfortably in a quiet room.
2. Close your eyes.
3. Relax your muscles systematically as described in the previous technique, beginning with the toes and working your way slowly up the body.
4. Once you're relaxed, repeat the word *one* or any simple syllable to yourself mentally with each exhalation of breath. After ten minutes, stop and slowly come out of your state of relaxation.

We feel on the basis of our experience with these and many other techniques that the best for achieving concentrated rest is the TM program as taught by qualified teachers at TM centers. It is expensive and you have to put up with a lot of needless philosophizing in order to learn, but the technique itself is worth it. Once you have learned the TM technique, you have a reliable method for gaining in a mere twenty minutes deeper rest than you can get during sleep, and the technique will last you a lifetime. You can practice it anywhere; it's easy and highly enjoyable.

None of these techniques is a substitute for getting a good night's sleep, but most people who have mastered the art of concentrated rest find that they need less sleep. The result is a dramatic increase in the number of days that you wake up feeling great, and a significant improvement in the ability to maintain a high energy level throughout the day.

Cultivate your ability to maintain a state of ease all day long.

This is a key to becoming a 200-percent successful person and enjoying every minute of your life. The largest companies spend millions on private dining rooms, limousines, helicopters, plush offices, and private gyms—all to help top executives sustain maximum inner ease amid high pressure and sometimes hectic days. If you're like most people, you don't have those resources at your disposal. Nevertheless, there is much you can do to lessen the impact of pressure on your inner life.

Don't overschedule.

Most people have a tendency to assume they can accomplish more in a given period than they actually can. The problem arises from planning a project without allowing enough extra time for things to go wrong (as they always do). Deadlines are valuable, because most people are more efficient and creative when they accomplish a task within a given period. However, you would be wise in setting your deadlines to allow an extra 20 percent for things to go wrong. When deadlines are so short that they cause anxiety and a last-minute rush, you and your work suffer unnecessarily.

Insulate yourself as much as possible from interruption.

Nothing is more jarring to the nervous system than repeated interruptions when you're in the midst of concentrating on an important problem. One of the worst mistakes is to get into the habit of taking every phone call no matter what you're doing. A good way to handle the telephone is to concentrate your calls in one time segment, say between nine and ten in the morning or four and five in the afternoon. During that time you take all calls, and call people back who called you. You aren't being rude to refuse a call because you are busy. You are being wise. If you are a victim of the telephone, telephone screening can change your work life.

Organize your work so you can always enjoy calm.

This is not as difficult as it sounds. The key is to be organized, and to have a system for keeping constant tab on your priorities. It helps to have four different files through which all your work flows. They should read "Routine Work," "Urgent," "Think," and "Work at Hand." Everything that comes across your desk should fall into one of the first three folders and remain there until you decide to move it to the position of work at hand. Once you start using this system, your work will take on a natural rhythm that will free you from unnecessary anxieties.

Consciously project ease and enjoyment.

For example, when you're at a meeting, sit back and relax. This is far more effective for listening than sitting on the edge of your chair. When you wish to speak, your movement forward will draw attention and quiet the group. Above all, don't hurry your speech. When you have something important to contribute, there is no rush! Your *words* are going to have an impact on your listeners. Take your time, be brief, and speak clearly. Intersperse pauses after key points. The value of silence is too often ignored. Be sure to enjoy yourself. That way you project maximum power and make others feel most comfortable. It's always a pleasure to listen to someone who is calm, speaks clearly, and projects a natural enthusiasm.

Put an end to five o'clock frenzy.

Many people waste so much time during the day on unimportant tasks that they habitually fall short of their projected goals for the day. The result is a mad flurry of activity just before the bell. Both the work and the person suffer as a result. If you set realistic goals, don't waste time with people you don't need to see or tasks you don't need to do, and pace yourself, then you can wind down each workday with a smooth sense of accomplishment. Of course, you won't always get everything done that you hoped for that day, but each day will be successful because you will have accomplished the most important tasks or at least their most important parts. Routine work that you may not have completed can be left for a catch-up afternoon that you schedule once a week. Once you have rid yourself of five o'clock frenzy, not only will your work improve, but you'll also be a much more enjoyable person to be around after work.

Remind yourself that creative intelligence, not hard work, is the source of your success.

The really valuable work you do in your job may be done in as little as five minutes a week! A brilliant idea. A pivotal decision. A simple solution. A telephone call that closes a big sale. In those five minutes you may accomplish more than in the forty hours you may have been trying to make those five minutes golden. This is not to say that you should strive to be inspired at each and every moment. That's obviously impossible. The point is to avoid getting caught up in working so hard that you lose your perspective and undermine your ability to be inspired.

Become aware of your natural optimum work/play cycles.

Just as you have a unique personality, you have an optimum work cycle that is likely to be different than anyone else's. Some people do their best work in the morning, others have an intense burst of concentration toward the end of the day. There are also people who have concentration bursts for brief intervals throughout the day. We call these periods of maximum alertness "prime time." Once you understand your prime time, you can schedule your activities so that you'll tackle the important and challenging ones at your peak creative periods and relegate mundane activities to your low points. Substantial evidence indicates that your prime time and optimum work cycle are biologically or even genetically determined. Trying to force yourself into an unnatural pattern (such as doing your most difficult work in the morning when you concentrate best in the afternoon) is a big mistake. You will cause needless tension, your work will suffer, and you will cheat yourself out of the most important thing of all—enjoying what you're doing.

Identify the conditions that help you get into a "state of flow."

Almost everyone has had the experience of starting work on a project and getting so immersed that they completely forget time, fatigue, even where they are. Many hours later, when the task is complete, they become aware that they've been functioning at a unique, high level where creative energies pour out effortlessly. Psychologists call this a state of flow. This wonderful and productive state is not arbitrary. You can learn how to create it and then use it at will to accomplish a great deal of work in the shortest time. The key is learning what conditions trigger the inner shift from ordinary functioning to flow. For some people, quiet is necessary. Most people must be well rested. Time of day is almost always a key factor. Flow is much more likely during your prime time than during a low period. Perhaps you need to be working at a particular desk or typewriter for flow to happen. There could be any number of critical conditions. Once you have learned what they are, you have made a major discovery. Flow is one of the basic means of "doing less and accomplishing more." It is also a natural state of inner joy, even ecstasy.

Don't put up with boredom.

Nothing is more stifling to the human spirit than hour upon hour of work that seems meaningless, unchallenging, unexciting. Many jobs are this way, but you don't have to get stuck in one! All you need is the courage to ask for what you want, presumably a job with more responsibility, more excitement, more challenge, more opportunity for promotion. You can get that job if you let other people know that you have the desire and the determination.

Value your time.

This may seem too obvious to mention. It would be if most people's actions reflected a true regard for their time. They don't. All too often, people fritter away time on unimportant activities; work overtime for an unappreciative boss who is taking advantage of a good nature and gullibility; sacrifice time that would be better spent enjoying their family rather than working late. Creating a new success profile requires absolutely that you seize control of your time.

Above all, you must stop wasting time.

One way, remember, is to ask a simple question periodically throughout the day: "Is this the most important thing I should be doing right now?" Don't worry about coming up with an answer. As soon as you ask the question, your inner voice will respond. Listen to what it says!

Spend a few minutes every day reviewing your priorities.

Make a list of everything you want to get done each day, then rank the items in their order of importance. Your order of attack will change throughout the day as new situations come up, but setting up your priorities at the beginning of each day will be a helpful guide.

Learn to make decisions effectively without consuming an inordinate amount of time.

For most people, decision making is the most difficult of

tasks. Failure to make decisions can consume endless time and cause endless unnecessary anxiety. Actually, decision making is a simple process. All you need is a systematic approach. Here is an excellent method that almost always leads to the best choice.

Let's assume you face a complex decision involving five possible choices. The first step is to consider each choice carefully to determine the worst that can happen as a result. Make a note of the disaster potential for each option. If any choice could result in a completely unacceptable outcome, that option can probably be ruled out right away. Now go on and review each option again to determine the best that can happen from each. Again, make notes. The best choice will usually be the one where the potential negative outcome is the least and the positive outcome the greatest, the middle course.

Set aside some time each day to enjoy a quiet period alone. You may want to take a walk, read, or just daydream. Collecting your thoughts in this way helps you keep perspective on yourself and what you are doing. Time alone is a mortar that holds the other parts of your new success profile together. You don't need a long time—fifteen or twenty minutes will do—but this period is very important. Do enjoy it!

Cultivate energy by getting things done.

Again this may seem obvious, but too many people ignore this simple principle. They take on big tasks and let them drag on day after day until they get no sense of accomplishment. They get so bored that they give up or finish halfheartedly. The best way to tackle your day is to break it up into discreet tasks—making phone calls, answering mail, writing letters or reports, making decisions. If you tackle each task as an accomplishment of itself and complete it before going on to anything else, you'll enjoy a burst of energy each time you finish a step. Energy rises with accomplishments. It sags with delay. Create your day so you can bask in many small accomplishments and draw on a continuous flow of energy.

Find time to cultivate friendships.

Many people make the mistake of assuming such a fiercely

competitive attitude that they fail to make close friends. Some people don't make friends because they regard friendship at work as a waste of time. Others hold themselves at a distance because they view the workplace as a battleground and themselves as combatants.

Failure to make friends at work is a big mistake for two reasons. First, you're passing up an important opportunity to add a bit more fun to your life. Let's face it, friendship is fun, so why not enjoy it? Second, if you need a payoff beyond simple enjoyment, you might remember that almost no one makes it to the top without allies. With the growing complexity of modern life, teamwork is a basic building block of success, and the importance of teamwork is only likely to increase in the future. Friends can help you tackle a job that is too big to manage alone, and when the job is done well, there is usually more than enough credit to go around.

Take the time to enrich your intellectual and spiritual sensibilities.

One of the best ways to develop your appreciation of your life is to rekindle your interests in literature, poetry, philosophy, history, or any of the humanities that may once have interested you. The less reason you find to visit a library, museum, art gallery, concert hall, theater, or park, the less human you become in the most important sense. Your life narrows and your satisfactions diminish. Without your even being aware of it, your ability to enjoy and to contribute to the world shrinks measurably day after day.

Let yourself dream.

Many people believe that daydreams are destructive flights from reality. Of course, that's what they can become if they're a substitute for effective performance. They are also essential components of a dynamic success profile. Many successful people readily admit that they daydream. They've discovered that dreams are a primary inspiration toward their goals. You can use daydreams in the same powerful way. The key is to link your fantasies to your personal goals.

Many people do this naturally during sex. Fantasies are often the initial stimulus toward erotic activity. Substantial evidence suggests that sexual satisfaction is directly proportional to the ability to enjoy fantasy and put dreams into practice. So too in the world of work. Your ability to succeed is in large measure proportional to your ability to envision the life you wish to attain, and your capacity to put your fantasy into practice.

The message: Set aside a few minutes each day for your dreams—constructive, creative, dynamic fantasy. Dream about what you want to accomplish, conjure up a vision of the rewards—money, fame, power, love, service or anything you choose. The more you enjoy your vision, the more energy you bring back to your work. Your imagination is a principal source of personal power. Use it wisely, and enjoy.

Finally, it's wise to remember that success is just another game and only a fool takes any game too seriously.

If there is one truth about living, it may be the old saying: "You win some and you lose some." No matter who you are —how talented, privileged, blessed—you can never win all the time. That being the case, your sense of humor is an invaluable asset. The ultimate sign of success may be the ability to laugh; to enjoy the simple pleasure of daily living, to appreciate the beauty of a flower or a sunset even at those times when things aren't working out as planned. Remember Murphy's law: "Whenever something can go wrong, it will." This is funny because it's so true. Things are bound to go wrong sometimes! With perseverance, determination, and desire, they are equally bound to go right once again. The key is to never give up, laugh often, and get as much enjoyment as you can!

V

Learning to Love Yourself (and Others) Fully

The whole theory of the universe is directed
unerringly to one single individual—namely
to you.

—WALT WHITMAN

No one can make you feel inferior without
your consent.

—ELEANOR ROOSEVELT

To get the full value of joy you must have
someone to divide it with.

—MARK TWAIN

PERSONAL ENTHUSIASM is indispensable to a full
life. When you meet people who radiate this zest, you're
naturally attracted by their charm. Their faces are bright,
their eyes keenly alert. At ease with themselves, they make
others feel more alive with exuberant vitality and energy.
Their delight in living is apparent in frequent smiles; their
laughter is contagious. Supremely self-confident, they share
their feelings freely and are willing to take the risks of
intimacy. You can never catch them complaining, but may

often find them sharing some encouragement. They give far more than they take; yet they usually seem to get what they want. These are the qualities that distinguish people who have learned to love themselves fully.

How do you feel about yourself? If you're like most people, you probably feel pretty good. The issue we want to raise in this chapter goes one step further than this initial self-assessment. Our point: There's a big difference between the moderate levels of energy and enthusiasm that come with feeling pretty good about yourself—and the unrestricted appetite for living that comes from loving yourself fully. Self-acceptance at the level of feeling merely pretty good is an anhedonic trap because you're capable of so much more!

Unbridled enthusiasm for living comes naturally to healthy children under the age of four. Young children have not yet learned to inhibit their spontaneous delight in themselves. They feel unabashedly that they are terribly important. They freely express their joys and sorrows. Psychologists often refer to the child's feeling of omnipotence, the belief that his/her small world is at his/her command. This robust self-appreciation is the incubator of the child's basic sense of self-worth and self-confidence that will later empower him or her to face all the challenges and opportunities of adulthood.

By age five, this golden age of childhood is already on the wane. The child has so many rules to learn about (controlling his desires and respecting other people's feelings) that inhibition of his natural self-love is almost inevitable. Self-inhibition and self-doubt reach peaks during adolescence. One psychological challenge of adulthood is to revive that unfettered childhood enthusiasm for life in the context of a mature personality. Few people meet this challenge, because they have learned all their lives that self-love is akin to conceit and selfishness, a personal quality to be held under strict control. This misguided belief is one of the primary anhedonic underpinnings of our culture. It's responsible for untold self-forfeiting behavior and self-made unhappiness.

Anaïs Nin once wrote about the debilitating effect of self-rejection and the liberating power of self-love:

> Every one of us carries a deforming mirror where he sees himself too small or too large, too fat or too thin, even you who see yourself so free, blithe and unscarred. One discovers that destiny can be directed, that one does not need to remain in bondage to the first imprint made on childhood sensibilities, one need not be branded by the first pattern.
>
> Once the deforming mirror is smashed, there is the possibility of wholeness, there is the possibility of joy.

Loving yourself fully is a key to taking advantage of all your possibilities. It is basic to your inner joy and enthusiasm for life. It is fundamental to your ability to love others. It is indispensable to your own dynamism and creativity. That's why learning to love yourself fully is a step worth taking.

Discover Your Deforming Mirrors

It's very difficult to discover your real feelings about yourself through introspection alone. Feelings can be remarkably deceptive. Take Hank, for example; he is thirty-three and gradually losing his hair. Ask him whether he feels any distress about it, and he'll tell you that he accepts his aging. Only if you sit him down and probe deeper, encouraging him to acknowledge all his feelings, does his shame and resentment surface. Judy is another example. She's a vivacious, attractive young woman who works as an assistant in the art department of a large department store. Her work involves setting up merchandise displays. She is quite creative and frequently gets compliments from store personnel about her work. Ask her how she feels about her ability and she'll say she thinks she's pretty good. Probe a little deeper and you find self-doubt. "I get a lot of compliments because people think I'm sexy," she says. "I'm not really that creative."

You may say that you feel good about yourself, but your behavior may speak otherwise. Here's a short list of common behavior revealing hidden feelings of self-rejection:

Feeling embarrassed about your abilities. ("It wasn't skill, just luck." "Today was just a good day . . .")

Giving credit to others when you really deserve it. ("Martha did all the work, I just drew a plan." You write a report and let your superior put his/her name on it first.)

Using cutesie-pie names that make you seem small. (Baldy, Cutesie, Shorty, the Kid, Fatso, Sweetie . . .)

Relying on others to support your opinion. ("The boss says . . ." "My husband says . . ." "According to *Time* . . .")

Failing to stand up for what you believe. (You criticize the president's policy; someone counters with a barrage of statistics; you back down.)

Passing up an opportunity for fun because you feel you don't deserve it. (Friends invite you to the beach/movies/ park but you stay home and work, even though you could spare a few hours for relaxation.)

Believing others can't find you attractive. (A man says you're beautiful and you respond, "Oh, sure, you say that to all the girls." A woman says, "You're handsome," and you feel embarrassed.)

Letting others put you down. (Someone yells, "Hey, stupid," and you turn around. Someone insults you and you take it.)

Saying yes when you want to say no in order to be a "good guy/gal." (A friend asks you to do an errand and you agree, even though it's really not convenient and you feel angry about it.)

Feeling that others are being kind or attentive out of charity. (You accept an invitation for a date but tell yourself he/she is only asking to be kind.)

Denying yourself orgasms.

Berating yourself when you make a mistake. ("How could I be so stupid . . .")

Putting up with poor treatment or poor service because you don't want to make a fuss.

Putting others above you when you're really their equal.

Do you indulge in any of these self-canceling acts? If you do, you have a clue about some of your inner deforming mirrors.

Self-nullifying behavior is an unconscious effort to hold yourself back. You learned in childhood to put the brakes on your feelings. You may still be running your emotional life with the brake pedal on. To love yourself fully you have to ease off the inner brakes and give your natural exuberance more play. You have to start affirming yourself when you might otherwise be putting yourself down. You must begin taking full advantage of your innate strengths when you would ordinarily make excuses with your weaknesses.

Here's how a self-affirming person operates. What actions might you want to start choosing for yourself?

- giving yourself approval
- talking to yourself gently, with affection
- trusting your inner voice and intuition
- developing your full potential and creativity
- understanding all your actions, giving yourself the benefit of the doubt
- forgiving yourself, overcoming guilty feelings
- having fun, lots of it; being free and easy
- taking responsibility for yourself, developing your own values and rules
- rewarding yourself when you deserve it (a great vacation, a hot bubble bath, your favorite piece of music)
- knowing when to say yes and when to say no
- taking risks for your own advancement
- letting yourself enjoy winning or losing
- affirming yourself, letting yourself succeed
- feeling pleasure fully, knowing you deserve it
- liking your body, taking care to look your best
- giving yourself permission to pursue your dreams, to experiment with your fantasies

- providing yourself with life-supporting and enriching people, food, ideas
- surrounding yourself with beauty, especially the natural
- accepting freely the affection and compliments of others, allowing others to be your friends

There you have the characteristics of the self-loving person. Note: Narcissistic behaviors (selfishness, disregard for others' feelings, total self-absorption with personal appearance) aren't included! Clearly, loving yourself fully has nothing to do with self-centered egomania. Quite the contrary: the self-affirming person exhibits healthy qualities that we'd all like to have.

A Question of Courage

The biggest problem in learning to love yourself fully is summoning the courage. Some people resist the idea because they feel it requires admitting a personal weakness. Others fear they may discover something "horrible" inside; to avoid such a self-discovery, they insist that they already love themselves fully. A third group of people feel there is something immoral about self-love. Having been taught all their lives to "think of others," they associate a sinful selfishness with what they see as total self-preoccupation.

Julia was in this group. The crisis in Julia's life began when her husband of nine months told her one morning that he wanted to end their marriage. She had been trying so hard to please him and make the marriage work that she was unaware of his real feelings and unable to see the problems growing in their relationship.

"I was caught totally by surprise," she admits. "It's as if the wind is knocked out of me!" Suddenly Julia, an attractive thirty-one-year-old woman, found herself alone in a new city, three thousand miles away from her family. She had no job or other means of support. She was heartbroken and terrified.

Julia grew up in a family that emphasized the satisfactions of self-sacrifice to help others. Her father was a social worker, her mother a nurse. A gifted girl, Julia heard throughout her childhood and adolescence about her responsibility to use her God-given talents for the benefit of mankind. "My first fantasy," she recalls, "was seeing myself as Florence Nightingale. Later I imagined working in Africa with Albert Schweitzer." No doubt these early lessons helped Julia develop admirable qualities, not the least of which are her compassion, her sensitivity, her strong desire to help others, and her intelligence. Yet she also learned to neglect herself, to deny her desires to be an attractive, vivacious woman.

"My parents weren't uptight about discussing sex," she says, "but at the same time, they had a funny way of making you feel ashamed about wanting to be sexy. One day when I was eleven my girlfriend called me over to her house to see a present her mother had just bought her. It was her first bra. She was very excited and I was curious. We took off our T-shirts in front of the mirror together to compare. I saw that I too had two tiny mounds. I ran home all excited to show my mother that I was ready for a bra too. When I told her, she laughed and said I shouldn't be in such a hurry. Her laughter made me feel terribly ashamed, but she didn't notice." Later when Julia expressed an interest in makeup, clothes, and boys, she met resistance from her parents. "These vanities can wait," she remembers her mother saying. "Your studies are more important now."

Julia went to a private girls' college where she did very well, and then won a one-year scholarship to study in England. She hadn't dated much in college; her parents' disdain for romance continued to inhibit her. When she arrived in England she stepped outside the circle of her parents' influence and was ready to fall in love. She met a young professor who swept her off her feet. He introduced her to the passionate exuberance for living that she had dreamed about. They read poetry and drove in auto rallies, studied Blake and went sky diving, took off on weekends and spent whole days in bed. When the school year came to a close Julia thought he would ask her to stay, and they would live happily ever after. It didn't work out that way. "When school ended, he took off to Greece. Before he left, he thanked me for a wonderful year and wished me well. I didn't say anything, but I cried for three days straight."

Julia's reaction was to turn within. The loss of her first love convinced her that her parents were right. She should stop thinking about herself and devote herself to others. Unable to cope with her hurt and mixed up about what she wanted to do, she sought refuge in an international spiritual movement. For five years her activities with this group satisfied her basic needs. She wanted to see herself as self-sacrificing. The messianic fervor for spiritually regenerating the world provided unlimited opportunities for feeling that she was saving humankind. The group behavior code (celibacy, devotion to a guru, and various dietary restrictions) provided an emotional bulwark against passions that caused her anxiety. With the approach of her thirtieth birthday, however, she began to recognize that she wanted something more than an ascetic life, after all. She met a young schoolteacher at a meditation conference. They fell in love and decided to leave the protected world of the messianic movement. They set out on their own, but within nine months their marriage collapsed.

Listen to how Julia describes her history and how she feels about her future. Her low self-esteem is plain.

It was immediately apparent that a first step to taking control of her own happiness was a massive dose of self-love. It would be wrong to think of Julia as an emotional cripple plagued by neurotic inhibitions. She isn't. She knows that she's an intelligent, attractive, capable woman. She has also developed a long-standing habit of self-neglect. She is never able to put her own desires first; consequently, she often lets herself down. The key to Julia's transformation is letting the passionate woman inside her take her place in the world.

One exercise worked particularly well for Julia. It is called affirmations. Julia's work with affirmations proved the major turning point in her transformation into the self-affirming person she is today. Affirmations are particularly useful because you can modify them to suit your exact needs. For example, you can use affirmations to increase your energy, improve your self-image, feel better about your body, achieve your goals, or enhance your relationships.

An affirmation is a positive statement that you choose to immerse in your consciousness to make a lasting and significant impression. Its purpose is to facilitate growth, so it's usually a statement that you do not presently believe but would like to be true.

If you have a low self-esteem, you might construct the following affirmation for increasing it: "I, [your name], like myself; I am a desirable, loving person." The point about affirmations is that they are statements that you might not ordinarily think possible. They may strike you as strange or even impossible. Therein lies their power to open you to a whole new vision of yourself and a greater appreciation of your inner joy and ability.

How well an affirmation works for you depends on how you use it. Don't just say it out loud as if you're practicing positive thinking. Write it twenty times at each sitting and record your response each time. By repeating this exercise several times per day for two or three weeks, you can give yourself a massive dose of self-love, targeted in just the way you may need. The result can be fabulous.

Here is a typical affirmation taken from Julia's file. This example shows you how to do an affirmation:

I, Julia, deserve love.	No, I don't.
I, Julia, deserve love.	Not me.
I, Julia, deserve love.	Who would love me?
I, Julia, deserve love.	Not really.
I, Julia, deserve love.	I'm ugly.
I, Julia, deserve love.	Selfish, selfish, selfish.
I, Julia, deserve love.	Can't believe that.
I, Julia, deserve love.	Maybe I'm not so ugly.
I, Julia, deserve love.	This is silly.
I, Julia, deserve love.	From whom?
I, Julia, deserve love.	From myself?
I, Julia, deserve love.	From my dad?
I, Julia, deserve love.	Maybe I do.

I, Julia, deserve love.	*Can I say so?*
I, Julia, deserve love.	*Do I dare?*
I, Julia, deserve love.	*Perhaps I do.*
I, Julia, deserve love.	*I do.*

One affirmation, practiced like this, does not appear to be very significant. Nevertheless, affirmations do gradually work. They can produce dramatic results in weeks.

As you work with an affirmation you trigger three developments:

1. Negative feelings emerge.
2. The affirmation takes root in your mind.
3. You gain insight into the sources of emotional distress.

This never happens overnight. You have to spend fifteen to twenty minutes a day on your affirmation and you must work with several applicable versions over a period of weeks, maybe months. In time, you will find that an affirmation no longer seems strange or impossible. Negative feelings and thoughts about yourself begin to fade. The reality of your affirmation becomes more apparent. You begin to see that, deep within yourself, the essence of your affirmation was true all along. You had simply been giving too much attention to negative self-images. Once you break this cycle, you begin to appreciate all the power of your inner joy.

Here are the affirmations Julia worked with during a three-month cycle:

- "I deserve love."
- "I like myself always in all ways."
- "I never have to apologize for being me."
- "My past cannot haunt me; I'm open to all my memories."
- "I am free to express all my feelings."
- "I deserve sexual pleasure."
- "I am sexy and it's good to let people know it."
- "I am beautiful and gracious. I can be totally open."
- "My breasts are perfect. They are full and luscious."
- "I don't have to prove myself to anyone."
- "I am creative and successful."
- "I have terrific orgasms."

Julia didn't start with all these affirmations at once. She used the first one for a while and in the process discovered her need for the second. This is what makes affirmations effective. It is a self-modifying technique that molds itself naturally to your needs and your personality. As you use one affirmation, your need for others will emerge and you will invent them naturally.

Within a short period after using affirmations, Julia's life began to change. You could see it first in her eyes. They had tended to look toward the ground. Now they looked at you directly with a bright self-confidence. She stopped mourning about her past and began to take charge of her present. One of her first steps was to go on a diet and start running. She lost twenty pounds in six weeks.

"For the first time," she says, "I started enjoying looking at myself in the mirror. I stopped feeling embarrassed with my clothes off. I always used to cover my fat belly with my hand when I saw myself naked. It was a reflex. Yesterday I caught myself doing it and put my hand behind my head like a model. I laughed with the pleasure of showing off. The feeling of freedom is terrific!"

Julia also gave herself permission to stop treating all her relationships so seriously and to start thinking of her own sexual needs. The more comfortable she became with herself, the less dominated she was by her old "should"s and "should not"s. She began looking at the values she had blindly accepted and discovered that she could be much more. When she met a man at a party, she let herself enjoy his affection and they hit it off right away. She could feel the sexual chemistry was good and decided she wanted to sleep with him even after he explained that he had a steady relationship and would only be around for three weeks. When they went back to her apartment, she discovered that her intuitions about their sexual chemistry were absolutely right. For the next three weeks, they became very close and shared fantastic sex. Julia began to radiate self-confidence and energy.

"I didn't feel guilty about it," she explains. "He said he loved the woman he was living with, and I wasn't trying to take him away from her. I was willing to risk falling in love knowing I couldn't have him. The relationship was good for both of us, totally positive, loving, and joyful. We shared love and beautiful sex for a brief period, and now we both have wonderful memories."

With her growing self-confidence and new radiance, Julia started aggressively looking for a job. Immediately after her husband left she had made a halfhearted attempt, but was so unhappy that no one would hire her. Not long after her affair she found an excellent job with a local advertising company and moved into a new apartment. Today she is single, divorced, and more enthusiastic about herself than she has been for many years. She is seeing several men but is in no hurry to get remarried. All you have to do is look at her, and you can feel her charm. She has learned it's OK to work on loving herself fully.

How to Get the Most from Affirmations

Using affirmations is one of the most powerful techniques for overcoming self-rejection. We highly recommend that you experiment with several affirmations for a week or two to see how much you can increase your inner joy with minimal effort. Here are basic principles for doing affirmations:

- Use at least one (preferably several) each day. Before sleep, on awakening, and whenever you feel down are the best times.
- Phrase affirmations in the present tense, not in the future. Don't write "I will be happier"; write "I am happier now."
- Write your affirmations in the shortest, most positive form you can. Don't write "I no longer get anxious," but rather "I feel at ease under all circumstances."
- Write each affirmation at least ten but not more than twenty times at each sitting. Try to create the feeling of belief as you write. You're not lying to yourself. You're counterbalancing the negative impressions you have been accepting for so

long. It is very important to write your response each time. Gradually the affirmation takes hold and the negative impression fades.

- Always remember to write your name in the affirmation: "I, John . . ." or "I, Sue . . ."
- Be patient and continue working with your affirmations until you begin noticing the results you want. You may work with a particular set of affirmations for a month or more before results begin to show up clearly.
- After the first ten days you needn't continue writing responses to your affirmations. All the negative material will have surfaced; you don't want to keep repeating it. Keep doing the affirmation and the negativity will fade; the affirmation will become a part of you.
- After ten days you may want to write one or two key affirmations on note cards and carry them with you for reference during the day. This helps imprint the affirmation in your subconscious.
- You can record your affirmation on a cassette for listening during the day. This is not a substitute for writing your affirmation on paper, but it can be a useful booster.

You can design affirmations to suit whatever goals you have. Here are suggestions for building general self-love:

- "I like myself always and in all ways."
- "It's OK for me to have fun and enjoy myself, and I do."
- "My opinion is as valuable as the next person's."
- "It's always OK for me to express myself and my feelings in an appropriate way."
- "I never have to apologize for being me."
- "I would not trade me for anyone."
- "I am wise and knowledgeable and have many talents."
- "I control my present and my future without apologizing to anyone, especially myself."
- "I forgive myself for all my mistakes."
- "My past cannot haunt me; I'm not afraid of ghosts."
- "I am not lacking; I have everything in me that I need for what I want to do."
- "I regard every obstacle as an opportunity to confirm and enhance my abilities."
- "I do not judge others . . . but accept them as they are."
- "I live and act in harmony with myself and others."
- "I love all things and am loved in return."

And here are affirmations to enhance your sexual self-image:

- "I deserve sexual pleasure."
- "I can ask for what I want in sex."
- "I can trust myself to go at my own speed."
- "I don't have to prove my masculinity/femininity. I am relaxed and can turn toward pleasure freely."
- "I can say no without losing my lover's love."
- "I am a terrific lover. I am open to giving and receiving pleasure in many, many ways."
- "I am sexually attractive and desirable."
- "I can freely express my sexual desires."
- "I can have orgasms and help my partner have orgasms in many ways. I don't have to rely on intercourse all the time."
- "It's OK for me to howl and growl and let it all hang out during sex."
- "I can abstain from sex for a while and still feel great about myself."
- "I can be active or passive during sex; changing roles turns me on and helps me get closer to my lover."
- "Any reaction during sex is OK."
- "Any feeling during sex is fine."
- "I am beautiful/handsome during sex. I can be totally open."

How to Use Your Inner Voice

If you really want to love yourself fully, you must be who you are. Simple enough? The fact is that most of us tie up enormous energy suppressing our feelings and trying to be someone we're not. There is a gulf between the self we show to the world and the self that we keep hidden within. The result of this split is an inner parade of doubt, fear, and anxiety every time those hidden feelings are threatened with exposure. As long as you let yourself remain burdened with these unacknowledged feelings, you inhibit your emotional freedom and diminish your inner joy.

The split between the inner and outer self begins when a

child first gets scolded with the line "You're a bad boy/girl."
What parents mean is that the child has done something
unacceptable to them. But that's not what children hear.
They can't make the distinctions, so the scolding registers
as "I'm bad," and a first crop of self-nullifying feelings is
sown. In the early teens it is very difficult not to succumb
to the media myth of the ideal person, like Miss Teenage
America, perfect in every way. No one talks about finding
perfection by developing unique talents and tastes, so almost all adolescents measure themselves against the myth-
ical ideal, and inevitably find themselves lacking in one or
more categories.

How about you? Were you upset about a facial feature?
Perhaps your nose or your chin? Maybe you thought you
were too short, or too tall. Were you happy with your
figure? Did you think your breasts were too big? Too small?
In the locker room, boys inevitably compare sizes of their
sexual organs and some always leave feeling underendowed.
The possibilities for self-deprecation at this age are nearly
endless. Strength, wit, intelligence, beauty, or athletic skill—
any quality at all is a potential source of anxiety about not
measuring up. By the time most teens reach young adulthood they have developed a two-tiered personality and the
inner joy of authenticity, freely being the person you are,
is lost.

This adolescent split in the personality peaks in the late
teens. Reintegrating the public and private selves is a primary task of adulthood, especially the twenties and early
thirties. This reintegration occurs naturally whenever you
risk sharing one of your hidden feelings and discover that
the feeling was never really justified or not nearly as important as you had made it.

A lover tells you that your breasts are not really too big,
but actually full and lovely. A boss compliments you on
your excellent work and sharp intelligence. You go out on
the tennis court with a friend and have a great time even
though you're not tournament material. Through experiences like these most people gradually empty their tote bags
of self-deprecating feelings held over from childhood and

adolescence. We want to show you how you can clear up self-nullifying feelings on your own without waiting for outside help.

Some people hide the belief that they are not intelligent. Others hold on to fears of sexual inadequacy. Perhaps you harbor distaste for some parts of your body. Many people hide feelings that they are unattractive. Couples commonly deny many sentiments about one another even after years of marriage. You may also be hiding from feelings about your job, your future, or your real level of personal happiness.

Whatever self-nullifying sentiments you may shelter, you don't have to go on putting up with them! You can clear out your backlog of self-deprecation by learning to hear and use your *inner voice*, that deep inward voice of your clearest insights and most accurate self-knowledge.

Everyone has an inner voice, but most of us are only dimly aware of it. The inner voice is the innermost dimension of the self. It communicates in the language of intuition, the bodily feeling and felt sense, not in words or images. If you're like most people, you have been conditioned all your life not to trust your feelings. That conditioning explains in large part why the inner voice is so often ignored. The greater the discontinuity between your inner and outer selves, the more difficult it becomes to hear the quiet messages of your inner voice.

To understand what your inner voice is, it may be helpful to know what it's not. It's not that part of your mind which engages in lengthy analysis. The inner voice speaks simply, not in complex arguments. The inner voice does not engage in dialogue. It isn't that part of you which generates the internal chatter that sometimes makes it difficult to make your decisions. The inner voice takes sides quickly in decision making, often through a simple and clear yes or no. Your inner voice also is not your will. It doesn't involve intention and isn't really subject to control; you can ignore it but you can't force it. For your inner voice to be useful, you have to listen to it and use your will to act on the insights you hear. Finally, your inner voice is not the undulating flow of emotions. Though the inner voice communicates through feelings, it is better understood as that part of the self where feelings and thinking meet.

The more familiar you become with your inner voice, the more you will appreciate the degree and personal power that you have been ignoring. Your inner voice is useful in overcoming self-nullifying feelings and resolving the discontinuity between the inner and outer self. That's only the first step. The inner voice is able to know what we can't rationally explain. For example, for some people it can provide creative ideas that far exceed their estimates of their own creativity; for others it can yield business hunches that result in remarkable payoffs; it can save time and energy by telling you exactly where to look for something you want; it can identify the smoothest path to achieve your goals.

Although your inner voice is natural, you must cultivate your ability to hear it. This may seem paradoxical, but it isn't. Walking is natural, but must be learned. Speech is natural, but also must be learned. So it is with your inner voice. It's natural, but you still must learn how to use it. Contacting your inner voice takes time and a specific technique is helpful. Once you get good at the technique, however, you no longer need it. You can pause for a moment anywhere, anytime, and tune in to the messages from your deepest self. The better you get at this, the more you find yourself operating from your deepest self all the time. At that point you are functioning with maximum power and inner joy.

Here's how to contact your inner voice. The procedure takes about ten minutes, so you need to set aside that much time to be alone in a comfortable and quiet place.

1. Begin by closing your eyes and settling into a state of relaxation. Use any of the techniques in chapter IV. After several minutes, when you're feeling at ease, begin to notice that you're able to sit back and observe the flow of thoughts and feelings in your mind and body. You can feel your state of being. At the same time you can step back from those feelings and be aware of your self.

2. Now you can clear an inner space, a quiet field of inner awareness that will allow you to hear your inner voice. As long as your mind is engaged in a constant inner flow of words and occupied with all your daily concerns, you won't be able to hear the quiet messages from your deepest self. To create a quiet inner space, make a simple decision to set all your problems and daily concerns aside. This doesn't require effort or forcing thoughts out of your mind. All that's really required is a decision. The idea is not to forget your problems but to put them in an orderly perspective (almost like making a list of all the things you have to do). Once you clear this inner space, you will settle deeper into yourself. You will begin to have a more intimate sense of your total bodily state. You may notice tension in a muscle; a worry may be nagging somewhere in the back of your mind. These subtle feelings indicate that you're clearing space to learn what's really going on inside you.

3. Now you're ready to choose a problem you want to work out. Choose any problem you like. It can be an emotional one having to do with your inhibitions or unhappiness. It can have to do with a relationship. If you're doubtful about a business decision or any other major decision, you can choose to work on that. The point is: Your total self has much more information to bring to bear on any one of your problems than you normally give yourself credit for! Now you're getting at that total body of information.

4. Bring your problem to mind. The trick is neither to focus on it too closely nor to hold it at too great a distance. Let yourself be aware of the problem and notice any feelings that begin to emerge from within. Don't hurry and don't try prematurely to label what may begin to come up. Let the feeling grow on its own in response to the problem you choose to focus on. If the feeling shifts, follow it, don't force it. Attend to it as if watching an interesting movie. Gradually the feeling will take on a recognizable shape.

5. The next step is to put your feeling into words. The feeling is giving you a new perspective on your problem, so don't be in a hurry to label it with stock phrases. Assume an experimental attitude. Words will come up. Gently

match them against the feeling. If there's an approximate match, you'll have a deep inward felt sense of rightness. There will be a click. Perhaps an "Aha." If the match is not good, the sense of rightness will be fuzzy. As you work with words to describe your feeling, use this sense of rightness as your guide. It is very similar to the sense of rightness you have when you adjust a crooked picture. When it's straight, you simply feel it's right. So, too, with finding the words to understand the new feeling from your inner voice. When it's clear, you'll feel it's right.

These are the outlines of the technique. The more you practice it, the better you'll understand it. Keep in mind that each step leads naturally to the next. If you try to exert too much control, you inhibit the whole process. Usually you'll find the entire experience pleasurable. If you're working on a difficult personal problem or repressed feeling, you may encounter a few rough spots. Go easy with any rough emotions that come up. Don't try to analyze them. Don't push them away either. If you let repressed feelings come to the surface, you'll find a great sense of relief. This experience is one of the most satisfying results of using your inner voice. The repressed pain of old emotional wounds can dissolve in one big flow of feeling. All at once an inner block dissolves. You feel a physical shift toward a new sense of emotional freedom and inner joy.

Until you become very practiced at listening to your inner voice, you may have to use this technique several times to get a clear answer to a particular problem. At times you may feel ambivalent about the messages you hear. Or you may get stuck on a feeling that won't move. Be easy with whatever comes up. Ask yourself: "What does this feeling mean?" Wait for a response. You'll probably find new feelings creeping into your awareness, changing your perception of the initial experience. If, after ten minutes, you feel no click of understanding, no sense of a rightness to anything that has come up, let it be. Come back later, do the technique again. Be patient! The breakthrough will come, and the change will be significant.

Saying Yes to All Your Feelings

Your inner voice is very real, if intangible and difficult to describe. If you're intuitive, you may already have a feel for it. If not, this case may help explain how it works.

George grew up in a Catholic, upwardly striving, lower-middle-class family in New York. When he was thirteen his mother bought him a guitar despite his father's objections. No one in his family believed that he would ever be the rock-and-roll star he dreamed of becoming, so both of his parents were angry and disappointed when he decided not to go to college. By his twenty-fifth birthday, however, he had already cut three platinum records and become the focus for the adulation of millions of teenage girls. He'd earned more money than his parents could dream of. His future appeared paved in gold.

George arrived at my office in a grand style choreographed to impress my staff and anyone else who might be watching. When he got out of his silver limousine he was followed by two bodyguards who stood outside my office door throughout our session. As soon as we were alone, he put up a smoke screen to avoid dealing with his reasons for seeking help. He wanted to know whether I had ever been backstage at a rock-and-roll concert (which I had) and insisted that I be his guest at his next concert. He began boasting about the women who would be there and the drugs that would be available for the asking. Only when I pressed him was he willing to admit why he had come to me.

"I've been thinking about ending it," he finally said. "An O.D. My life stinks."

The better I got to know George, the more clearly I understood the tremendous disparity between his inner and outer selves. To the world and all his friends, he is the idol of millions of screaming young people. He projects an image of the male superstar with flamboyant clothes and enormous sexual energy. He has learned to be "on" almost all the time. Behind his facade he is a very different person. He feels lonely and incomplete. Despite his apparent self-confidence, he harbors many fears about his career. He fears that he isn't really talented; that he can't trust his manager; that his star will fall as fast as it has risen. He also has many sexual complaints. Though women are eager to come to his bed two and three at a time, he fears he's never able to satisfy any of them. "They're let down," he says. "No one would tell me, but I can feel it. It never turns out all that great."

The focus of George's sexual fears is the belief that he is sexually underendowed. He has bitter memories of his older brothers and their friends teasing him about his penis. Later, in high school, he compared himself unfavorably to other boys in the locker room. When alone, he pulled on himself in the hope of "stretching it." His fear is so great that he makes it a practice never to take off his clothes with women unless he has a full erection. Whenever he makes love, he is always plagued by the fear that he will become flaccid and be exposed as the weak, frightened boy he harbors inside.

In the course of our conversations George tried to find any excuse for avoiding his real feelings. At first he wanted me to believe that the problem was too many drugs. Then it was his manager, who he thought was looking out for the other members of the group and not taking his star status into account. Next it was the hectic pace of the rock scene—too many appearances and not enough time to be alone and be himself. The more George resisted accepting his real feelings, the more apparent it became that those hidden feelings were the real problem. I suggested that to get at the truth he needed to get in contact with his inner voice.

The first time George tried the inner voice technique, he learned how little contact he had with his inner life. I asked him to sit quietly with his eyes closed for two minutes. After thirty seconds he became restless and started complaining that the whole thing was a waste of time. I pointed out that he'd been sitting for only thirty seconds. He didn't believe me. I had him time himself so he could begin to see how long two minutes really is—and, not so incidentally, how little time he had been allowing for his inner life.

The first responses George started to get were very general. "I'm unhappy, but I'm not supposed to be unhappy." "Millions of people would give anything to trade places with me, but I hate myself." When these ambivalent feelings came up, George felt stuck. He wanted a quick answer to his unhappiness. I explained that he would have to be patient. The goal was to get behind those general statements to discover the hidden feelings at the root of his self-rejection. I suggested that he continue to try the inner voice technique at home, but that he be very patient and gentle with himself, allowing the feelings to emerge on their own. I also suggested he learn the Transcendental Meditation (TM) technique to facilitate his relaxation and to increase his ease in experiencing his inner world.

George finally precipitated a breakthrough when he stopped trying to label the feelings that were coming up and just learned to patiently attend to them with the gently probing question: "What is the feeling all about?" George let himself experience his sadness until the words came to describe it.

"No one loves me for me" was the phrase that brought the release and the tears. He began sobbing as he felt himself feel all the pain of the lonely boy who always had to hide how he really felt. I encouraged him to be with the pain for as long as he needed to be. After a time the relief began to show visibly on his body. His shoulders relaxed. His breathing eased. A smile began to appear on his lips.

This inner shift became the basis for a significant transformation over the next several months. George learned from direct experience that he could say yes to all his hidden feelings, no matter how painful they might first appear. He began to understand that the way to break down the barrier between his inner and outer selves was to accept his feelings and the risk of expressing them. He was able to see that his big fear (that he had a small penis) was another self-rejecting feeling that could control him only as long as he fought it.

To end this inner battle, I suggested he practice affirmations in front of a mirror and work on getting the felt body sense of his penis as a part of his body that he accepted and loved. Once the process of self-acceptance began, it snowballed on its own. George began to discover that he didn't have to be "on" all the time or rely on a facade. Once he started appreciating his own inner joy, he began feeling more confident in his ability to have a good time with his friends without any strain.

George's relationships also changed. No longer did he feel threatened by other members in the group. He worked on sharing his feelings with his manager and group members. With a noticeable reduction in tension, he began enjoying his concerts. He believes his music has become more creative. He also changed his sexual relationships. He still has women chasing him, but he no longer feels the pressure to prove anything. He is less invested in a macho image, more open to sharing pleasure and love. He is much less phallically oriented in his sexual encounters and much more open to other pleasures such as massage.

George's case is significant because the change that resulted from contacting his inner voice was so dramatic. We could have spent months talking about why he felt miserable without accomplishing a quarter of what he achieved through his direct inner experience of his repressed feelings. Note that George was doing more than practicing the inner voice technique. He was also in the TM program, and our therapy sessions helped him in self-discovery and self-acceptance. But the core of George's transformation was his contact with his inner voice.

Learning to Love Yourself (and Others) Fully

Accepting Your Body

Body image is very important to loving yourself fully. Learning to accept and appreciate every part of your body is a tremendously liberating experience. Everybody seems to have something that they'd like to change but can't. What is your complaint? Your nose, your complexion, your height, your eyes, your legs, your hair, your teeth? Holding on to these bad feelings about your body is a trap you don't have to accept. The strange thing about physical beauty is that people are more sensitive to the feelings you radiate about yourself than they are to your characteristics. When someone meets you, he sees the whole you, and doesn't focus on that part of you that you don't like. If you radiate the feeling that you are an energetic, attractive person, people will see you as one.

The best way to begin loving every part of your body is to practice affirmations with a mirror. Take off all your clothes. Stand in front of a mirror. Look at yourself, front and back. Sit down and make a list of what troubles you. Here are a few terms taken from my clients' lists:

- "hair doesn't look cool"
- "forehead too narrow"
- "really ugly under it all"
- "potbelly"
- "breasts sag"
- "breasts too small"
- "not enough muscle"
- "dry skin"
- "penis too small"

Be honest and complete; admitting your self-deprecating feelings is the first step toward change. The next step is to face an item on the list and try to love that part of yourself. Recognize that whatever you're rejecting is really part of you and deserving of your love. You might affirm "I love my breasts; they're beautiful because they're part of me." You may gag at this exercise at first, but if you do it with honest feeling, you're likely to be surprised by its power. Work through your whole list. In a short time you may achieve a major inner transformation.

If you have a friend who enjoys growth games, you can do this exercise together. You'll find it a surprising relief to confide all your hidden misgivings about your body. Many people are surprised when their friends give them positive feedback about parts of themselves that they thought were unattractive. This exercise can be great fun and truly liberating.

Of course, there may be aspects of your physical appearance that you can change. If you're overweight and want to reduce, then the self-loving thing to do is shed those unnecessary pounds. Or if you have bags under your eyes from lack of sleep, then you ought to take some time off and get the sleep you need. Anything you do to increase your physical health and vitality is an act of self-love; keeping yourself in healthy physical condition is an essential part of loving yourself fully. If you have difficulty sticking to a diet or exercise routine, affirmations may help to boost your resolve.

Cultivate trusting your body's ability to feel at ease and pleasantly alive. If you practice contacting your inner voice, you can discover that your body has enormous wisdom. It has the natural capacity to be perfectly at ease every moment, if you let it. The key is your ability to learn that you don't have to fight inner feelings of tension or anxiety. Because you have been conditioned to suppress your feelings, you have developed the reflex of tensing your muscles in reaction to any unpleasant feelings that arise. This is the direct expression of your lack of trust in your body. What you have to learn is that every feeling of tension or disease is an indication that your body feels out of balance and *wants to shift back into a state of balance*. This is the absolutely critical point. Your body's feelings of tension is the sign to you that it knows the right way to adjust itself to feel better. The tension is the body's signal that it needs you to give it the opportunity to make an adjustment.

At first you may need to take a few minutes to tune into

your inner voice, perhaps using the technique we have described. The more sensitive you become to your inner voice, the more capable you become of sensing when your body is out of balance, and taking thirty seconds or a minute wherever you may be to allow the adjustment to occur and the feeling to come to the surface. Eventually you'll learn how to allow yourself to enjoy maximum ease and vibrancy virtually all the time.

Loving Others

Perhaps the most wonderful result of learning to love yourself fully is the growth in your ability to love others. The principle involved is simple. When you're in contact with your inner voice and can accept all your feelings, you are able to be yourself without pretense. That gives others the freedom to be themselves. If you can be open and honest, others will respond in kind. An open and loving attitude is highly contagious. The more at ease you make others feel, the more everyone can freely share what we all want: honesty, caring, and love.

Fundamental to loving others fully is mastering the basic principle of loving communication. Attunement to your inner voice is an important step because the same principles for communicating with your deepest self also apply to communicating with someone you love. Here are the basic principles:

Choose to communicate your deepest self.
It's very easy to slip into a pattern of taking any relationship for granted and let communication drift into superficialities. The habit of suppressing feelings is well ingrained in most people. To keep love alive, you must make the conscious effort to keep in touch with your inner voice and share what you are hearing with your lover. Only then does communication remain most honest, meaningful, exciting.

Sustaining a loving relationship takes effort. If you're not willing to make the effort, you can expect the communication to become banal, and then love will fade.

Cultivate your ability to listen.

To hear your own inner voice, you have to develop your ability to attend to your feelings without interpreting them or adding on anything to what may come up. You have to "get" what you're feeling as plainly and simply as possible. The same kind of listening is critical to loving communication. Your lover wants you to understand how he/she feels, not how you think he/she feels or what you think he/she ought to feel. In other words, you need to cultivate your ability while listening to create an air of acceptance so your lover feels free to share whatever may come up. Most people don't know how to listen this way. Instead they interrupt because they are so involved in their own thinking. They can't hear what someone else is saying without adding something to it or making an interpretation. If this is your listening pattern, you'll be a much better lover if you change it.

Give up your need to prove other people "wrong."

Most people spend enormous energy trying to prove that they're right and someone else is wrong. If you're in a business meeting this tactic may be appropriate; in loving communication it is highly destructive. This doesn't mean that lovers can't have disagreements. The point is: Most often two people with opposing views are both right to a degree. Trying to prove one or the other wrong is a destructive exercise in ego inflation. If you have to be right all the time, you may never give anyone else an opportunity to share real feelings with you, because no one wants to be proved wrong! Your need also makes you argumentative about your own feelings. If you're out to prove others wrong, you expect that others are out to do the same to you. Nothing is more destructive to loving communication than having to be right all the time.

Favor the positive whenever you can.

Love grows in an environment where two people are sharing many good feelings as frequently as possible. When you first meet someone, the instinct to favor the positive is natural. You offer compliments, you find areas of mutual interest, you do things together that you both enjoy. After a while, romance wears thin. It becomes easy to take positive feelings for granted. Gradually you slip into a pattern of unloading the negative. This subtle switch takes place without most couples noticing it. They begin to dump frustrations on one another because each expects the other to offer sympathy, a solution, or some magic way to feel better. In the resulting environment most conversation is about problems. What happens to the joy in most relationships? You can usually find it lost in this avalanche of daily negativity. It's subtly allowed to take over. The alternative is to remember that loving takes constant commitment. Part of that commitment is choosing to be as positive and optimistic as you can.

Accept the fact that anger and tension will come up in your relationship and learn how to deal with them.

The more two people love each other, the more easily they can hurt each other. When you are hurt by someone you love, anger is inevitable. These are basic laws of human psychology; there is nothing you can do to change them. They mean that anger is bound to be part of any love relationship. (See chapter VIII.)

Share your real feelings, but beware of "dumping."

Love can't grow in the soil of dishonesty. If you hold back your feelings, you create barriers that make it impossible for your relationship to grow and evolve. So the courage to share your feelings is critical to sustaining a love relationship. This does not mean that emotional honesty should be casual. It does not mean that the next time you have something on your chest, you blurt it out at the earliest opportunity. That's dumping, the release of pent-up feeling without regard to the setting, time, or readiness of your lover to respond. If you have difficult feelings to share, ask your lover to set aside time when you can be together in peace and quiet without interruption. Allow more than enough time to work the situation through to a satisfying close, and then have some time left over for a little fun.

Acknowledge those you love as often as you can.

Many people seem to believe that love is supposed to grow on its own without help from the two people involved. They get into the habit of forgetting to say "Thank you," "You look lovely," "That was beautiful," "I appreciate what you did for me," "You make me feel great when you do that," and so on. All these acknowledgments are very important to the growth of love! Without them, you're left in the dark about how your lover feels about you. An essential part of loving is wanting to nurture the growth and happiness of your lover. You can't know how you're doing unless you and your lover make it a point to tell each other often. Try acknowledging your love more often—you'll see the relationship take on a new sparkle.

The Dividends of Self-Rejection

How can there be a psychological reward for not loving yourself fully? What can the payoff possibly be? No matter how illogical it may seem, there has to be a reward for holding on to self-nullifying feelings—otherwise no one would. To be sure, the rewards are unhealthy, but some people would rather settle for the security of self-rejection than risk change. Here are a few reasons why self-nullifying feelings persist:

Self-rejection is a built-in excuse for not accepting responsibility for your own happiness.

Instead of recognizing that the degree of satisfaction you experience in your life is wholly up to you, you can complain about how you were shortchanged in childhood. Your parents weren't good to you, your brothers and sisters got more than you, your teachers were no good. It doesn't matter who you blame, as long as you find someone to stick with the responsibility for your poor self-image. That allows you to deny any responsibility for your own happiness.

If you feel you're not worth very much in your own eyes, you can avoid taking the risks of sharing your real feelings.

Friendship, love, and intimacy are terribly frightening because they can lead to rejection. Rather than risk that calamity, many people prefer to reject themselves. That way they keep all the hurt inside and they can always try to make others think they're happy by wearing a false smile.

You can be lazy about maximizing your growth.

A positive attitude toward your life means putting a lot of energy into your own growth. If you're in the habit of keeping your energy output at a minimum, you may find it more comfortable to hold on to your self-rejection because these feelings exempt you from the need to grow. This exemption is your reward.

Some people hold on to a bag full of self-putdowns in an effort to endear themselves to others.

They carry their self-rejection around like a conversation piece. By making themselves seem small they hope to win others' affection, perhaps in the hope that everyone roots for an underdog. This may work in getting plenty of pity and some compassion, but only at the cost of denying your own possibilities for becoming a winner.

You have a perfect justification for continuing to be dependent on others rather than face your life on your own.

If you belittle yourself, you naturally can't trust your own decisions, much less your intuitions and your creativity. Instead, you have to adopt the childhood stance of asking someone else what you should do when you face an important decision. Parents, friends, your spouse, anyone will do as long as they let you lean on them without challenging your carefully worked out strategy for maintaining a low self-esteem.

Poor self-regard can be an excellent justification for failure.

If you start a project at work or school and it proves more difficult than you expected, you can drop the project with the perfect excuse: You just weren't up to it. You can drag up any number of self-putdowns ("I'm bad at math" or "I'm just not that smart") to justify giving up.

Your low self-esteem can be a valuable reason for indulging in self-pity.

Everyone suffers childhood hurts. Healing those hurts isn't always easy. Rather than work on mending those injuries, some people take the easier route: feeling sorry for themselves. This self-pity is the payoff; holding yourself in low esteem is justification for feeling that you can't do anything else but feel sorry for yourself.

All these psychological rewards for self-rejection feed on themselves. They're vicious circles. If you accept your self-negating feelings as a basic part of your personality, you're bound to make choices that lead you to feel bad about yourself. These choices then reinforce feelings of low self-esteem. To get out of this self-nullifying trap you have to make the decision to challenge your feelings of self-rejection. You must discover for yourself through direct experience that all these feelings are remnants from the past and have no reality in the present except the reality you lend them. If you stop feeding your poor self-image, self-nullifying feelings will lose their strength and you'll discover new personal power and inner joy.

More Techniques for Building Self-Love

It's impossible to radiate enthusiasm unless you give yourself permission to enjoy your life freely. This is the indispensable first step in the practice of self-love. You must decide to set aside any old encrusted beliefs that loving yourself is wrong or something like conceit. The essence of loving yourself fully is being 100 percent committed to your own growth, and that's a positive step you can take not only for yourself but for everyone else you know or will ever meet. Only by becoming the most energetic, loving person you can be, do you have the most to offer others. If you're fully enthusiastic about yourself, you're bound to be a giver rather than a taker—even while you get almost everything you want out of life.

Here are additional techniques effective for building self-love. Some will be useful for you, others won't. Find out what strategies suit you best, then try them wholeheartedly. You're likely to be amazed at how quickly you get results.

If you're feeling stuck, contacting your inner voice may be the best way to sort out your confusion and discover why you're rejecting yourself. Understand: Contacting your inner voice won't eliminate your self-nullifying feelings; it will illuminate them so you can deal with them. It's a good idea to contact your inner voice when you're feeling upset but don't know exactly why. Once the feeling is out in the open, you will experience relief just from knowing why you're distressed. Insight into your self-rejection lets you take steps to change.

Practice developing congruence between your inner and outer selves.

One way to do this is to make a habit of periodically "checking in" with your inner voice to see if you are putting on a mask or hiding something important. The idea is to develop your confidence in your ability to be yourself and have others appreciate you for it. Signs that you need to "check in" are feeling unnatural, cramped, inhibited, or tired. If you feel you have to monitor everything you say or if you tend to be serious all the time, then "checking in" may also help you relax and open up. Important: This "checking-in" exercise is to be practiced in addition to and along with the exercises for becoming more comfortable with your inner life. The TM technique (chapter IV) and the inner voice technique (this chapter, above) are fundamental.

Stop putting yourself down!

If you frequently say "I'm sorry," or if you use cutesie-pie names to make yourself seem small, or if you have difficulty accepting a compliment, you've got to change. Next time you put yourself down, a bell should go off in your head: "There I go again, the same old anhedonic thinking!" Right then and there, correct your error out loud. If you apologized unnecessarily, say "Wait a minute, I'm not really sorry!" If you've dodged a compliment by attributing your success to luck or someone else, say something like "There's my false modesty again! Thank you for the compliment." Changing your habits of self-putdowns is a very important step and requires intelligence. Try it. Within weeks you'll see that the effort is worthwhile. You'll start getting in touch with a personal power that you neglected for years.

Recognize that the most basic pleasure in life is the simple experience of self.

You don't have to do anything to deserve that pleasure. The joy of self-love is perfectly natural. There is no reason to be ashamed about it. The energy for self-confidence, enthusiasm for having an uninhibited love, is the greatest gift you can give others. The better you feel about yourself, the more love you have to share. This is a very old idea well worth making a part of your life—by cultivating inner joy.

Start giving yourself the credit you deserve.

For example, you might try making a list of the ten things about yourself that you are most proud of. Include possibly your abilities to interact with others, your creative ability, your physical skills, your appearance, or any other personal attributes. Tack the list up in your bedroom where you can look at it every day for a week. It may seem a foolish or embarrassing thing to do, especially if you are in the habit of approval seeking—after all, what would other people think if they saw your list! But the whole point of this exercise is for you to give yourself permission to fulfill your own approval needs. Experiment with this exercise for a week and you are likely to be surprised at your increased self-confidence and emotional independence.

Stop trying to win appreciation by putting yourself at everyone's beck and call.

You're only setting yourself up to be taken advantage of.

Learning to Love Yourself (and Others) Fully

Like it or not, we live in a world where self-interest abounds, and you'll get stepped on if you let appreciation become so important to you that you're willing to do anything to gain it. Your effort to win people's appreciation may in part be due to a fear of your own desires. You may have been taught that it's wrong to stand up for yourself because of your responsibility to others. Disarm this inhibition by recognizing your own value. Your greatest contribution to others will come from developing to their fullest your unique abilities, and this requires that you devote most of your energy to your own growth.

Accept the fact that you're going to encounter plenty of disapproval in your lifetime.

You can't please everyone, no matter how hard you try, so trying to win universal approval is an absurd waste of time. A random sampling of one hundred people would show that about 50 percent are likely to disagree with you on any given issue. Take comfort in the knowledge that everyone reaps their share of criticism along with their share of applause.

Make an effort to trust your own opinions.

When you go to buy clothes, don't ask your spouse, friend, or the salesperson how you look. Look in the mirror and see for yourself. If you're pleased with what you see, then go ahead and make the purchase. Also, stop asking your friend or spouse for corroboration of your opinions. "Isn't that so?" and "Ask her, she'll tell you" must forever be deleted from your speech.

It's very important that you take time alone.

We have said this before, but we say it again for reemphasis. One half hour alone per day is a minimum, and one day off a week for rest, recreation, and rejuvenation is essential. Are you skeptical about the principle of "doing less and accomplishing more"? Try taking time off; you'll be amazed at how much better you feel and how much more you get done!

Pamper yourself every once in a while.

If you want a new dress or new piece of sports equipment,

buying it can be a very self-loving thing to do. Or take a vacation you've dreamed about. The point is: You have a right to feel you deserve to be surrounded by beauty and to fulfill your desires. If you have this positive attitude, you're going to radiate the confidence necessary for success. Believing that you deserve what you desire is very important to getting what you want.

You must stop complaining about yourself.

When you complain about your past, about how you look, or about how you feel, all you do is reinforce your negative self-image. You accomplish nothing except to spread your own unhappiness into the lives of others. No one likes to hear personal complaints; it just spreads personal misery. When you feel like complaining, stop yourself. Instead, do something about what is troubling you! For example, if you're tired, don't complain about it; excuse yourself and go to bed. If you don't feel well, go to bed or go to the doctor, whichever seems most prudent. This doesn't mean you shouldn't ask for assistance when you need it, but there is a big difference between asking for help and complaining. Complainers often decline help when it's offered because that ends their reason for complaint.

Stop measuring yourself against a prefabricated ideal that you carry around in your head.

When you were a child, it was appropriate to try to emulate parents, teachers, and others whom you admired. All of us carry around a set of expectations we've internalized from our parents, and we often criticize ourselves for not living up to all those expectations. The next time you engage in self-putdowns for not living up to some internal ideal, ask yourself: Who am I trying to please? It could be your mother, your father, a sibling, or any other adult who was a major influence on you during your childhood. Set those expectations aside. Now that you're adult, you'll achieve maximum personal satisfaction by tapping parts of yourself that you're barely aware of. You have great inner resources of creativity and intelligence that you can spend the rest of your life discovering and expressing. This is the self-loving view of your future—an adventure in self-discovery. You'll live your life, in the words of Oliver Wendell Holmes, "not like doing a sum, but like painting a picture."

In the final analysis, loving yourself fully is a matter of appreciation. Are you going to continue falling for the anhedonic trap of our narcissistic commercial culture by trying to be like everyone else and punishing yourself when you can't? Or are you going to risk standing away from the crowd and saying: "This is me; these are my special talents and abilities"? William Saroyan summed up a major source of personal strength when he advised: "Be grateful for yourself. Yes for yourself. Be thankful. Understand that what a man is he can be grateful for, and ought to be grateful for."

How about you? Isn't it about time you began appreciating all the things about yourself that you have reason to be grateful for? This is indispensable to a life well lived.

VI

Getting Unstuck: Joyfully Recreating Your Life

Whatever you can do, or dream you can do, begin it. Boldness has genius, power, and magic in it.

—GOETHE

Our doubts are traitors
And make us lose the good we oft might win,
By fearing to attempt.

—SHAKESPEARE

I feel trapped. I spend my days wiping runny noses, preparing meals that get cold before they get eaten, doing dishes, clipping supermarket coupons, cleaning house. No matter how hard Jim works, we always seem to be scrimping to get by. This isn't what I had in mind when I said "to have and to hold till death do us part." Some days I get the urge to pack up and leave. Other days I feel depressed, sort of sorry for myself. Most of the time I'm just bored.

These are the words of a young mother, married to a young aerospace engineer. They live in a quiet residential area, have a small house, two cars, and a future that promises them all the comforts of the suburban American lifestyle.

Jim and Barbara love each other, and their marriage has

been stable. Neither raves about their sex life, but neither has sought extramarital sexual contact. Casually appraised, they are beneficiaries of the American dream, both college-educated, both products of middle-class families. Nevertheless, Barbara feels she is suffocating; Jim feels too pressured by his work to be of help. Both feel stuck . . . good and stuck.

The "I'm stuck" syndrome, an anhedonic emotional trap if ever there was one, is reaching epidemic proportions. It's widespread among young marrieds, but the same feelings of depression and resignation are showing up among adults at every stage of life. Perhaps you're feeling stuck in your job. If you're older, you may feel cornered by inflation or illness. Many a mother going back to work soon feels stifled by the limited opportunities. Having played out the singles scene, you may be pessimistic about your chances of finding a lasting relationship that will work. Or you may be twenty years into a bad marriage and unable to get out. The common denominator is the feeling of being caught by a situation beyond your control; it leaves you depressed about the present and resigned to the future.

If you've been bitten hard by the "I'm stuck" bug, you can marshal any number of reasons to justify your frustrations. You may get angry at the company that doesn't recognize your ability and give you the promotion you feel you deserve. You may complain about the government, which mishandles the economy and allows inflation and taxes to keep rising through the roof. If you're a woman, a black, a Chicano, or a member of any other group that has suffered discrimination, you can blame the system that denied you your opportunities. Spouses make excellent targets to blame for your distress.

The frustrations of the "I'm stuck" syndrome may be more or less legitimate: you are facing a very difficult and perhaps oppressive situation. But that insight doesn't accomplish very much other than to justify indulging in self-pity. The important questions are: Why do you let difficult situations make you feel powerless? What can you do to start molding your life to suit your desires?

Who Makes the Rules?

Do you have a set of values, standards you can call your own? Or do you (like many people) make your important decisions and set your personal goals by consulting a tote bag of "should"s and "must"s? These are important questions—among the most important in this book. A favorite way for people to rob themselves of their own power and wind up stuck, frustrated, and unhappy is blind adherence to a list of "should"s gathered during early life.

Jenny is one of these people. Jenny came into the hospital emergency room one night because she was having what she called one of her panic attacks. She was afraid she was freaking out. She was not psychotic, but suffering from a moderately severe anxiety and phobic neurosis. A little reassurance and a mild tranquilizer were enough to alleviate her immediate emotional crisis. She began therapy because she felt she had lost control over her life and was frequently anxious. She complained of anxiety attacks occurring at any time of the day under almost any circumstance—at parties, at home alone, at the food store, while making dinner, even while doing the laundry.

A tall, dark-complexioned woman, Jenny does her best to wear a warm smile. At twenty-seven she is the mother of a six-year-old son and spends her time taking care of her husband and child. Talk to her when she is feeling at ease and you can't help but be impressed by her obvious charm and intelligence. If you look closely at her smile and listen to her voice, you can sense the strain.

Jenny's emotional crisis had been building for years and the event that finally touched it off was minor: she got into a squabble with her mother-in-law over some drapes. Listen to what Jenny says about it, and the power of her "should"s becomes clear:

"What a silly reason for a fight! My mother-in-law was so adamant that those drapes were the only ones that could go with the furniture and carpet. I hated the damn drapes, and this time I couldn't put up with her pressuring me. I got angry and told her I would put up the drapes that *I* chose. She got insulted and stormed out. When she left, I began feeling terrible. I shouldn't have gotten angry at her!"

There it is: Jenny's "should" about how to deal with her mother-in-law. As soon as she violated it, she made herself so anxious that she wound up later that evening with a panic attack.

Jenny's whole life is a list of "should"s and "must"s. "I got married when I was nineteen because mom and dad thought I should. I wanted to go to college, but they thought a college education wasn't important for a woman." Children: "We're Italian, and so is David's family. When you get married, you're supposed to have children right away. That's the way it is. I never questioned it."

Jenny's "should"s were not limited to the traditions of her family background. She was also suffocating herself with a catalog of "should"s about how to be an ideal wife and mother. Here's a partial list:

- Serve terrific meals every night.
- Keep the house spotless.
- Never get angry, especially with David and her son, Mark.
- Always look lovely when David comes home.
- Never be in a bad mood.
- Take Mark to the park every day.
- Be warm to David's mother.
- Be a terrific lover.
- Be liked by everybody.

Jenny's "should"s make her a totally other-directed person. Everything she does is for someone else; never does she allow time or energy to find out what she really wants out of life. In place of her own desires she substitutes her long list of "should"s to guide her every waking moment. No wonder she feels sick and has so little inner joy.

Completely out of touch with her own needs, Jenny set herself up to be dominated by her husband. "David never takes anything I say seriously. He's always pushing me around," she complains. The fact is that Jenny invites David's dominance by refusing to take herself seriously and ignoring her own intelligence. "I'm not very bright," she say, echoing the archaic "should" about women sticking to the home while men face the challenges of the business world.

The destructive effect of Jenny's "should"s is nowhere more clear than in her sex life. She has a long list of sexual "should"s that make it impossible for her to enjoy sex. "I know I should want to have sex more often," she tells herself. She fails to see how her anxiety to be a better lover interferes with her sexual desire. Jenny is anxious because she doesn't "come very often when David is inside me." She feels she "ought to be more sexually responsive."

When Jenny began trying to come to terms with her anxiety, she showed the typical reaction of a person burdened with "should"s. She had great difficulty sorting out what she really wanted out of life. She also had difficulty appreciating her abilities. An early turning point involved a decision to get a college degree. Jenny's initial reaction to the suggestion that she had the intelligence to do well was predictable. "I can't," she said. "David wouldn't like it. My parents would think I was deserting my son Mark and my other responsibilities. David's mother would be furious. It would be crazy." We explored these objections one by one. Eventually Jenny began to see that her protests were more disguised "should"s based on other people's wants and needs. I suggested Jenny begin asking herself who makes the rules in her life and who were the rules for.

Jenny finally decided to enroll in a local college and pursue a degree in elementary-school education. As expected, her announcement of her intentions brought a chorus of criticisms and precipitated a marital crisis. Jenny had prepared herself for the tirade of "You're deserting me," "You can't do that," "I won't let you," and "A woman's place is in the home." Doors slammed and phones rang as the whole family became upset. Jenny's strategy was firm. She insisted that she was determined to give college a try. She hoped

David and her family would support her. "Who made the rule that I can't get a degree and be a good mother?" she asked. She also asked David to join her in therapy.

Like Jenny, David was initially reluctant to confront the "should"s in their marriage. Jenny finally broke through David's resistance by telling him frankly how unhappy and sexually frustrated she felt. David's sexual ego was wounded. "I didn't realize it was so bad for you," he said. Once the facade that hid their sexual relationship was gone, David was ready to begin examining the "should"s that he had been imposing on the marriage.

Who made the rule that the housework and the children were all Jenny's responsibility? Who made the rule that Jenny couldn't have her own friends? Who made the rule that they could only have sex his way? The harder they looked at their lives, the more clearly they saw that they were living according to rules that they didn't make and didn't really accept. For Jenny and David this was a key to change and a major step toward inner joy.

By the end of Jenny's freshman year, she and David had worked through their marital crisis and were starting to celebrate their new emotional strength. Each began feeling free to make friends and spend time pursuing their own interests without always worrying about the other. They discovered that their love was far more durable than they had thought. They didn't need protection from a blanket of "must"s and "ought"s. "Our great realization," Jenny and David now explain, "is that the more freedom we have to grow as individuals, the more deeply we grow in love. We can create our lives any way we decide."

Jenny's case illustrates the difference between a life grounded in "should"s and an effort to create your future according to your own values and desires. Your experience is different from anyone else's. This doesn't mean that you can't learn from others or you must reject all traditions and values held by your family. "Should"s become destructive and anhedonic *when you accept them as rules to be obeyed without question*. Examine each one carefully in light of your own experience, desires, and goals. You need a set of values that will nourish your individuality, not confine it.

Coming to terms with your "should"s is not likely to be easy. For Jenny it was a lengthy struggle that uprooted her basic sense of herself and transformed her marriage. She had to confront her fears and stand up to the pressures of her family. She often wanted to quit and return to the security of her "should"s. Now well on the way to creating the life she wants, she can look back on her struggle and congratulate herself for having the courage to take the risks necessary to reap the rewards of her new emotional freedom. She has an abundance of inner joy.

OK, Go for It!

Our culture values comfort over fulfillment. Most of us have been exposed to a barrage of messages to discourage risk taking and encourage conformity. The good life equals the money made, the size house owned, the cars driven, the vacations taken. Young people are encouraged to choose careers not according to what they want to do, but according to the future demand for their skills and the money they are likely to earn. This leads to an obsession with security at the expense of satisfaction. This fear of taking the risk of going all out to do what you really want can lead into a dismal anhedonic trap.

Dan grew up programmed to get caught in it, but managed to find a way out. He's from a staid New England family. Risk was regarded as a four-letter word. His grandfather had begun in the mailroom of a Wall Street brokerage house and wound up running the company. His father followed in his grandfather's footsteps. Well before Dan was conceived, it was assumed that the grandson would also tread this same path, now paved with gold. No one ever asked Dan what he wanted to do. It never occurred to anyone in the family that Dan might want to find a path of his own. Who could ignore the prospect of a six-figure income served on a silver platter by age thirty?

Dan started going away to prep school shortly after John Kennedy won the Democratic nomination for the presidency. On that crisp January morning when the new president enjoined all to ask themselves what they could do for their country, Dan listened raptly. Though Dan was barely fourteen, the president's words made a lasting impression. Dan still remembers them with a thrill. "I wrote home to ask what I could do for my country," Dan recalls. "My father wrote back that he wouldn't put up with my wasting time and that I'd better put all my attention on getting into Harvard."

When Dan moved to Cambridge, he steered clear of the protest movements and the counterculture because his family never let him forget his responsibility to the family name. "Grandfather told me I wouldn't get a dime if he ever heard the slightest rumor that I was experimenting with drugs or demonstrating against the war." Dan was not ready to risk losing his tie to the family purse strings.

In the autumn of his senior year, Dan met Judy. Boston blue blood. Wellesley senior. The perfect mate. They fell in love as naturally as the golden leaves falling in the wind. By Christmas, they were meeting each other's families. In June they wedded. When they moved to their first large apartment in New York, they seemed to be the ideal couple, with futures as secure as a blue-chip stock. They had been given a tidy sum by Dan's grandfather as a combined graduation and wedding present. When they decided to invest it, rather than spend the summer in Europe, everyone was pleased. Dan and Judy were so sensible!

Dan set out to learn the brokerage business. Judy started having babies. They had two children in close succession and bought a co-op. Approaching their twenty-sixth birthdays, Dan and Judy delighted both their families. They were settled. Their lives stretched before them like a smooth superhighway. No bumps, no stop signs, few exits, and no surprises. No one seemed to notice that Dan was slowly, almost imperceptibly beginning to show signs of suffocation. "I started realizing that I was becoming locked into a life that wasn't my own. I had always had a dream of creating something, making a contribution that was mine; in the back of my mind, I kept waiting for something to happen. One day I realized that all I was learning to do was trade someone else's property. At home Judy talked about clothes, furniture, travel, and schools for the children. Our marriage was becoming an incredible bore."

Out one night with an old college buddy, Dan met Inga, a Swedish graduate student in anthropology on fellowship in the United States. She was tall, blond, and blue-eyed, but most of all—exotic. Fluent in four languages, well traveled, independent, she talked about ideas, not things. "She was incredibly attractive," Dan remembers. "I was fascinated. She was open and honest. We both sensed a mutual chemistry, and she didn't seem disturbed at all that I was married." For once Dan threw security to the winds. He asked to see Inga again—the lock on his life had snapped. Within four months, Dan had fallen so hard for Inga that he could no longer keep his affair secret. He told Judy and suggested they separate until Dan could make up his mind. After tears, threats, and recriminations, Dan moved out to a small apartment of his own and Judy took the children back to Boston.

"This was the first time in my life," says Dan, "that I did something without a plan. My family was outraged, but eventually they saw there was nothing they could do. At least I was sticking it out with the firm."

But that was not to last. Inga was the first person Dan loved who was interested in finding out what was really going on inside him. When she found out that ever since college he had dreamed of going to law school so he could get into public service, Inga's enthusiasm fanned the flames of this old desire. At twenty-eight Dan finally gathered the courage to step off his assigned path. He enrolled in law school. When Judy came back from Boston seeking reconciliation, Dan asked her for a divorce. Judy was crushed, but didn't protest. Except for the children, Dan had no regrets.

Against his family's wishes, Dan and Inga took an apartment together near the university. Over the next three years they lived the life of students. "For the first time I was feeling a rush of excitement about my life. There were no preconceived plans. We studied, and read, and talked, and made love. A whole new and important world was opening up to me. Nothing affects people's lives more than the law. I was finally discovering a way to make a contribution." Dan presumed that after his graduation he and Inga would marry, but that was not to be.

"The month before graduation, Inga dropped a bomb on me. She said she had been seeing another guy, and had fallen in love with him. She didn't want to talk about it, and she wasn't about to change her mind. A week later, she moved out. There I was on the receiving end of what I had dished out to Judy. I was devastated," he remembers.

Dan moved down to Washington to take a job with the Justice Department, and for the first time in his life was truly alone and on his own. Panic set in. "I started looking frantically for someone to fill the void, and wound up sleeping with a different woman every weekend. I must have dated more women in that year than in all the years before. I bought a sports car, grew a mustache, played the stud trip to the hilt. My emotional gyroscope had gone haywire. I don't think I would have recognized what I was looking for if I found it." Holding out the bait that he was looking for a permanent relationship, Dan had his pick of the young women who ply the halls of Washington office buildings. Finally Dan began to realize that what he was looking for was not to be found in someone else.

"How little security we have," wrote the essayist William Hazlitt, "when we trust our happiness in the hands of others." Or in the possession of things! This simple wisdom, learned through a decade of efforts to declare his independence, proved to be the key to Dan's final escape from the security trap. *The fundamental human need for security becomes a trap whenever security, economic or emotional, is sought in someone or something outside of your own self.* The only real security is knowledge that you have the power to create your own life joyfully.

With this realization, Dan and his life-style changed. He stopped trying to find another woman to lean on, and began directing his energies toward making the contribution that had always been his dream. He loosened up, and stopped trying to fit into a mold. No longer did he need to play a role: Young Harvard man, Justice Department young Turk, stud, or any other of his stylized selves. He started being himself, unafraid to let people know what he was really feeling, confident that he could handle any failure or success. He became active in the environmental movement and eventually left the Justice Department to work full-time for an environmental action group. He also remarried two years after he met a woman who works full-time as an independent television producer. Together they are now working on a documentary on the potential hazards of nuclear power. For the first time in his life, Dan is brimming with inner joy.

You *Can* Beat the System

In our world of inequities, unequal opportunity is still a fact of life for women, blacks, Mexican-Americans, and others despite the progress toward eliminating discrimination based on race, sex, color, or national origin. The wealthy still have a better chance of avoiding conviction for crime than do the poor. Huge companies, especially the oil conglomerates, have enormous power to create shortages and raise prices. Your employer, your spouse, your children, the government, your landlord, anyone at all may be taking advantage of you or trying to keep you from taking control over your life. The issue is whether any amount of injustice justifies your feeling stuck. The fact is that it doesn't. Mistreatment at the hands of a person or organization is reason to act, not to wallow in self-pity.

Standing up for your rights is never easy. It may risk losing your job or being threatened; it can cause family turmoil; it always results in emotional upset. But anyone who has felt stuck and dared to challenge the system knows the sweet rewards of exercising personal power.

Marjorie took on the system, and won. "I'm not a crusader," she states. "At thirty-eight, I'd just gotten tired of being taken advantage of by a company committed to treating women as second-class employees. I've been a senior analyst in the systems analysis department for five years. In that time I watched the director of the department get promoted or transferred three times. Each man told me I'd be most likely to succeed him when he left. Three times I saw the position filled by a younger man hired from outside the company. The first time I took it silently; the second, I complained, which didn't do any good. Finally I was fed up, so I decided to fight."

Marjorie is a happily married mother of three. She had worked for the same company for fourteen years, and regularly received praise and promotions until she reached the level of senior analyst. Her next promotion would have advanced her into the ranks of management and opened opportunities to rise in the management hierarchy, but her company had few female executives and held on to a strong bias against women in promotion policies.

"I had a friend who was involved in a women's group. She had tried to get me active, but I was always too busy with my family. Every time I complained about how I was getting used at work, Betty told me I shouldn't take it. She wanted me to file a class action suit with other women in the company. For five years I listened and did nothing. I thought I had too much to lose. We needed my income

INNER JOY

and I didn't want to lose my job. I also didn't want to embarrass my husband or our three sons. You can't do something like that without it getting in the local papers.

"When I got passed over the third time, it was really a blow. I was depressed and angry at the same time. I started berating myself and was grouchy at home. Perhaps I was taking my anger out on my husband, I don't know. Anyway, my sexual desire disappeared. I felt like I had been used and there wasn't anything I could do about it. I had to do something or feel stepped on for the rest of my life.

"My husband was aware of my disappointment, but I hadn't told him all my feelings. I was afraid he'd think I was becoming too pushy or losing my marbles. My fears were groundless. When I told him I was thinking of contacting a lawyer, he gave me his full support. The boys thought their old mom was getting weird, but they came around. We had a family meeting to explain what I was doing and that we might get unfavorable publicity. Once the boys understood what we were fighting for, they were gung ho."

With the help of a local women's group, Marjorie filed suit against her company, charging discrimination against women in hiring and promotion. "I never worked so hard in my life," she recalls. "We didn't have the money to just go out and hire a top-notch legal firm that would do all the work. The women in our local group served as the foot soldiers. One of the first steps was finding other women in the company who had also been unfairly passed over and were willing to fight. Then there was the long and tedious process of gathering the evidence to prove our case. We spent hundreds of hours working on the suit.

"It wasn't easy for my family. There was local publicity and my boys took some razzing about their weird mother. What shocked me most was the reaction of some of the women who I thought were my friends. I was accused of everything from trying to become a local heroine to advocating lesbian rights. It's impossible to cope with all the misunderstanding. Some of it you have to ignore. Throughout the ordeal, my husband was a godsend. He cooked dinner when I couldn't; he took the boys away for weekends. And most of all, he gave me support and encouragement all the way.

"Looking back, it's clear to me now that the suit had positive effects on the family. The boys learned a tremendous amount about how our system works, and I think they gained an appreciation for women's rights. My husband and I became closer. I know his respect for me grew, as did my appreciation of him. We talked about our feelings and our hopes more openly than we ever had before. We became stronger individuals, and more united as a couple."

After two years of struggle, the case finally came to court. Marjorie won in the lower court, and the case has now gone on to the appellate level. Shortly after winning the case, Marjorie was offered a management position with another local company. She took the offer because she felt her future would always remain clouded with her former employer. Now at the crest of forty, she has become an active local leader in the women's movement and she radiates energy. She shines with the inner joy of having taken control of her life.

Putting It Off

Some people get themselves stuck with what may seem to be the best of intentions. They don't want to make trouble for others, or don't want to risk losing what they have in order to create something better. Rather than take control of their lives and accept the risks of growth, they choose to put up with stifling jobs, lingering health problems, collapsing marriages, or destructive habits. It's an anhedonic trap. The longer they procrastinate, the more difficult change becomes, and the more desperate they are likely to feel.

Dianne, a thirty-six-year-old mother of three, spent the last sixteen years trying to convince herself that her marriage could work. When she finally came for help, she was living what Thoreau called a "life of quiet desperation." At her first visit, her eyes were red and inflamed from crying and lack of sleep. She looked drawn, had a bruise on her left arm, and was visibly anxious about seeking assistance without her husband's permission. In an outpouring of feeling pent up for years, she told her story:

Our marriage has been miserable for as long as I can remember. This isn't the first fight or the first affair. He was seeing another woman the first year we were married. When I found out, I was devastated, cried my eyes out until he promised to be faithful. I believed him because I was young, I loved him, and I wanted our marriage to work more than anything else in the world.

I've tried to get him to open up and make our love grow. It never worked. He always kept his feelings inside. There's always been a distance. We haven't had sex for over a year now, but I really don't miss it because it was never any good. Steven wanted to think he was a real macho lover who could drive me wild. I learned to put on a great performance. Maybe he knows, or just got bored with me. I don't think we were real lovers for more than a few months after the honeymoon.

The children came and that gave Steven the excuse he needed to stay out of the house. He earned the money; I raised the children. Sounds corny, doesn't it? But that was our arrangement. He said he couldn't work at home, so he spent several nights a week and most weekends at the office. I actually convinced myself that he was working all those times. Even when I practically knew he was seeing another woman, I wouldn't admit it to myself. Just after our seventh anniversary, a friend of mine told me she saw Steven in a restaurant with a young blonde. I had to confront him. We had a terrible fight that ended with Steven telling me he didn't mean anything and pleading for me to stay. Like a fool, I did.

Two years ago Steven lost his job. He was out of work for six months. Ever since then our relationship has been a quiet hell. We never spend any time together, never even go to the movies or watch TV. Steven is always out or in his den. We still share the same bedroom, but never exchange more than a kiss hello or goodbye. That's more for the children than for us. Steven makes all the decisions about money and never asks me about them anymore. I no longer know how much money we have or even how much he is making.

Last week he came home late. He called to say not to wait up for him. I did anyway. When he came in the door, I could tell right away that he'd had a few drinks. He said he'd stopped at a bar on the way home. Then I noticed a long red hair on his coat. I'd ignored these things before. I don't know what made me ask him about it, but I did. We wound up in a shouting match and a terrible fight. He has never struck me before, but this time he flew into a rage and knocked me down. Said I was an albatross around his neck and he wished he'd never met me. I was shaken, and frightened. I locked myself in our bedroom and cried all night. The children must have heard everything. They got themselves off to school the next morning. Steven is now pleading for me to forgive him again. He admits he's been seeing another woman, and is giving me the same old line.

"Why did you wait so long to do something?" I asked.

"I loved Steven and I was afraid of what might happen. There were the children to think about. I kept hoping things would get better. I told myself maybe Steven would change. If I tried to please him, our relationship would improve.

From the first year of her marriage, Dianne's inner voice was telling her that there were serious problems in her marriage. Year after year she chose to ignore those inner messages and to rely on make-believe. She assuaged her anxiety with the classic self-deception: "Maybe things will get better if I just wait it out." By choosing to ignore her inner voice and hold on to wishful thinking, Dianne created sixteen years of unhappiness. Recognizing her complicity in her misery was a first step toward change.

Dianne eventually convinced Steven to join her in counseling. He professed to want to save the marriage; Dianne took a stand. Either they tried together or it was over. Over the course of ten sessions, Steven's insecurities and Dianne's years of hurt came out in the open. Steven asked for reconciliation, Dianne asked why she should trust him again. The more Dianne learned about her husband, the more doubtful she became about remaining married.

"For the first time," she said privately, "I see how much

growing up Steven has to do." She finally summoned the courage to face what she had avoided for so long. "I'll be better off on my own," concluded Dianne. "I've already wasted sixteen years. I can't afford to risk any more."

She filed for divorce and spent the next two years recovering the power she had long put in mothballs. She had three children to care for and no means of support other than alimony. She did not want to remain dependent, but finding work was not easy. For sixteen years she had cultivated the skill of putting things off and turning a blind eye to her real feelings. Many times she had talked about going back to college. Many times she had thought of getting a job. Never had she chosen to listen to those quiet urgings from within. By cultivating the "put-it-off" syndrome, she had dulled her confidence, sensitivity, and will. Once out on her own, she had to learn how to mobilize herself again.

Today Dianne is a single mother with a house and a job of her own. She is working in the public relations department of a large law firm that handles celebrities, including many sports figures and entertainers. After completing her B.A. at age thirty-nine she plans to get her law degree. She is managing to complete her education through a combination of night study, leaves of absence from work, summer school, bank loans, tremendous support from her children, and the fantastic new energy she has discovered surging forth when she chooses to act from her deepest self and go for what she really wants.

The next time you find yourself putting off dealing with a source of unhappiness in your life, ask yourself: Will hoping for improvement really do any good? The answer is no. The longer you put it off, the worse it's likely to get—whatever "it" may be. Gather your courage and choose to get unstuck. Now!

"I've Always Been That Way"

Another way many people get themselves stuck is by fore-closing on change with the reassuring rationale, "I've al-ways been that way."

Edith is a forty-two-year-old widow whose husband died of a sudden heart attack two years ago. After a prolonged period of mourning, she is reaching a point where she is ready to love again. Yet she holds herself back. A lovely woman who looks more like she is in her early thirties, she is not lacking in interested men. When her relationship with a man begins to heat up, however, she puts on the brakes. "I'm afraid of sexual involvement," she says in therapy. "In all my years with Roger, I never had an orgasm. I've always been that way. I can't help it." Sex wasn't so important to Edith when she was married, so the belief that "I'm not orgasmic" wasn't a problem. Now things are different. She is single again, and awakening to new desires. Only after she decided that she has the power to break free from her past was she able to begin rediscovering sexual joy.

John, a college student, complains, "I can count the num-ber of dates I've had on one hand and not run out of fingers." He's obviously got a sense of humor, but he is afraid to be himself around women. "I'm shy," he says. "That's my nature." John recalls his mother telling people that he was "the shy one." He never realized that his mother had an emotional investment in keeping him tied to her apron strings. John spent his childhood and adoles-cence living up to the family label of "the shy one." No doubt he had a tendency to be shy as a little boy, but with their labeling, his parents helped him develop that tendency into a full-blown personality characteristic. The question is whether John is going to continue justifying his fears of women with the rationale: "Shyness is my nature." When-ever you resort to a label to explain a negative personality characteristic, you're only making excuses for avoiding the challenge of growth.

Gloria is twenty-six and overweight. She has tried every imaginable diet, managed on several occasions to lose over thirty pounds, but always put the weight back on. She says she wants to shed her excess poundage forever, but in the same breath she reveals why she has always been unsuccessful in her attempts up to now. "I've always had a weight problem, ever since I was a little girl. I must have too many fat cells or a low metabolism or something." Gloria keeps herself stuck with the classic recall to her physiology. What she doesn't see is the hidden payoff. As long as she is fat, she has a built-in excuse for feeling lonely and unattractive. Terrified by the prospect of rejection, she avoids it by rejecting herself, then hiding her self-rejection ("I've always been that way"). You may be tall, short, fat, thin, big-bosomed or small-breasted, bushy-headed or bald as a snowball. None of these physiological characteristics is justification for keeping yourself stuck and unhappy. They just aren't that important. Far more significant is your vitality, your friendliness, your self-confidence, your inner joy. These are the qualities you can choose to make outstanding in your life.

Vanessa at twenty-eight has been offered a major promotion at work. A vice-president has asked her to become his administrative assistant. The new job requires that Vanessa polish up on her basic math. Vanessa wants the job, but she is afraid to take it because she has always had difficulty with math. "I barely passed math in high school," she says. "Numbers make me nervous. I can't even balance my checkbook." For sixteen years Vanessa used this "I've always been" to avoid the extra effort required for her to become proficient in basic math. Now she has a choice. She can continue to use her "I've always been that way" as an excuse, or she can decide to focus whatever energy it takes for her to develop her math skills. The first choice is guaranteed to keep her stuck; the second opens broad new possibilities for success. Who knows why she has had difficulty with math in the past? It really doesn't matter, because she has the intelligence to acquire the skills the new job demands. All she needs now is the courage to challenge her "I've always been."

Tim is known for a short temper and frequent angry outbursts. His boss has told him that if he wants to make any kind of progress with the company he will have to learn to control his temper and develop his interpersonal skills. Tim's response has been consistent. "Sure, I have a short temper! I'm Irish." Ever since Tim got into fights on the school playground, his parents indulged his temper with this excuse. Now Tim sits at his desk in a sullen rage; his boss has told him that due to economic pressures on the company, Tim will be out of a job. His boss did not hide the fact that Tim, of all the junior executives, was dismissed because senior management found him hard to work with. This blow was finally enough for Tim to realize he had to make some changes. The alternative was to get stuck not only emotionally, but also economically. Having put all his excuses aside, Tim is now working on developing the emotional skills he needs to be a better manager. (See chapter IX.)

If you want to know where your "I've always been" comes from, have a talk with significant people of your early life (parents, long-time family friends, teachers, grandparents). Ask them how they think you got to be the way you are. You'll hear a list of labels you've learned to apply to yourself. If you tell them you're determined to change, you're likely to meet considerable doubt ("You can't change, you've always been that way"). But why go on living up to labels others have put upon you? Sören Kierkegaard wrote: "When you label me, you negate me." By accepting labels others pinned on you, you negate yourself. You're saying: "I'm a finished product, I can't change." This is an anhedonic choice, because it is a denial of your potential for growth. *No one is ever a finished product!* You are bigger than all the labels you may hang on yourself. Anytime you wish, you can choose to get unstuck by putting your past behind you. All it takes is courage and determination.

The Dividends of Self-Immobilization

Like all anhedonic behaviors, your choice to stay stuck also brings rewards. Here are several:

Once again, avoidance of responsibility is a primary pay-off.

The choice to remain the way you are is always a choice to live by the dictates of others, so you can say "They're responsible for my unhappiness!" When you choose to exercise your own power, you forfeit this ready-made system for blame. For some people the prospect of assuming full responsibility for their happiness is so onerous that they prefer to suffocate their own creative potential with the weight of others' expectations. This dubious bargain is the essence of being stuck.

Keeping yourself stuck can help you remain self-righteous.

It doesn't matter how stultifying your "should"s may be; you can pride yourself on remaining exactly the way you are. You can even look down your nose at others who experiment with new life-styles and violate your sacred rules ("They aren't doing it the right way").

Remaining stuck permits you to indulge in psychological regression.

By following your "should"s and living up to your labels, you can take solace in being a "good boy" or "good girl." You can take satisfaction in your obedience. It doesn't matter that mommy and daddy are no longer around to pat you on the back for following their rules. If you refrain from questioning your childhood "should"s, you can recreate the comfort of having someone else make your important decisions. You avoid having to think for yourself.

Keeping yourself stuck lets you avoid the risk of failure.

If you've been well schooled in the merits of safety, boredom is likely to seem preferable to defeat. You assume that your self-esteem is so fragile that you could never pick yourself up after a fall and try again. For people convinced of their own weakness, avoidance of failure is an alluring reward.

Keeping yourself stuck creates fertile ground for self-delusion.

"Nothing is easier than self-deceit," said Demosthenes. Especially when you stifle your impulse toward growth, we add. By remaining the way you are, you avoid a confrontation with your dreams. You can hold all your options in abeyance while you ponder your possibilities. By planning your first novel but never getting around to writing it, you can keep telling yourself how much potential you have as a writer. By refusing to work on a difficulty in your relationship, you can convince yourself that the relationship is basically sound and will last. Peaceful delusion is the reward.

You create opportunities to substitute complaining for doing.

When a problem doesn't go away, no matter how much you hope things get better, you can complain that you never get any breaks. If you remain in a relationship that's going sour, you can complain about how your lover mistreats you. You're putting up with an unsatisfying job? Berate your boss, the company, and your fate. You were mistreated by your parents? It is so much easier to blame mom and dad than it is to take concrete steps toward becoming the person you want to be. Complaining may not seem to be a reward to you, but some people make a career out of it.

Choosing self-abnegation protects you from fear.

Whenever you take a step in a new direction, as we've often said, you are bound to experience some anxiety. Anxiety is natural when you move into a new job, challenge a failing marriage, go back to school, decide to have children, or venture into any unknown emotional territory. You can't expect to be an explorer of your full potential without encountering a measure of fear. Some people would rather continue believing their lives must inevitably remain flat rather than risk making an adventure of the future.

Reread these reasons why people persist in self-immobilization, and you may have difficulty regarding them as rewards. Under the cool scrutiny of rational analysis, they are obviously self-destructive. Nevertheless, these emotional payoffs constitute the support system for choosing to be less than you could become. This is anhedonia in action.

Some Steps Toward Self-Direction

Once you have decided to take control, you *have* the power to create your own life according to your personal vision. You *can* establish your own values based on your own experience. To get unstuck, you need to seize this power to break free from your past and transform your intuitions into realities. The decision to take control of your life is a first step. Transforming that decision into action is the real test. Here are some suggestions that you may find useful:

Stop thinking of yourself as fragile.
Behind every anhedonic choice that keeps you stuck is the belief that you (or your life) will fall apart if you challenge the rules. This is a powerful myth! It can keep you absolutely paralyzed! The only way to rid yourself of it is to put your psychological strengths to the test. Few people realize how strong they really are until they stop putting up with the problems in their lives and take some steps toward change. It won't be easy. You may get knocked down a few times, but you won't fall apart. On the contrary, the more

you assert your ability to take control over your life, the stronger you'll become. Developing psychological strengths is just like developing physical abilities. The more you exercise, the stronger you become.

Once and for all, you must eliminate the words wish, hope, *and* maybe *from your vocabulary.*

These are sedatives you administer to yourself to numb your sensitivity to your emotional realities. Like any narcotic, wishing and hoping weaken your power to take control of your life. In place of wishing and hoping, you have to substitute a new confidence in your willpower.

Substitute "*I will make it happen*" for "I hope things get better."

Substitute "*I am going to do x, y, z, so I'll feel better*" for "I wish things were better."

Substitute "*I will make my marriage work*" for "Maybe my marriage will still work out."

Start considering yourself too important to put up with anxiety about the obstacles in your life.

The best antidote for anxiety is action. Instead of bemoaning your problems or worrying about the long way to a major goal, take the first step. If your job is suffocating you, stop complaining and put together your résumé. Get any assistance you need to make certain it's the best résumé you can possibly write. If you're in a relationship that is faltering, gather up the courage to have a long talk about your future with your lover. Don't put it off until tomorrow. Do it today! Action, even one small step, breaks the illusion that makes personal problems seem insurmountable. You can only solve your problems one step at a time. Taking the first step has the amazing effect of reducing any problem to life size.

If you're feeling ambivalent about your life, try this little experiment.

Imagine you have only one year to live. Now ask yourself whether you're doing what you'd like to be doing given this sudden abbreviation of your life. If the answer is no, better get busy and start making changes. Whether you have one or fifty years ahead, your life is too short to waste.

The habit of putting up with a life that you have failed to make your own grows more difficult to break each year. Don't risk looking back on a life of regrets. Dare to challenge yourself now.

Choose one of your bigger dreams and start making it a reality.

One of my clients had always dreamed of exploring the Inca ruins in Peru. She had never been out of the United States and, as a secretary, didn't earn a large income. Nevertheless, this was the dream she chose. I suggested she contact travel agencies, museums, and local universities to explore all possibilities for her trip. The cost of a commercial tour was out of her reach, but she did discover that she could for a modest cost join an archaeological expedition from a local museum. She paid for some of her expenses and joined in the work as a volunteer. The result was the most rewarding vacation of her life. More: by actualizing just one of her dreams, she broke the cycle of defeatism that was keeping her stuck. Now at twenty-seven she is back at school to study archaeology. Fulfilling a dream is an exercise in discovering personal power. It can turn your life around.

Stop feeling you always have to have a plan.

Plans have their place, but planning involves only half of your brain, the verbal, analytic hemisphere. There is a huge silent dimension of your personality, the intuitive dimension, and you're probably not using it. Scientific research on creativity shows indisputably that the creative process depends just as much on the right brain functions (intuition) as on the left brain operations (analysis and language). If you insist on always having a plan, you cut yourself off from your intuitive self and the inner joy it provides. To break planning addiction, indulge in one freedom. Decide to spend a day exploring a park or a neighborhood with curiosity as your sole guide. Enroll in a local university and take a course that strikes your interest. You never know, it may lead you into a new occupation. The next time you feel attracted to someone you don't know, and want to introduce yourself, go ahead. You're likely to make a new friend. By giving yourself freedom to follow your hunches, even in small ways, you develop your sensitivity to your inner voice. You learn to hear the quiet messages that can make your life an adventure.

Once and for all, eradicate your tendency to put things off.

Procrastination is a habit easily broken. First, make a list every morning of everything you have to do that day. Divide the list into areas: telephone calls, letters, housework, reading, writing, appointments, and so on. Make your list early every day so it becomes a habit. Throughout the day, consult your list and cross off what you accomplish. Whatever remains at the end of the day becomes part of the next day's list. If an important item remains for several days, tag it and allot a special time of day to do it. This simple technique can help you end procrastination forever.

Don't be ashamed to ask friends for support when you consider a major change.

You may have legitimate concerns about leaving your job, going back to school, moving to another city, or doing whatever seems necessary to create the life you really want. From some people, you may get very conservative advice: "Don't take risks," "Don't rock the boat," "A boring job is better than no job at all." But you're also likely to get encouragement and help. People will respond to your courage. Doors will open. Try it. You'll be surprised how helpful people are when you ask.

Decide to forego the crutch of old labels you've pinned on yourself to make excuses for remaining the way you are.

Instead of saying "I've always been that way," try a new affirmation: "Until today, I have chosen to be this way. Now I am choosing to change." You have the power to create your life as you wish. Important techniques are spelled out in every chapter of this book. For any technique to work, you have to begin with a firm commitment to make it work.

Remember that "should"s have only as much influence over your life as you give them.

If your "should"s have been weighing heavily in many of your important decisions, the time has come to declare your independence. Ask yourself who is making the rules in your life: your parents, a teacher you once had, an aunt or uncle, or you. Take an inventory of the "should"s that are causing you the most trouble. You might even write them down. Then choose to override those "should"s and choose new behaviors. For example, Annette wasn't allowing herself to have orgasms because of all her sexual "should"s—"A woman shouldn't have to tell a man what she wants; it's not romantic," "I should be able to come with intercourse alone, or else there is something wrong with me," "A woman shouldn't be too aggressive during sex." These "should"s are popular misconceptions. When Annette began asking who was making these rules, she began recognizing the absurdity of letting them dominate her. She discovered that she has the power to create an ecstatic sex life if she listens to her needs and gives herself more freedom. You can make the same choice in any area of your life.

Have faith in yourself, your ability to succeed at what you attempt and to get back up if you fail.

William James wrote: "It is only by risking our persons from one hour to the next that we live at all." Often faith in an uncertain result makes the result come true. The greatest rewards of living come when you step out of the bounds of your ordinary existence and extend yourself beyond what you believe are your limits.

Don't let yourself be crippled by the fear of failure.

If you hold back and never depart from your routine because you fear failure, you're letting approval needs get the best of you. The worst part of failure is what others will think. This is a terrible anhedonic trap! It's the basis of all performance anxiety, whether on the tennis court, in bed, in the classroom—wherever someone may watch how well you do. The only way to end performance anxiety is to stop worrying about the audience and do whatever you're doing for the sake of your own enjoyment. This is when you absolutely *must* be selfish! Remember: Pleasure is a sign of optimum functioning. If you follow your own desires to enjoy what you are doing to the maximum, you'll do the very best you can, and that is all you ever need ask of yourself.

Spend more time being a doer, less being a critic.

Many people fool themselves into thinking they are not really stuck by engaging in criticism whenever possible. They have a harsh word for almost everyone, friends, neighbors, movies, books, politicians, doctors, lawyers, the washer repairperson, anyone at all. After criticism comes complaint. What they're really doing is disguising their own unhappiness because they don't know how to create more satisfactions in their own lives. Beware of wasting your own time as a critic and listening to others engage in this usually fruitless activity. When you're caught listening to a critic, ask: "Is any of this going to help either of us right now?" Chances are it won't, so you'll go on to a more satisfying conversation.

Learn to master fatigue.

One of the most common responses to an unpleasant task is a sudden onset of drowsiness. If you're like most people, the first time you experienced this psychosomatic reaction was as a student when you had to do some homework. You sat down full of energy, but twenty minutes into studying, your eyes started to droop. But do you remember how this reaction abates as soon as you start doing something else? Let someone suggest going to a movie and the energy surges. Clearly, your energy level is governed by your attitude. If you get tired trying to complete a difficult or unpleasant task, it's best to take a five-to-ten-minute break. Get up and exercise vigorously or nap in your chair. Either way, you can choose to master this type of fatigue so that you get the difficult task accomplished in minimum time.

Decide once and for all that your happiness or unhappiness is primarily up to you.

There are no guarantees in this world. No matter who you are, living has its ups and downs, wins and losses. Maturity is the ability to derive deep satisfaction from your life whether or not your efforts are yielding full fruit for the moment. Every time you let your happiness depend on others, you surrender a portion of yourself. You reinforce childhood beliefs that someone else will take care of you. Isn't it time to give up these childhood beliefs and discover your own power of inner joy?

VII

Guilt and Worry: Self-Punishment You Don't Deserve

> "It's a poor sort of memory that only works backwards," the Queen remarked.
> —Lewis Carroll

> Life can only be understood backwards, but must be lived forwards.
> —Sören Kierkegaard

FEELING GUILTY about something that happened in the past isn't going to change it and worrying about something that may happen in the future is certain to prove equally unavailing. You don't need a Ph.D. to understand the futility of these feelings. Then why are guilt and worry so commonplace? Why in any group of a hundred people do you find over half either inhibited by guilt or troubled by worry? Why isn't insight into the pointlessness of guilt and worry enough to eradicate these ubiquitous joy-killers? These questions don't have easy answers, but if you're willing to look behind your ways of feeling guilt and worrying, you may discover how to conquer them once and for all.

Guilt is self-punishment for inability to change the past. Worry is self-punishment for inability to change the future.

Both are particularly destructive causes of anhedonia because they so often turn the best of times into quagmires of emotional distress.

Kay has been living with Roger for over a year. They're talking about marriage. He is a geologist; she recently graduated from business school. They share many common interests and are deeply in love. Their only problem is their sexual chemistry. Having grown up in the Midwest, Kay learned very early from her mother what "good" girls did and didn't do. Roger seems to prefer what "bad" girls do. Kay realizes his desires are perfectly normal. She desperately wants to ignite the magic in their sex lives, but despite her rational insights, she can't shake her feelings of guilt. Now Kay and Roger worry about what they should do.

Guilt and worry are difficult habits to break because both stem from healthy functions of the psyche. Guilt is the child of conscience, worry an offspring of concern. The argument can be made that some guilt and worry are inevitable for a fully integrated personality. The capacity to feel guilty is basic to differentiating between right and wrong, and living according to a set of personal values and ideals. Complete absence of guilt is the primary characteristic of the psychopath, who proceeds through life cheating, stealing, and swindling without regard for others. Worry is an almost inevitable consequence of love. The more you love someone, the more concerned you are for their well-being. The boundary between worry and concern is vague indeed.

Our point is not that all guilt and worry are bad and to be eliminated. Problems arise when guilt and worry become *excessive*, serve no useful purpose, and pointlessly diminish inner joy. This chapter will help you eliminate anhedonic guilt and worry that are so common and so destructive.

Guilt and Worry

Action vs. Immobilization

The first issue is: Are your guilt and worry useful, healthy products of conscience and concern? Or are they destructive, misdirected means of unnecessary self-punishment?

If you're like most people, you'll find examples of both types of guilt in your life. You may have become inappropriately angry at your friend. Later you feel guilty about your blowup. To alleviate your guilt and restore the friendship, you apologize. On another occasion, a friend may ask you to do a favor that you honestly don't have time to do, even though you would like to help. You say no, but feel guilty about it. The same two types of worry are found in most lives. On one occasion, perhaps, your worry about the possibility of getting pregnant may prompt you to use birth control. Another time you may not take precautions, and you wind up worrying *after the fact* whether you're pregnant.

The difference between a healthy conscience and anhedonic guilt, or between appropriate concern and destructive worry, is one word—*action*. Do your feelings prompt you to act to alleviate them? Or do they lead to immobilization, pointless self-made emotional pain that only makes you inhibited or anxious? This is a criterion to apply to determine whether guilt and worry are a problem in your life. If they lead you to action and are therefore short-lived, they're normal and healthy. If they lead to immobilization and tend to linger, they're anhedonic and you've got work to do.

The Madonna Prostitute and Other Stories

It is fashionable in this era of sexual freedom to believe that sex-related guilt has become antique. The evidence is otherwise. If anything, the new public exposure to sex, including a whole range of techniques and practices (cunnilingus, fellatio, group sex) long regarded as immoral, is exacerbating sex-related guilt. For many people, far more than you might imagine, the adage "Doing it more but enjoying it less" applies.

Paradoxically, sex-related guilt is among the easiest to overcome if you're willing to admit the problem and can summon even a little courage to do something about it.

Ed, for example, was extremely troubled by sexual guilt, so much so that sex with his wife had always been a source of anxiety. Recently it had also become very infrequent. "I love Karen dearly," Ed explains in my office. "She's the ideal wife, pretty, intelligent, supportive. She manages to keep the house beautiful and still look great when I come home from work. We don't fight very often and when we do, we can make up without holding grudges. All that's great, I couldn't ask for anything more, except there's this major problem. I can't fuck her. When I do, I feel terrible, really rotten, and I can't explain it."

Ed's problem becomes comprehensible when you explore it. He married Karen when she was a sophomore in college, barely nineteen. Raised in a strongly Catholic family, she was still a virgin on their wedding night. "I wanted it that way," Ed says. In keeping with the old double standard, Ed had lost his virginity with a prostitute at twenty. Since then he'd gratified many of his wildest sexual fantasies. "I dated a lot of girls who were fun to take out but you wouldn't want to marry," he admits. Now, due to his own Catholic upbringing where virginity was prized as one of the highest virtues, Ed still harbors the belief that you can't have sex with a woman you love without losing your respect for her. Ed views Karen as a madonna and feels terribly guilty about his sexual desires for her because he fears turning her into a prostitute.

Productive fantasy frequently proves effective in reducing sex-related guilt, and Ed and Karen used it with excellent results. Each was asked to write down in detail one sexual fantasy. The fantasy didn't have to involve each other, but after writing it down, they were to insert each other's names as participants. This was crucial for Ed because he felt too much guilt to fantasize about Karen. Each came up with exciting scenes. Here is Karen's dream:

> I undress myself in a very seductive way, trying to arouse Ed just by taking off my clothes. When I take off my bra, I do it very slowly, touching my nipples, getting myself excited as well. I cup my breast in one hand and rub my clitoris with the other . . . then slip off my panties. Ed is just watching and getting excited, so I go over and begin undressing him. I slip off his shirt and then unbuckle his pants. With one hand I grasp his swelling organ. Massaging his swollen shaft, I whisper what I want him to do, which is bring me to climax with his mouth.
>
> He responds eagerly and lays me down on the floor very gently. He kisses my mouth, my shoulders, and works his way down over my bushy mound. He kisses and sucks gently until I begin writhing out of control. I yell "Yes, yes, I'm coming" and I have a wild climax. Before I can recover, he is fulfilling the second part of my wish. I feel his rigid penis filling my anus while his finger is entering my vagina. He thrusts hard for a long time, driving me to renewed ecstasy, until he explodes inside me and I come in a second wild frenzy. We lie together exhausted.

Ed's fantasy is quite different. He imagines taking Karen out to the woods on a picnic with their favorite foods and a portable stereo. The sun is shining and they take off their clothes. Ed is excited by the possibility of discovery because they are in a public park. They kiss and caress for a long while, each growing aroused. Karen begins kissing Ed's belly, then works her way down to his erect organ. She kisses and licks him, blows gently, drives him wild. She takes him into her mouth and begins sucking, slowly at first, then more vigorously. She holds his buttocks with both hands and sucks wildly until he explodes in her mouth. They lie in each other's arms, completely satisfied.

Needless to say, sharing these fantasies generated considerable initial anxiety. At first Ed refused to read his fantasy to Karen, but she finally convinced him she wanted to hear how he wanted her to please him. She read her fantasy first and that helped Ed let go. Both Ed and Karen were surprised at how excited they became hearing each other's fantasies. "It sounds so beautiful," Ed said in astonishment.

The guilt also surfaced as we talked, but the immediate joy of sharing their fantasies created a new sense of freedom. The old guilt seemed less significant. Eventually Ed and Karen were able to act out their fantasies. This is crucial for the exercise to be productive. Only when the fantasies and the newly discovered pleasures become real does the new sense of emotional freedom develop. After trying this exercise once, Ed and Karen were eager to try it again.

Productive sexual fantasy is effective because it breaks the immobilization of guilt. As long as you allow guilt to stifle your feelings, the guilt remains unchallenged. With sexual fantasy you get your sexual feelings moving; guilt gives way under the pressures of newly discovered joys. To preserve guilt, you have to keep telling yourself that you're bad. It's hard to go on believing you're bad when you start feeling terrific.

It's My Life

One of the most difficult developmental tasks of adulthood is coming to terms with the values and expectations imposed by parents. The seminal stages of this struggle occur during adolescence, but the process of declaring independence can go on well into the third, fourth, or even fifth decade. It is almost impossible to go through this process without suffering some pangs of guilt. "I'm letting them down," "After all they've done for me, look how I'm treating them," and "I want to respect you but I've also got to respect myself" are typical guilt messages that result. If it remains unresolved, this guilt can lead to a permanently crippled sense of self.

Parent-inspired guilt is especially painful for two reasons. First, your parents are your primary teachers of conscience, the basic sense of right and wrong. Very early in your life, you learned to trust your parents' guilt messages. When your parents said, "You're letting us down," you were usually doing just that and needed guidance to change your behavior. Second, your parents are also the guardians of family and cultural traditions, social roots that may extend far back in history. It is the nature of each generation to hope that the next generation will perpetuate its traditions. Major emotional and family crises erupt when children choose to adopt values and traditions different from those of their parents. Often parents use their power to inspire guilt as a last resort for controlling their adult children.

A crisis erupted in Sara's family when her mother happened to pick up a letter from Sara's fiancé, David. Sara is Jewish and David, Methodist. In his letter David explained at length that he had decided he did not want to convert. Sara and he had discussed the problem many times and agreed they would both follow their consciences and not let religious differences stand in the way of their marriage. Neither was particularly religious, so they decided to postpone dealing with the issue of religious education for the children they hoped to have.

Sara met David at school in Michigan. David is a medical student, Sara a graduate student in education. They met early in the school year and by May had become engaged. Each went home to discuss plans with parents before arranging to visit prospective in-laws together during the summer.

Sara had explained many times the possible objection of her parents unless David agreed to convert. When they parted in May, David was still struggling over the idea. While at home in Ohio, he made his decision and wrote Sara in New York. Though disappointed on receiving the letter, Sara resolved she would marry David no matter what. "I'd never met a man like him before," she says. "Intelligent, sensitive, very funny. We're both into art and literature. And he's also gorgeous. The sexual chemistry is terrific. I've never experienced anything like it. I want to share my life with him."

Sara's mother happened to "stumble across" the letter while straightening up Sara's room. The volcano went off immediately. "What's this?" was her mother's opening line, as if Sara had just brought home a loaded revolver.

"How dare you read my mail!" Sara retorted, indignant that her privacy was being invaded and her mother was treating her like she was still underage. From there the battle lines were drawn and emotional artillery set in place.

Over the next two days, Sara's mother and father used every possible weapon to destroy Sara's love with guilt. They began with lightweight salvos like "It'll never work, your families are worlds apart" and "How can you do this to us? We sacrificed everything for you." In a more rational moment, they argued, "This is a five-thousand-year-old tradition you're throwing away." Finally they escalated to:

- "We named you after Aunt Sara for nothing!";
- "She died in a camp and you're a disgrace to her memory";
- "The Nazis will have their revenge after all";
- "You're killing us"; and
- "The rabbi's daughter married a gentile and he never saw her again. Do you want to be dead to us?"

Under this constant pounding, Sara finally took refuge in a delaying tactic. She agreed to postpone her plans until "things can be worked out."

Sara spent the summer avoiding further confrontation and tried to come to terms with her guilt. She discussed the issues with a close friend, met with a local Reform rabbi, and sought short-term counseling. By summer's end the issue crystallized in her mind. Every part of her body and soul told her that David was the man she loved and that they could make their marriage work. The issue was whether she had the courage to trust her feelings and to stand up to her parents without losing them forever.

Before going back to school she sat down with her parents and had a long discussion in which she explained her decision. Each time her parents tried to bend her with guilt, Sara responded with a loving and rational reason why she wanted to go ahead and marry David. The discussion closed on a very sad tone when Sara was forced to explain, "It comes down to whether I'm living my life or yours. The deepest parts of me tell me that my happiness lies with David, so I've got to marry him even though it hurts you. I pray you'll forgive me one day."

Three years later, Sara and David are very happy. They were married in a small civil ceremony attended only by a few close friends. They have one child and David will soon be finishing his residency in family medicine. Sara is working for a consulting firm and pleased with her future. They finally agreed that the children would have a Reform Jewish education because Reform Judaism seemed most congruent with the values they wanted their children to have.

Despite its inauspicious beginning, the marriage is working extremely well. With the birth of their child, the ice began to break with Sara's parents. Unable to resist seeing their first grandchild, they came to visit and discovered their daughter happier than they had ever seen her before.

There is no easy way to deal with the guilt that follows when you declare your independence from your parents' values and expectations. The very fact that time makes generations see the world differently makes this pain almost inevitable. In his novel *Damien*, Hermann Hesse refers to this when he writes: "Sooner or later each of us must take the step that separates him from his father, from his mentors; each of us must have some cruelly lonely experiences . . ."

Courage and compassion are elements essential to coming to terms with manipulative parent-inspired guilt. Without courage and compassion, this guilt may lead to a lifetime of self-suffocation and resentment. The ultimate question you have to ask is: "Whose life am I living?"

"I Can't Do Enough"

In this time of inflationary expectations people keep pushing to get more out of themselves to get more out of living. Not since ancient Greece have so many people been so determined in their pursuit of the "perfect" body. Running, tennis, and racquetball have progressed beyond fads into the mainstream of American life. The economic pressures of a stagflationary economy have doubled the pressures on millions of men and women to climb the ladder of their careers. The traditional family where one person works outside the home and the other takes care of the family is an endangered species (16 percent of American households now fit into this category). Men are under more pressure than ever to share the burdens of child care and domestic responsibilities; women are making unprecedented headway in business, science, and government. We are swept up in social transformations that are likely to alter the American home and lifestyle for decades to come. Caught in the conflicting push of divergent social and family pressures, many people are falling victim to feelings of guilt for their inability to live up to all their expectations. The magic in their lives is lost in the self-punishing admonition, "I can't do enough . . ."

Valerie is a bright young woman with a husband, two children, two cats, a dog, and a large apartment, and an excellent position with a local public relations agency. Her husband is an assistant bank vice-president, her children are in a nursery school/day-care center five days a week, and she has a housekeeper Mondays, Wednesdays, and Fridays. She runs two miles every other day, serves her family low-cholesterol meals, and keeps up to date on the latest health news. Meet her and the first thing you notice is her abundant energy. It radiates from her large blue eyes. Talk to her for a short while, however, and you find she is torn by inner turmoil. She feels terribly guilty for not providing her children with the homelife that she had when she was a child.

"My mother was always home," she recalls. "If I got sick at school or came home unhappy after a fight with a girlfriend, she was there. Like all children, I took her loving, secure presence for granted. In retrospect, I'm sure it was very important to me in ways that psychologists haven't yet been able to measure. I can't provide that same kind of home atmosphere for my children, and I feel guilty about it.

I worry that I'm letting them down, that I'm not fulfilling my responsibilities as a mother."

Compounding Valerie's guilt is a belief that she may be sacrificing her children to pursue what she sees as a selfish desire for a career. "I don't have to work," she explains. "That makes it worse. My career is my choice, and it provides me with a great deal of personal satisfaction. It's a purely selfish decision."

She resents her husband for not feeling the same guilt she does about the children: "What a cruel joke! Now I've got the career I've wanted, but I'm plagued by this guilt. Michael says not to worry about the children, but that's easy for him. Men have never taken responsibility for children, so he can take that attitude."

Valerie's dilemma flows from her inflated expectations. There is no way for her to be exactly like the mother of her own childhood memories and still achieve her career goals. Somewhere she has to compromise and accept her limitations. Her guilt is self-punishment for not being able to live up to all her dreams.

To end her war against herself, Valerie had to do some deep soul-searching. Would she be better off staying home with her children, trying to be the model mother of her memories? Or should she continue to pursue her career? Could she compromise and do both? She was finally able to make her decision when she began to accept her own emotional realities. "If I give up my career," she decided, "I'll be miserable, and that would be worse for my children." She rejected the idea of working part-time because she felt that would leave her in a nebulous middle ground.

Today she isn't entirely free of concern about her mothering, but she is learning to relish her dynamic life-style without constantly undermining herself with guilt. In practice, she has become more conscious and appreciative of the time she spends with her children. "I am learning that it isn't just the amount of time but the quality of it," she says. To make certain she doesn't let career pressures shortchange her children, she sets aside time each evening for play and conversation with them. She and her husband also make a point of taking the children on an outing at least one afternoon per week, usually Saturday or Sunday. "I'm finally realizing that I can't create the home my mother did. The times have changed, but it doesn't mean our family life is any less fun or any less loving." Indeed, now that Valerie is setting aside her anhedonic guilt, she has more inner joy to share than she thought.

Feeling Guilty for Feeling Good

Innocent until proven guilty—that's a fundamental premise of our culture, but you'd never know it by looking at how some people treat themselves. Somewhere in the back of their minds they maintain a belief that innocence is the very sign of guilt. Whenever they have an occasion for deep personal gratification or even a little relaxed fun, they're on the alert for reasons to cut their joy short. They treat themselves like prisoners who steal pleasure to which they have no right. Here are examples:

"What about my friend?"

Edith has received word she's been promoted to department manager. Overjoyed at first, she suddenly suffers pangs of guilt because her promotion means that Anne, her best friend, doesn't get the job.

"I'm escaping from my problems."

Paul has been struggling with a set of serious business problems for the last two weeks without a break. He decides to take an evening off for dinner and a movie, but by the time the movie begins, he's getting a knot in his stomach because he feels he is being "escapist."

"What about my husband?"

Nancy's husband is in the hospital for gallbladder surgery. She visits him every day, but visiting hours are over at eight. Trying to be helpful, a neighbor invites her over for a drink and to meet some new people. She's not tired, so she goes, but once she gets there, she can't enjoy herself because she keeps feeling guilty about her husband.

"I'm terrible for letting my boss/friend down."

Janet has a date this evening. Just as she's about to leave work, her boss asks if she'd mind staying late. This is not the first time. Her boss has commended her many times for her willingness to ignore the clock and work until the job gets done. But tonight she has tickets to a play and no way of reaching her date. She explains why she can't stay; her boss is completely understanding. Nevertheless, she feels guilty all evening.

"I don't deserve it."

Steven, an artist, has his first one-man show. All his paintings sell. His gallery wants him to exhibit regularly. After struggling for five years, he finally appears to have a future as an artist, but he can't rejoice freely in his success. Somewhere deep inside he keeps hearing, "I don't deserve it."

"It should have been me."

Judy and her friend Martha were on their way to the shopping center. A car hit them from behind. Judy was driving and wasn't hurt; she was wearing a seat belt. Martha wasn't wearing a seat belt and was seriously injured when she hit the windshield. Police reports confirm that Judy was in no way responsible for the accident, but that isn't enough for Judy. She can't shake the feeling that the accident wouldn't have happened if she'd been more alert. Every time she thinks of Martha, she feels terribly guilty.

"I'm being silly."

Anne and her husband Tony are at the beach with their friends Joan and Tye. It's a Wednesday afternoon. The beach is completely deserted. Anne would like everyone to toss off their bathing suits and go frolicking in the surf, but she can't bring herself to make the suggestion. "It's so child-ish," she tells herself, feeling guilty for her wish.

Behind each of these guilt messages lurks the old puri-tanical notion: hard-working, moral, virtuous people keep fun to a minimum. Enjoyment, according to this philosophy, is the first sign of sin. If you're having fun, you can't be taking your responsibilities seriously. You can't be caring adequately for those you love. You can't be showing compassion for other people's hardships. If living is serious business, any sign of frivolity means you're trying to escape from reality.

If this self-forfeiting philosophy has even the slightest grip on you, you have changes to make. The roots of this anhedonic attitude extend far back into your childhood when you learned that grownups take life very seriously and the sooner you start doing so, the better off you will be. That's part of life's deal. What you *weren't* told is that enthusiasm, enjoyment, and fun are every bit as important to effective living as hard work and responsibility. You can't possibly be enthusiastic about living if you start imposing guilt on yourself whenever you take a break from your responsibilities.

You've got to start asking: *What am I actually accomplishing with my guilt?* Only then can you take steps to eliminate it.

The Psychological Support System for Feeling Guilty

Here are some hidden payoffs for making yourself feel guilty:

The discomfort of guilt can bolster your self-image.

You can hold up your self-censure as proof that you're a genuinely caring, responsible, hard-working person who shuns "frivolous" enjoyment. You can tell yourself that others live for themselves alone while you put all your efforts into serving humanity without thought of personal gratification. The more anguish you inflict on yourself, the better a person you can believe yourself to be. Taken to the extreme, this holier-than-thou attitude can make you feel truly superior.

By choosing to feel guilty, you can avoid the risks of de-

claring your own uniqueness and standing up for your personal values.

You probably have misgivings about some of the traditional values you learned as a child. Do you have the courage to challenge them and define the values by which you want to live your life? It's easier to punish yourself with guilt for breaking a childhood rule than to challenge the validity of that rule and stand up for what you think is right. Guilt keeps you safely tied to your past and spares you the anxiety of looking into your own future.

If you make yourself miserable enough with guilt, you can hope that you'll exonerate yourself for past misdeeds.

The only way to make amends for the past is to do something in the present to repair the damage or right the wrong. Taking such steps is not easy. You may not know what to do; you may be ashamed to face the person whom you hurt; you may feel too embarrassed to admit you did something wrong. One answer is to punish yourself silently with your own guilt and hope that this self-punishment will somehow make amends for you. Of course, it won't. All you're doing is avoiding your fear of publicly admitting your mistake.

If you tell others how guilty you feel, you're using your guilt to win pity.

This allows you to trade your own discomfort for comforting words from others. You can hear the sweet words of praise for the virtue you display by making yourself feel so miserable. (What no one notices is that your guilt accomplishes nothing more than to make you an object of pity.)

Guilt can help you hide from your own fear of pleasure.

When your life is going well and you're feeling great, your enjoyment may start causing you to feel anxious about feeling "too good." Rather than face your fear of pleasure, you can inhibit further enjoyment by imposing a measure of guilt. This stamps out your joy and spares encounters with ecstasy, an experience that might change your comfortable view of yourself and your world. For some people, anything is preferable to the anxiety of personal growth. Guilt helps you stay the way you are.

If you're clever, you can use your guilt to transfer blame for your discomfort.

You can complain about how other people manipulate you into feeling guilty so you'll do their bidding. This allows you to adopt the posture of the innocent victim made miserable by big powerful others who always have their way.

Guilt is a highly effective way to fill your time with ruminations about the past (so you can avoid the challenges and anxiety of the now).

When things go wrong, it's so much easier to consume your present moments with guilt than pick up the pieces in the present. Guilt immobilizes you, allows you to sit back and hope that things will get better by themselves. If they don't, you can deny responsibility. After all, you were busy feeling guilty.

These psychological rewards constitute the basic support system for your self-chastising behavior. Note that each transforms guilt into something else. Guilt immobilizes you in the present or ties you to the past. It's a trade-off against the anxiety inherent in the challenge of growth. Trading guilt for the opportunity for self-affirmation is not a very good deal. If you're ready to start making a better one, you're ready for strategies to eliminate self-defeating guilt.

Some Steps for Reducing Guilt

The key to overcoming needless guilt is learning to give yourself permission to be a unique individual with distinct interests, ideas, values, preferences. The more freely you express your individuality, the more satisfaction you'll get from work, the more joy you'll experience with others. Guilt is self-punishment aimed at keeping you tied to other people's ideas about the right way to live. Your happiness lies in discovering your own right way. The following strategies can give you the permission and freedom you need:

Stop trying to make decisions according to some abstract idea of right and wrong.

If you get five people together and ask them about important decisions in your life (whom to marry, whether or not to quit your job, where you should live, what your responsibilities are to your parents), you're likely to get five different answers. *For most of the decisions you face, there is no absolute right and wrong!* There are merely different courses of action with varying consequences. The self-affirming way to make a decision is to look at the consequences honestly and determine which are most in accord with your desires and intentions. This gives you permission to be who you are. People who look for an ultimate right or wrong in everything they do often feel guilty no matter what choice they make. They have difficulty making up their minds because they can't see their decision in terms of the likely consequences. They turn inward, hoping for mystical insight into the "right" way. When a decision doesn't work out, they feel guilty for having listened to the "wrong" inner voice.

Recognize that no one is perfect, and that you (like everyone else) are entitled to make mistakes.

"Aversion training" means learning through punishment. If you insist on punishing yourself every time you make a mistake, you're gong to train yourself never to take risks, never to stray from the norm, never to dare stepping outside your routine. Which inhibits joy by repressing your creativity.

Let yourself put the past behind you once and for all.

Make a list of everything you've done in the past that still causes you to feel guilty. Don't rush! Give yourself a couple of days to make it complete. Then take a look at each item. Is there anything you can do to make amends for any unhappy incidents? If so, go ahead and do it. Now! With the remaining list, ask yourself: is your guilty feeling going to accomplish anything? The choice is yours: Are you going to continue wasting time on the past? Or will you put these old guilts behind you once and for all?

Confront your values honestly and decide which you believe in and which you don't.

Some people say, "I understand intellectually that I shouldn't feel guilty, but I still feel that way." This is a common self-deception. If you really understood that you shouldn't feel guilty, then you wouldn't. If you feel guilty about some behavior, then you still believe that what you're doing is wrong, though you may tell yourself otherwise. Let's examine a case to make this clear:

Dorothy is a young woman with a sexual interest in other women as well as men. She came for help because she kept feeling guilty about her relationship with her sister's girl-friend. "I know intellectually I shouldn't feel guilty," she said, "but after I leave her, I start getting down on myself about what I'm doing. I can't help it."

An attractive, dark petite woman of twenty-nine, Dorothy has had satisfying relationships with men and professes an interest in marriage if she meets "the right guy." She discovered her love for women one summer weekend when she went on a canoeing trip with two female friends. "I suspected they were getting it on together," she explains, "but I wasn't sure. Out there in the woods, we all went skinny dipping and that led to more. They coaxed me into it; it all seemed so natural. I opened up to feelings of love that I'd never experienced. Making love with a woman is so different from being with a man, so much more tender, so slow and gentle."

Dorothy had two choices in dealing with her guilt. First, she could abstain from further relationships with women. This choice she completely rejected. The second alternative was to stop intellectualizing about her guilt and uncover the real feelings behind it. Once she stopped telling herself that sex with women was all right, her suppressed feelings emerged. She feared that she would lose all interest in men. She also felt shame for engaging in what she labeled "perversions."

Having coaxed her true feelings in the open, Dorothy was

able to face them. She was encouraged to listen to a tape of herself describing her lovemaking. Did it sound shameful? "No," she said. "It's not dirty at all. It's beautiful!" She also asked herself whether she was still attracted to men and she recognized that she was. Through this difficult and direct exploration of her experiences, she was able to establish new connections between her true feelings and her beliefs. Through gentle and gradual self-exploration, she eliminated the roots of what she saw as her self-destructive guilt. She now feels proud that she freely expresses her desires for love and sexual sharing with women. "The new feeling of freedom is ecstatic. It's wonderful," she says exuberantly. "Sex has become for me a ritual of completely joyful self-expression."

Make a point of taking time for some "frivolous" fun when you might normally feel guilty about doing so.

If you're struggling to get through a load of work and would feel guilty for taking a break, go ahead and take an afternoon off. Be sure and spend a few hours doing something you truly enjoy like swimming, reading, ice skating, or just watching TV. Think of it as a minivacation. If you've given yourself permission for pure enjoyment, you'll notice a great surge of energy when you go back to work. Learning to take minivacations without feeling guilty is fundamental to "doing less and accomplishing more."

Stop letting yourself be manipulated by your boss, friend, or spouse.

If you can be easily manipulated with guilt, those around you will quickly spot your weakness and take advantage of it whenever they need your help. Your boss will ask you to work late, your friend will keep asking too many favors, your spouse will expect you to pull twice your share of the household tasks. No one will give a moment's consideration to your needs and desires. This is not a cynical view of human relationships; it is factual. You bring on this disregard for your needs by putting out the message: "I want you to see how kind and virtuous I am, so I'll drop everything to help you out. Just ask." If you're tired of being at everyone else's beck and call, or if you want to stop feeling guilty when others ask you for favors, you've got to stop sending out this message. You've got to start letting people know that you are busy, your needs also deserve your attention, and you aren't available at the drop of a hat. You'll find that people respect you far more for taking this stance than they do for making yourself a human doormat.

Learn to express your feelings confidently.

When someone is trying to make you feel guilty, they can only succeed if you cooperate by suppressing your real feelings. If you speak out frankly, the inner tension necessary to guilt will be released; both of you will then see your relationship in a broader context. The following dialogue between a mother and daughter illustrates the key points to keep in mind. It is taken from a role-playing exercise. The daughter was learning how to cope with the mother's efforts to manipulate with guilt.

MOTHER: Don't you feel it's time to settle down? You know what I mean. Find a husband and get married. If you don't have children soon, I'll never be a grandmother.
DAUGHTER: I think you're still worried that I'll never have a husband or children. Why don't you ever ask whether I'm happy with what I am doing?
MOTHER: Your father and I have given you everything you've wanted. Now we want to see you settled. You can't go on with this acting career forever, you know.
DAUGHTER: You tell me you're worried about me, but it sounds like your real worry is for you and dad. I'm only twenty-five and my career is getting better every year.
MOTHER: After all we've done for you, the least I'd expect is that you'd want to make us happy now. Your father is so dearly looking forward to having grandchildren.
DAUGHTER: You want me to settle down in the suburbs with a husband and children just like you did, but that isn't what I want out of life. Would you please try to understand that my dreams are different from yours?
MOTHER: You insist on making us unhappy! Such ingratitude! And your father has a weak heart, remember?
DAUGHTER: You're telling me you can only be happy if I live my life according to your script. I understand you feel I'm ungrateful for wanting to live my own life, but surely you can understand I have to follow the dictates of my own

conscience. I think dad will be more proud of me for doing what I believe is right than just trying to please him.

MOTHER: How can you be so stubborn and cruel?

DAUGHTER: You know I love you and dad very much and don't want to hurt you in any way. What you see as stubbornness, I see as passion for my work! I hope one day you'll appreciate that passion and recognize how grateful I am for all you've done. Without your love and support all these years, I could never have come this far.

The conflict is self-evident. The daughter wants to pursue her career; the mother wants to see her daughter settled with a husband, children, and a secure future. The real problem arises when the mother tries to manipulate her daughter with guilt. The mother has been very effective using this device to control her daughter's behavior. Over the past few years, the mother has gradually lost control. The daughter sought help to cope with the guilt her mother could still engender and improve her relationship with her mother.

This dialogue illustrates five keys to expressing your feelings when someone is trying to manipulate you with guilt:

1. Restate the other person's feelings in *you* language. The daughter says "*you* are worried," "*you* want," and "*you* feel." This helps make clear that the distress is primarily the mother's problem, not the daughter's.

2. Ask the other person to appreciate your feelings. When the daughter says "Please try to understand that my dreams are different from yours," she succeeds in letting her mother know that there are two sides to the story and she affirms her right to have her own feelings and dreams.

3. Let the other person know that you appreciate their feelings. When the daughter says "I understand you feel I'm ungrateful," she is telling her mother that she is taking very seriously everything her mother has to say. Having heard her mother, she can still hold to her own viewpoint.

4. State your reasons for following your course of action. The daughter says she must follow her own conscience, that her career is improving, and that she has a passion for acting. All these statements reinforce the daughter's right to her own viewpoint.

5. End the discussion with positive feelings, if possible. By closing with an expression of love and hope, the daughter can walk away from the conversation without residual feelings of bitterness and can feel compassion for her mother.

Temper your personal expectations with reasonable appreciation of your limitations.

With the accelerating pace of living, you're bound to be pulled in many directions. Work, family, friends, your own interests all compete for your time and energy. The larger-than-life character in some novels and movies would have you believe you can do it all. This is the superman (superwoman) mentality. It's fine for exciting entertainment; it can make you miserable if you try to emulate it in your daily life. There is wisdom in recognizing that there are conflicts in your life you won't be able to resolve. Punishing yourself for not being able to is an exercise in false pride.

Worry (the Other Side of Guilt)

For every ounce of needless guilt there is another ounce of useless worry. Guilt and worry, hand in hand, are masters of self-punishment, two sides of the same coin. Let guilt play an inordinate role in your emotional life and there's depression. With worry, you make anxiety a constant companion. Neither is inevitable; you have to choose to give them power over you. Just as you can choose to eliminate anhedonic guilt, you can decide to put destructive worry out of your life.

Why do you worry? Well, there's a lot to worry about. The six o'clock news brings you the day's disasters. Inflation keeps driving prices up and it seems harder every month to keep pace. Our streets aren't safe during the day, much less at night. The energy crisis keeps getting worse and the politicians seem paralyzed. And still beyond are all the personal causes for worry: your health, your job, your marriage, your weight, a car accident, a plane crash, or your graying hair. And how about the weather?

Make a worry list. Question: Are these the true sources of your worry? Mark Twain wrote: "Worry is like a rocking chair. It goes back and forth but gets you nowhere." Perhaps this thought has occurred to you. Obviously, no amount of worry is going to bring down the inflation rate, ease the energy crisis, reduce crime in the streets. Worrying isn't going to save your job, protect you from cancer or a heart attack, or stop your hair from graying. This simple insight should convince you that the real reason for your worry is not on your worry list at all. It lies elsewhere. Discover that cause and you'll own the key to eliminating worry forever.

Worry vs. Concern

First, distinguish between effective concern and useless rumination. On your worry list are many causes for genuine concern. If something isn't done about the energy crisis, the national economy will become more disabled. If you don't exercise and eat a high-fat diet, or if you continue to smoke cigarettes, you are very likely to suffer a heart attack or get cancer. Valid reasons for concern, no question.

The difference between concern and worry lies in your ability to do something about potential disasters that may lie ahead. Concern leads to action. If you're concerned about inflation, vote for leaders you think can stop it. If you're concerned about your health, make changes in your diet and life-style. Concern is a natural expression of your own appreciation of your ability to control your own destiny. Only a fool goes through life free of concern.

Worry is very different. When you worry, your power to do something about potential disaster never enters the picture. The opposite is the case: worry arises from feelings of powerlessness. When you worry, you may start thinking about all the difficulties your family will face if you lose your job. Or you envision a panic in your household when you can't get gas to go to work or enough heating oil to keep the pipes from freezing. Or you imagine the crushing pain of a heart attack. In all these mental pictures is you, sitting in the middle of calamity, incapable of acting.

Fundamental to all worry is a fear that you have no control over your future. Worry is a disguise and a self-inflicted punishment for that fear. Few people like to look fear in the face, especially fear of their own powerlessness. Worry is a convenient mental escape mechanism. At the same time, no one is proud of trying to escape from fear. Bring on old reliable worry! It disguises your fear and punishes you for refusing to confront it honestly. Escape mechanism plus self-punishment for running away—that's what worry is about.

Karen is pregnant and worries about having a normal child. No family history suggests she has a high risk of bearing an abnormal child. She worries anyway. "Every mother worries about that," she tells herself. Ask her whether she could love and care for an abnormal child and the real cause of her worry surfaces. "I don't know what I'd do if the child isn't normal," she says fretfully. There, Karen says it. The real cause of her worry is her own fear of being emotionally paralyzed should her baby be abnormal.

Dana and his wife have stretched their credit to the limit and now worry more than ever about their bills. "Anyone with my income has got to worry about bills," Dana insists. Is Dana in any danger of losing his job? No, but explains, "If I get some unexpected expenses . . . an illness, a problem with the house—I don't know what I'm going to do." There it is again, the phrase "I don't know what I'm going to do." Dana fears he won't be able to find any way out of financial catastrophe if he gets one unexpected bill. Making plans for that eventuality doesn't enter his mind. Instead, he worries because he can't face his fear of an inability to pay his bills.

Nancy is planning a big party. It'll require using her patio and deck as well as the first floor of her house. She's worried about the weather. "What will I do if it rains?" she asks. Again fear of immobilization takes precedence over sensible concern. Instead of making plans to accommodate her guests in case of rain, she consumes her present moments with worry, adding one more unnecessary ounce of anxiety to her life.

Joan's husband is a traveling salesman. She worries every time he comes home late, even though "I know the worrying doesn't accomplish anything." Ask her to imagine how she'd feel if her husband didn't come home one night, and the real cause of her worry surfaces. "I couldn't stand being left alone! What would I do?" She's *concerned* about her husband. But she's *worried* about herself.

To eliminate worry you have to eradicate your fear of having no control over your life in difficult circumstances. You have to learn to appreciate your own power. Before you can do that, however, you have to understand the psychological rewards you derive from worry.

Some Benefits of Worry

Worry allows you to think you're accomplishing something when you're standing still.

Worry consumes a lot of energy. Your fatigue is proof of your efforts. Even though you may plainly see that you're not accomplishing anything, the constant rumination about a potential problem can look like progress. At least you're exploring all the possibilities in your mind, or so you may tell yourself.

Worry can add to your feelings of self-importance.

Busy people face many problems, so they would seem to have lots to worry about. By making sure to keep a few worries at hand, you too can be one of these busy people. The only flaw with this reasoning is that truly busy people are far too busy to waste time worrying.

Worry can help you avoid unpleasant tasks.

Perhaps you have a report to finish, but you just can't get to it. Rather than face your procrastination head on, you can find something to worry about—your children, your bills, your spouse, the weather—anything will do as long as you can tell yourself "I'm too worried to get to work."

Some people use worry as a sign that they are truly caring, loving people.

The logic is that if you love someone, you absolutely must worry about them. Little does it matter that the worry accomplishes nothing except to make you anxious. The more you worry, the more you can tell yourself what a good friend, spouse, or parent you are.

Worry can send you to the doctor or even put you in the hospital.

Valium is the most prescribed drug in America because we live with an epidemic of worry and anxiety. Hypertension, ulcers, and nervous breakdowns may all result from incessant worry. While these may not seem like rewards, some people depend on illness to get pity from others and escape from their problems.

Worry can be a very effective justification for all kinds of self-nullifying behavior.

You may have a problem with overeating. No doubt you eat more when you are worried. If you just keep worrying, you won't ever have to go on a diet. How can you diet when you're so worried? The same holds true of smoking, drinking, lack of exercise, other self-destructive habits. Worry is a wonderful excuse for avoiding the challenge of growth.

These are not the only rewards for worry. You can probably find others of your own. Once you've diagnosed the psychological support system that upholds your own worrying, you're ready for strategies of change.

Eleven Ways to End Worry

Ask yourself what you're avoiding by consuming your present moments with worry.

Perhaps you're putting off a difficult task. If so, put your mind on constructive activity that will help you finish the task as swiftly as possible. If you're avoiding a confrontation with a destructive habit like overeating or smoking, resolve to stop wasting your energy on worry and start using it for personal growth. The key is to transform worry from a signal to do nothing into a sign to get moving.

Take an inventory of your worries and see what they accomplish.

Did your worry about any of the items on your list ever alter their outcome? How many of the catastrophes that you have worried about actually occurred? These questions should demonstrate the futility of worry.

Label your worries as anhedonic thinking undeserving of your attention.

For your worry habit to persist, you have to invest energy in your worries by allowing each one to dominate your awareness. Next time you get all wound up in worries, tell yourself, "There I go again, worrying, the same old anhedonic thinking. It means nothing at all." This statement is enough to end your bout with worry. You become aware that you have a choice. Instead of dwelling on your worries, you can choose to favor something positive, such as making plans or setting to work on a creative project. Make a habit of *labeling* your worries as anhedonic thoughts; you'll be surprised how quickly your worry habit fades.

Next time you worry about someone you care about, do something constructive to show your love instead.

If your spouse is coming home late and you're worried, do something around the house that your spouse will appreciate. Bake a cake, do some cleaning, get out some wine and music for a little romance when your spouse comes home. It doesn't matter what you do as long as it's something concrete to express your love rather than sitting and idly indulging in your worry.

If you're an absolutely confirmed worrier, you may find it necessary to use affirmations to break your habit. (See chapter V.)

Here are two affirmations you can use: "I am free from needless worries" and "I am confident that I can take care of myself in every circumstance." Use both of these affirmations twice a day for a month or two; you'll have made a major step in eliminating anhedonic worry.

Face your fear of powerlessness.

If you're worrying about some potential disaster, ask yourself what's the worst that can happen. Get a clear picture in your mind of this calamity. Now ask yourself: What would you do if it occurred? Don't suppress your feelings of fear. Do consider what options you might have. Instead of worrying, make concrete plans for action. This will transform your worry into concern.

Beware of the belief that you need worry as a motivator.

One of my clients, who suffered from an ulcer, told me, "If I don't worry about what worries me, then what I fear is likely to come true." This means she believed her worrying was essential to accomplishing the important tasks in her life and to avoiding any personal catastrophes. She believed she had to worry about grades, or else she would get F's. If she didn't worry about bringing her grandmother flowers in the hospital, she would forget. If she didn't worry about getting a summer job, she wouldn't get one. She had developed the habit of *treating herself like a mule she had to whip to keep moving.* I explained that she was expending as much energy in self-punishment as she was in achievement. To break her worry habit, I asked her to make a conscious effort to find some enjoyment in everything that she was doing and let the enjoyment be her motivator. In that way, I explained, she would get twice as much done with twice as much pleasure because she would be able to use all the energy she was wasting in needless worry. The same strategy can work for you.

Try to turn your worry into an opportunity for healthy laughter.

Try setting aside ten minutes a day to do all your worrying. If you catch yourself worrying at another time, just tell yourself to wait until the designated time. Try this once or twice and your worry period will soon become full of belly laughs because you will see how ridiculous worrying is.

If you catch yourself worrying, tell yourself to stop, then do something that will bring you pleasure.

That way you'll reward yourself for cutting short your period of immobilization and doing something constructive instead. You'll learn that taking a break from your troubles and having some fun is much preferable to wasting time making yourself unhappy with worry. Beware of feeling guilty for not worrying.

If a worry won't leave you alone, use a technique called "thought stopping."

This makes use of your ability to control the thoughts that pass across the screen of your awareness. To stop a worry cold, take a few minutes to sit down in a comfortable place, close your eyes, and either silently or quietly tell the worry, "Go away" or "Get out of my head." Usually repression of feelings through willpower is not helpful, but with the worry habit it can be very helpful. Feel free to do this as often as you like.

Recognize the wisdom of accepting life's uncertainties and confusion.

There are many aspects of your life over which you have little or no control. So why get worried or anxious? It's wiser to treat these uncertainties like the weather. Accept them and go on to other things.

These simple strategies can banish worry from your life. All you need is the commitment to put them into practice.

A Matter of Choice

In the final analysis, the key to eradicating guilt and worry is recognizing that you have the power to eliminate them. Our culture teaches you that guilt and worry are emotional states you can't avoid. This is pure fiction. Behind all guilt and worry are hidden psychological payoffs. For most people choosing self-defeating actions has become so habitual that they feel guilt and worry are inevitable. Under examination the error in this belief becomes clear.

In his essay "Golden Day" Robert Burdette wrote several famous lines that sum up the key to living free from guilt and worry: "There are two days a week about which and upon which I never worry. Two carefree days, kept sacredly free from fear and apprehension. One of these days is yesterday . . . and the other . . . is tomorrow." These lines became famous because they ring so true. Whether you inhibit your life with guilt and worry or choose to live wholly and unhesitatingly in the present is up to you.

VIII

Making Anger
Work for You

I was angry with my friend
I told my wrath, my wrath did end.
I was angry with my foe:
I told it not, my wrath did grow.
        —WILLIAM BLAKE

Nothing on earth consumes a man more
quickly than the passion of resentment.
        —FRIEDRICH NIETZSCHE

ANGER is frequently maligned and often misunderstood. Many find it frightening. For most, it's troublesome.
On the receiving end of an angry outburst you're likely to
feel defensive, threatened, and unjustly under attack. If
you mete out an emotional tirade, you may well wind up
feeling drained, tense, guilty about losing control. Giving as
well as receiving, anger seems most often destructive. In
fact, getting angry is fundamental to being human; denying
anger is as destructive as expressing it excessively.

In this imperfect world, anger is often the only sensible
response to a nasty situation. Consider:

- A friend betrays your trust by blabbing something you had
  asked to be kept strictly confidential.
- Your boss fails to acknowledge your assistance with a report
  that gets highly praised by the company president.

- Your parents continue to berate your spouse even though you have asked them many times to stop.
- Your child gets caught shoplifting in a drugstore.
- Your lover leaves you without saying goodbye.
- Your best friend dies because of a design flaw in his car.
- You get fired without warning.
- Your spouse agrees to help you with an important project, then forgets to do some things you are counting on.
- You get mugged or your house gets broken into.
- A cab driver takes you ten blocks out of your way and you wind up late for an appointment.
- You get passed over for promotion because you're a woman, black, Mexican-American, or a member of some other group that's subject to discrimination.
- You come down with a serious illness.
- People at work keep barging in on you with their problems while you're trying to work on yours.

Anger is a perfectly natural response to such emotional injury. You have absorbed negative energy that has been projected at you with varying degrees of intensity. To balance your emotional scales and create an opportunity for resolution of the hurt, anger is important and healthy. If you suppress your anger, you add insult to injury by denying your own feelings and your right to stand up for yourself.

The price you pay for suppressing anger is reduced sensitivity to all your feelings. The only way to deny a strong feeling such as anger is to mask it with another. With anger, the usual disguise is indifference. To make the denial convincing, especially to yourself, you have to put a lot of energy into your indifference with elaborate intellectualizations of why "it doesn't matter" or why you "ought to just forget it." You also have to keep a careful watch on all your emotions lest one persistent feeling rupture your facade and break the dam holding back your anger.

To reinforce your fortifications, you must limit your awareness of your world by turning away from what you're afraid to see and becoming a little deaf to what you don't want to hear. You become a highly defended individual with little room for spontaneous responses because you put more energy into controlling your feelings than into dealing openly with others. You weaken yourself in the name of self-control and you inhibit your passion and your inner joy.

It is not that you ought to go walking around with a chip on your shoulder or that anger is easy to master. If you set yourself up to take offense every time your wishes are frustrated, you could remain angry almost all the time. That would obviously be silly and destructive. Also, if you're hurt deeply by someone close to you, throwing a tantrum and stomping out of the room in a rage isn't going to be very helpful. Anger is natural, but you have to learn how to use it, just as you have to learn how to use language.

We want to help you become comfortable with anger and learn how to make it work for you. At bottom, anger is a source of power. It puts your system into overdrive when and if you need it. Far from a useless emotion or a genetic mistake, anger can serve the growth of your relationships and the expansion of inner joy. Maybe this seems paradoxical. Hold on! The better you understand the constructive functions of anger, the more clearly you'll see its relationship to inner joy.

Destructive vs. Constructive Anger

There are two ways to get angry and they differ in intent, quality, and outcome. You can explode because you want to repay another person for the hurt he or she caused you. Whether you scream in rage or walk out in cold silence, the goal is the same: to punish the other person for an offense. Or you can use heated words and gestures to communicate your hurt and explain how you want the relationship to change. You may yell or curse, but you don't back down or walk out until you get your point across.

In the first case, your anger adds hostility, creates additional bitterness, and freezes the relationship around an event of the past. In the second case, your anger releases tension, facilitates an emotional breakthrough, and helps the relationship evolve to a new level of mutual respect, understanding, and appreciation. In the end, anger that punishes is destructive; anger that communicates is constructive.

When anger becomes infected with the desire to punish, it becomes twisted. Its effects on you and others are wholly negative. Destructive anger—

- weakens self-esteem and creates a feeling of impotence because it only exposes lack of self-control
- masks your real feelings of hurt with cold indifference or a furious assault
- inhibits communication and leaves you feeling tense or bitter
- creates emotional distance, destroys relationships, increases feelings of isolation
- defeats its own purpose by making other people turn away from you while you wind up compounding your own tension and frustration
- leads to ulcers, high blood pressure, and headaches when you get locked into a defensive and chronically angry pose
- accumulates over time and contributes to general hostility and distrust that seep out in nasty bits and pieces

Anger becomes constructive when its specific characteristics contribute to healing the underlying emotional injury. Constructive anger—

- empowers you to stand up for yourself and stop putting up with the pain you've been caused
- helps you communicate your hurt so that you're free to say "I feel let down, betrayed, disappointed, pushed around"
- allows you to share the intensity of your hurt with appropriately forceful language
- enables you to break through a fixed and destructive pattern in a relationship
- aims for mutual understanding so the relationship can be restored on a new footing where your feelings are given more weight
- has the stated purpose of changing the relationship in specific ways that will help avoid future hurts and misunderstandings
- prepares the emotional ground for forgiveness and forgetting once the relationship begins to shift to its new footing

Making Anger Work for You

Many people are frightened by their own anger and intimidated by anger in others because their experience is largely with the negative variety. Here's what one typical group had to say about anger:

- "It's a waste of energy."
- "When I get angry, I'm afraid the other person will fall apart."
- "I've got to keep the lid on or I'll lose control."
- "It's childish."
- "I'm afraid of what'll happen in response."

There you have the common rationales for avoiding anger and denying the personal power that only anger can give you. To the degree that your experience with anger is negative, these attitudes may make sense. If you get angry and wind up feeling bitter, or if you get into an angry argument that ends up destroying an old friendship, or if you explode at your boss and lose your job, you learn to distrust anger. To change your attitude toward anger and learn how to make it constructive, you must first understand the difference between anger and its expresssion.

Anger per se is neither positive nor negative. It's a simple emotion with specific signs and symptoms. When you get angry you feel a surge of energy, your blood pressure increases, your muscles tense, and you may feel warm. You're likely to have destructive thoughts such as "I'd like to wring his neck!" or "I'd like to show her up for what she is!" Many people are uncomfortable with these powerful feelings: "I get nervous when I get angry," said one of my clients; "It makes me feel guilty," said another. These feelings lead to an internal struggle that inhibits the natural experience of anger and makes it more difficult to control.

Stop for a moment and look objectively at the sensations of anger. What's wrong with feeling a surge of energy, or a muscle tensing, or a wave of warmth, or a violent thought passing through the mind? These components of anger in themselves are neither good nor bad. They just are. Whether anger becomes destructive or constructive depends on how you channel the energies that anger releases in you. To control your anger, you must allow yourself to feel it. Paradoxically, the more you experience the power in your chest, the rising energy in your body, and the heightened alertness of your mind, the more control you have over your anger, and the less grip it has on you.

Sometimes it's useful to think of anger as a chemical reaction. When you apply heat to a piece of wood, carbon compounds react with oxygen, and the wood bursts into flame. Given enough heat and an adequate oxygen supply, the fire is inevitable. It's the same with anger. Given enough emotional hurt or frustration, the human psyche responds with anger. Adrenaline pours into the bloodstream, creating a surge of energy. Blood pressure increases along with alertness and body temperature. You can't turn this response off; you've got to do something with it. If you fight it and lose control, it comes out in a destructive display. If you block it with other emotions, it goes underground but continues to smolder like a fire doused with water but not put out. The third possibility is to accept the anger, let yourself feel it, then collect yourself and use the energy to deal with your hurt.

Anger becomes positive when you shape your expression of it with these characteristics:

Warmth. You release your feelings honestly and openly with strong words to let the other person know that you have been hurt.

A *clear goal.* You want the person who hurt you to acknowledge your hurt and to agree on how you can avoid future misunderstandings.

Release. It allows you to feel better, forgive, and forget. You completely release the tension that accompanied your anger so you can see the relationship in a new light and be magnanimous about forgiveness.

Brevity. You get your anger out in five or ten minutes by expressing it as directly and honestly as you can. This doesn't mean you'll move to understanding and forgiveness so quickly. The angry outburst may open doors to many issues that need examination. Their discussion may take time, but the hostility will be lessened quickly and the atmosphere becomes conducive to reconciliation.

Sorting Out the Slush

Some people express their anger frequently but rarely wind up achieving any positive outcome. When an angry outburst leaves them feeling tense or bitter, they blame the world for being unfair, insensitive, cruel. You hear them calling others stupid, selfish, and dishonest. Even when they're in a "good" mood, anger may slip out in bits through acerbic remarks and nasty comments. These people can't go into a store without getting into an argument with a salesperson or get their car repaired without having a bout with the mechanic. They claim that trouble follows them. They never consider the possibility that they may be creating the conditions for all the hostility in their lives.

The underlying problem is a confusion of present irritation with past hurts accumulated over a lifetime. Each of us carries around a reservoir of emotional slush of old, never fully healed hurts. The response to those hurts was anger that got buried. These old hurts and unresolved anger become sources of personal sensitivity, emotional red buttons that lead to blowups when they get pushed by somebody's thoughtless comment or action.

Anger that stems from emotional slush is almost always destructive. When someone pushes an emotional red button, the explosion is often completely out of proportion with real injury. Accumulated slush also can poison a relationship gradually by seeping out in bits at every opportunity. Either way the result is hostility that serves litle purpose, because it's not related to the present.

To make anger constructive you need to learn to recognize when your feelings are coming from old hurts and to set them apart from anger that fits a current situation.

Once you become aware of your anger slush fund, you can begin to empty it gradually, safely.

"I got so mad I was ready to explode," said Chuck, a forty-two-year-old father with two sons and a managerial position at a large manufacturing firm, when he described a recent run-in with a bank teller. The teller had made an error on a deposit receipt. Chuck had difficulty pointing it out. "I don't know how they can have someone so stupid working in that kind of position," Chuck went on, his face becoming red as he recalled the incident. "Finally I told her to give me the goddamned receipt and my check so I could go over the whole thing with the manager." Eventually Chuck got the error corrected, but as usual with him, only after a tremendous waste of energy and considerable embarrassment and ill feeling. The bottom line was half an hour lost at the bank and a knot in his stomach for the rest of the day. And he's still fuming!

He's looking for help because his boss suggested that Chuck might not go much further in the company unless he learns to control his temper. Like most people who suffer from a heavy load of slush-fund anger, Chuck is relatively unaware of why he finds the world so hard to deal with while others don't seem to find half as many reasons to get irritated. He has a reputation as a hothead, his few close friends joke about his temper, so he doesn't pay much attention to it. He gets along well with his sons and rarely quarrels with his wife, who accommodates his short fuse. Until he learned how his superiors viewed him, Chuck thought he had his life and himself under control. Now he is willing to look deeper.

Chuck's blood pressure is elevated. He frequently comes home with a stiff neck and a tension headache. He can't stand waiting in line. Should a waitress be slow, he soon begins seething. It takes considerable time for Chuck to develop enough trust to open up, but when he does it becomes apparent that he isn't very happy. He's suspicious of most of the people at work. "They'll stab you in the back if you blink for a second," he says bitterly. Nor is he complimentary about most of the people he meets. "Most people are stupid," he says. "I can't stand stupid people." His relationship with his wife has grown cold, their sex perfunctory. "She just agrees with me about everything," he explains. "She doesn't enjoy sex much anymore either. It's gotten stale." Only through reexamination of these feelings was Chuck able to begin seeing that he was living in an emotional world of his own making, and that he would have to work unloading his old anger if he really wanted to change.

The bottom of Chuck's anger slush fund bubbles with emotional wounds he suffered from his parents' divorce when he was seven. Chuck and his natural father were very close. The separation was intensely painful. These shocks were compounded when his mother remarried and his new father had him sent away to military boarding school. He recalls the climate in his new home as very cold, his stepfather as distant if not outright mean. After the remarriage, Chuck's natural father moved to a distant part of the country. Chuck felt abandoned and mistreated by everyone he loved most.

While this is helpful in understanding the source of his bristling hostility, it isn't the first place to begin work to help him transform his anger into a positive force. You learn best through direct experience that it *can* be transformed. Lengthy excursions into old hurts delay this crucial step.

First Chuck had to come to terms with his own desire and commitment to take control of his anger. All his life he had justified his frequent angry outbursts by blaming other people for being stupid or threatening. Only when he decided that he not only could, but was determined to bring his anger under control, was he able to begin making any progress at all. Once he was clear about his goal, he became willing to start a running program to lessen his overall level of hostility and increase his baseline feelings of ease and well-being.

One technique, Anger Desensitization, proved especially effective in helping Chuck bring his angry outbursts under control. It involves using the imagination to recreate situations that pushed his red buttons, and then defusing the slush-fund anger that sets them off. Chuck made a list of fifteen situations that normally caused him to explode, including waiting on line, receiving an angry memo from his boss, and finding the toothpaste uncapped. Then, as instructed, he sat in a comfortable chair and used a relaxation technique (see chapter IV) to become as calm as possible. Once he was fully relaxed, he described each of the incidents in detail. (At home, he recorded the list on tape so he could play it back to himself.) Chuck's goal was to hear the situation, systematically relax himself, and then respond reasonably, sorting out his slush-fund reaction from the moderate irritation that the situation would normally call for.

This technique helped Chuck gradually empty his emotional slush fund accumulated over the years. The more he became able to imagine an upsetting situation without becoming excessively angry, the more insight he gained into his red buttons and his capacity to temper his anger according to the situation. For the first time be began expressing his anger in ways that helped him deal effectively with specific problems and left him feeling better.

Finally Chuck agreed to begin a Transcendental Meditation (TM) program. TM exposes mind and body to a unique state of deep rest that appears to have a profound healing effect on the psyche. Just as bed rest helps the body repair physical wounds, the inner rest achieved through TM appears to facilitate healing of psychological wounds. The process occurs naturally and requires no analysis or self-exploration. It's very useful for the long-term growth that Chuck needed.

As Chuck made progress, the quality of his dealings with other people began to change. The first time he was able to handle an inept salesperson without creating a nasty scene, he was proud as a boy who first masters a bicycle. Here's what happened. A piece of merchandise was on sale. The salesperson was having difficulty calculating the discount. Two months earlier Chuck would have stood there, feeling his blood beginning to boil, finally exploding with a mean comment and a call for the manager. This time he was surprised to find he felt a little sympathy for the salesperson's difficulty. He offered, "Perhaps I can help." Chuck took out his calculator, quickly figured the discount, and walked out of the store with his merchandise—and many thanks from the salesperson!

Sorting out slush-fund anger and defusing your emotional red buttons does not mean becoming a pushover or denying your real feelings. Chuck's efforts to get comfortable with his anger took time and required a commitment to work with the techniques prescribed. Running and TM continue to be important to his growth, and he worked with Anger Desensitization for two months before he began to notice a real change in his relationships. When he finds himself becoming hypersensitive he uses the desensitization technique to defuse the slush-fund anger that may still be left.

Learning to Express Anger

The best way to express anger is to be simple and direct. In plain language charged with your real feelings, tell the person who hurt you that he or she did so. If you respond with the thought, "I can't tell someone that they hurt me!" you've already discovered the principal cause of your discomfort with anger. Fear and insecurity keep you from giving vent to your hurt.

That's Debbie's problem because, like many people, she's been told all her life that people aren't supposed to get angry and if they do, they risk losing control or losing a friend. Debbie is a nurse who shares an apartment with Melissa, another nurse who works in the same hospital. Debbie and Melissa were friends for several years before they started living together. Talk to Debbie, and it's clear that Melissa usually assumes the dominant role, often taking advantage of Debbie's compliant nature. Melissa's dominance has never been a major concern in the past because Debbie has many other friends and the relationship was not constricting. Now the situation has changed. Melissa is taking advantage of Debbie, who is hurt but conceals her anger. Debbie forces her anger underground, but it's reappearing in the form of hives and headaches.

Melissa walks all over Debbie in many ways, but nowhere more obviously than in their financial and household dealings. Because they eat different foods, Debbie and Melissa agreed to set aside separate shelves in the refrigerator and buy thir own food. Oblivious to this agreement, Melissa regularly raids Debbie's food and never replaces it. When they go out to eat together, Melissa almost always leaves Debbie with the check and forgets to pay her share later. Melissa also has visitors at all hours without ever asking Debbie if the noise is disturbing her.

"Melissa is my friend," says Debbie, already apologetic for telling me how she feels abused by her roommate. "I can't get mad at her. What if she hates me and walks out?" Anger, she believes, is the kiss of death to friendship, and she desperately wants to hold on to all her friends. She fails to recognize that when a friend hurts her, the anger happens automatically. It can't be stopped. It can only be suppressed (as she's doing) or expressed, which I proposed that she learn.

First Debbie had to get comfortable with the feeling of being angry. When I first asked how she felt about Melissa's behavior, Debbie answered blandly, "It upsets me, but it's hard for me to get angry about it. I'm not an angry person." Like many people who have difficulty expressing anger, Debbie is unfamiliar with the sensations of this emotion. She hasn't experienced the feelings of tension, rapid heart rate, warmth, and excitement, so she views them as dangerous steps toward complete loss of control. To change this perception, Debbie worked on getting angry under the safe conditions of the office.

Debbie made up a simple sentence to express her hurt and then practiced saying it to me as if I were Melissa. The sentence she finally felt comfortable with was: "Melissa, you've been taking advantage of me by ignoring our household agreements; I feel hurt and angry." When Debbie first tried to say this sentence, it came out without the slightest bit of passion. Her tone was flat. She looked at the floor. I could hardly hear the last few words. Debbie was mouthing a complaint, not expressing anger.

To change her tone, I asked Debbie to imagine herself acting the part of an angry roommate. With encouragement, she gradually began to let go and act out her angry feelings. She experimented with standing up, using gestures, pounding her fist on the table, and speaking loudly. Eventually, as the anger began to surface, Debbie discovered that anger is not such a terrible emotion after all. The more comfortable she felt with the power of her anger, the more she wanted to continue this exercise. On her own, she added some additional sentences:

- "I'm tired of you eating my food when we agreed to buy food separately!"
- "When you eat my food, I'm the one who has to go out and replace it!"
- "I have just as tight a budget as you do, and it hurts me that you show such disregard for my situation!"
- "If we're going to go out together, let's both be sure we have money before we go out the door."

By the end of the session Debbie was elated by her newly discovered energy. "I never realized anger could be so much fun," she said.

Expressing anger involves risk. Before Debbie had her showdown with Melissa, we discussed the range of Melissa's responses. She might deny all Debbie's complaints, justify her actions with rationalizations, or get angry in return and begin heaping up counteraccusations. To express anger constructively you must be prepared for the risk and be willing to ride through the storm to a positive outcome. That means giving the other person plenty of opportunity to vent his or her feelings without denying your own. Again Debbie practiced with me by playing the role of Melissa.

Here's a practice dialogue. Melissa tries to deny the issue.
Debbie keeps the conversation focused on how she's been
hurt:

MELISSA: C'mon, Debbie, it's not such a big deal!
DEBBIE: It is to me, because I'm the one who has to spend
the extra money and do the extra shopping.
MELISSA: But I don't do it that often.
DEBBIE: How often isn't the point, Melissa. The point is
that you do it without even a thought of me! You never even
mention it. You never make an effort to replace anything,
and that says you don't care about me. That's what really
hurts!
MELISSA: I didn't realize that's how it was coming across
to you.
DEBBIE: Now I hope you can appreciate my side and that
you're willing to make some changes so we can get rid of
the tension around here.
MELISSA: I'm sorry if I've hurt you. I do want our friendship.

Note that Debbie kept the conversation focused on the
fact that she felt hurt by Melissa's indifference. It didn't
get bogged down in specifics about how much food Melissa
ate, what it cost, or when it happened. All that needed
to be established was that Melissa did engage in this selfish
behavior and that she hurt Debbie through her thoughtless-
ness.

Debbie's confrontation with Melissa proved a success.
Voices were raised, tempers flared, firm words flew, but
after it was all over both were able to move off their anger
to a new level of mutual appreciation and friendship. Melissa no longer takes advantage of Debbie's good nature. No
longer does Debbie set herself up to be Melissa's doormat.
The tension in their friendship has been replaced by new
respect.

Debbie's discovery that anger can be a useful, even enjoyable emotion that serves the growth of a relationship has
changed her in many ways. Above all, her hives and headaches have disappeared. She also feels better about herself
and her ability to go after what she wants out of life. Hav-

ing lifted the lid on her angry feelings, she's pleased to discover that she's much more energetic and passionate than she had imagined. She is enjoying her sex life more and is also more assertive at work; she no longer lets everyone push her around. In every way Debbie is more able to stand up for herself and project her interests. What surprised her most was the warm response and new respect she received.

Asserting Yourself with Your Family

Expressing anger is particularly difficult with people you believe you're always supposed to love. Expressing anger toward your parents can be extremely difficult if you've been conditioned to believe that to be angry at your parents always means lack of respect and is therefore wrong. Parents, like anyone else, can hurt you. When they do, you're angry. To deny that anger is to poison yourself and destroy the chance of an evolving relationship. Expressing your anger constructively is one of the most difficult emotional tasks.

George married Linda with his parents' grudgingly given blessing. George's father is a physician. His mother graduated from Vassar. George went to Harvard and later to law school. Linda comes from a poor family in West Virginia and worked as a model before George met her. The wedding was small and entirely paid for by George's family. His mother has quietly (and sometimes not so quietly) been trying to destroy the marriage ever since. Linda is a beautiful woman, friendly, sensual, alluring—very different from George's mother. Clearly there is an element of jealousy in George's mother's feeling about Linda.

Five years after the marriage, George's mother is still bitter and makes destructive comments whenever she gets the opportunity. It doesn't matter that George and Linda now have two children. Her own unexpressed anger keeps coming out in bits. Linda always feels uncomfortable around her mother-in-law. George winces at the prospect of the three of them being in the same room. For five years, George has quietly put up with his mother's acerbic comments. Finally, when George and Linda received an invitation to spend Christmas at his mother's, Linda refused to go.

"I can't take her," said Linda, leaving George caught in the middle. Only when Linda remained adamant in her refusal to put up with her mother-in-law's abuse did George face the fact that he had to confront his own feelings or else break off his relationship with his parents altogether. He sought help.

It didn't take long to find out that George and Linda have a happy marriage with abundant satisfactions. Clearly the mother-in-law's comments were not based on any accurate perception of the relationship; they were intended as destructive thorns. Understandably, George had difficulty accepting that his mother was being intentionally hurtful. He had never faced the possibility that his mother felt so jealous that she wanted to hurt Linda for taking her son and to get even with him for "running off" with Linda. These feelings are nevertheless precisely those that some parents are capable of feeling when their adult sons or daughters choose to live in ways that conflict with the parents' values or expectations.

George *had* to let himself get angry with his mother. Only then was there any hope of dispelling the hurt felt by all and moving to a new level of love and understanding. Here's the dialogue I rehearsed with George:

MOTHER: George, please tell Linda not to wear that hideous black dress to the Christmas party. It makes her look as cheap as she is. I'd be mortified to have our friends see your wife has such poor taste.

GEORGE: There you go again, mother! The first thing you have to say to me is something mean about Linda. I've never told you this before, but every time you say something like that you hurt me very deeply!

MOTHER: The truth does hurt, doesn't it, George?

GEORGE: Mother, stop reveling in your mean wit and listen to me! I *am* hurt, and I *am* angry about the way you treat

Linda. I don't know why you want to be so destructive, but that's what you are. You're not destroying my love for Linda. You're destroying my love for you!

MOTHER: Come now, George, stop being so sensitive.

GEORGE: I wish you'd try to hear what I'm saying. You've hurt Linda and me again and again, and I want you to stop it! Five years is long enough! I'm not going to take it anymore! I don't expect an apology, but if you want our relationship to continue, then you'll have to change.

MOTHER: Are you threatening your own mother, George? Is that what you're doing? Threatening me with that cheap whore?

GEORGE: I'm not threatening you, mother. I'm just telling you that I love Linda, I'm committed to her. That's a fact you'll have to accept. I'm also telling you that you've *got* to stop trying to hurt us with nasty comments. It's cruel and destructive. I'm asking you not to destroy my love for you with these continued attacks on my wife.

George and Linda ended up not going to his parents' for Christmas. George later made a special trip to see his mother and try to work things out. Having admitted his own hurt and anger, George was eventually able to make his mother comfortable enough to express *her anger at him.* When her hurt and disappointment came out, George was able to sympathize with her but point out that, as an adult, he had to live his life according to his own values. This is the classic schism between parents and their adult children. Anger is an inevitable part of it. If the anger is allowed expression, the relationship can move to a new level of mutual respect, understanding, and love. The task isn't easy, but it can be done, and the rewards will be felt by all.

Getting Angry with Your Lover

The freedom to get angry is important to every healthy love relationship. When two people fall in love, they open themselves so completely that they expose the most sensitive parts of their personalities. Love by its very nature creates fertile soil for hurt, and consequently for anger. When you love someone deeply and he or she reciprocates with the same feelings toward you, you will on occasion almost inevitably push each other's buttons, ignore each other's feelings, and let each other down. The result is hurt, which yields anger. It's an irony of love: it almost guarantees some degree of anger.

The biggest mistake of all that couples make—it really is the biggest!—is to believe they can protect their relationship by holding back their anger. Here's what really happens: When the hurt is denied and the anger is suppressed, the whole relationship is threatened with a gradual poisoning from bitter feelings that seep to the surface in destructive ways and at destructive times. A relationship remains free from a buildup of resentments only as long as both people feel they can open up to express their feelings. A good relationship may even be defined as a safe place to express any feelings. Not that love is a license to express anger indiscriminately. The closer you are to someone, the more skilled you must be at expressing anger if your anger is to be constructive.

When a couple suppresses anger, one of the first signs may be loss of passion. John is a film producer, his wife Julie a set designer. They have no children and no plans to have any. Married for three years, they have what everyone around them believes to be the "ideal marriage." They have exciting careers, make plenty of money, and have all the freedom they want. Yet they came for help because, as John said, "We haven't made love in six months."

It often takes a while to discover the source of the problem in a case like John and Julie's. They don't have many overt complaints to begin with. They talk about how much they love each other, what they do for each other, how much fun they have, what their plans are. But gradually a picture emerges of two people afraid to share their real feelings and their real hurts. The tip-off to their problem was Julie's point-blank statement: "We never fight."

They do have what can be described as a terrific relationship. They have many interests in common and care about each other deeply. Over their three years of marriage, however, they have both been accumulating a list of minor resentments and hurts that neither has been able to acknowledge. Julie gets irritated when John doesn't call if he's going to be late for dinner. John can't stand it when Julie takes all the pencils off of his desk. Julie is hurt when John spends a whole weekend working. John is hurt when Julie accepts jobs in New York that take her away from him for a week at a time. Julie is messy and throws her things around the house; John is compulsive and gets upset when he's constantly picking up after her. The list goes on, minor issues spiced with major ones. All are denied in the hopes that the irritations will somehow go away. They don't. Passion does.

John and Julie need lessons in getting angry with each other. Neither can separate anger from memories of bitter fights between parents. I wanted to show them that fighting can be done in a way that allows anger to surface but winds up being fun, even enjoyable. Two techniques proved most helpful.

The first is called Role Reversal. The point is to let two people put themselves in each other's shoes. John was irritated by Julie's disregard for his desire to maintain a neat desk well stocked with pencils and paper. Julie was constantly stealing his pencils, and John couldn't get her to stop. Role Reversal begins with John clearly stating his hurt: "Julie, you keep swiping my pencils even though you know I like to keep things neat. Your disregard for my feelings hurts, and I'm angry about it." The next step is for Julie to see it from John's side. Julie sits down at John's desk and assumes the role of John trying to hold on to the pencils. John takes the role of Julie swiping them. John proceeds to demonstrate all Julie's pencil-swiping techniques until Julie finally gets the message of how John feels and how her own behavior appears to him. By acting out Julie's role, John is able to release his anger fully. Julie is able to see the need to change her behavior. Usually this exercise ends in laughter because so many minor irritations among couples are idiosyncratic and funny.

The second technique is useful when there is a major buildup of tension. This is called Push-Pull. The idea is to create a safe space for the physical expression of hostility. John and Julie take off any rings, earrings, shoes, belts, and other clothing that might cause injury. They then stand at arm's length and put their hands on each other's shoulders. Once firmly set, they begin pushing and pulling at each other. When they get into it, they begin verbalizing their feelings as well. Comments like "I'm angry at you!" "You piss me off!" and "I'm not going to get pushed around anymore!" come out. This exercise, like the previous one, usually ends in laughter and the feeling that the initial source of the argument isn't so serious after all.

Here is the irony of anger among couples. When it remains repressed, it builds up until there's a destructive explosion or, worse, a gradual erosion of love through constant sniping and biting. When anger is fully released whenever it arises, the initial tension is followed by relief, trust, warmth, love, and mutual respect. Once a couple becomes confident about getting angry constructively, the exchange of angry feelings assumes a playful quality because both know that the anger will leave them feeling stronger and more committed to one another.

Expressing anger is crucial to sustaining a passionate sexual interest. Nothing is more destructive to erotic feelings than the systematic suppression of anger. Couples with boring sex lives are often the ones that claim they never fight. You can almost translate "never fight" as "never make love." Repressed hostility literally blocks the sexual chemistry. When these couples do have sex, it's usually hampered by ambivalent desire and silent tension.

If you are in a relationship where sex is dying due to repressed anger, the Push-Pull exercise may be particularly helpful, because it gets you back in physical contact with your lover in an open and honest way. Don't be surprised if it awakens your dormant sexual feelings and you wind up going to bed together. It can be a great breakthrough.

The techniques outlined so far are not enough for serious conflicts. Major disagreements about children, money, careers, and other critical areas of conflicting needs are very different from the minor tensions we've been discussing. For major conflicts, you and your lover need skills to *stand up* for your feelings so you don't get pushed around and later feel resentful, and also to *compromise* so you can negotiate an agreement you can both live with. The alternative is destruction of the relationship.

Janis and David have been married for three years but still haven't learned how to resolve major disputes. The result is an accumulation of resentments and disappointments that are threatening the marriage. Their sex lives have begun to suffer, so David finally insisted that they seek help. Both are in their early thirties. David is an architect. Janis is interested in horses and horse training. Both are so involved in their careers that they sometimes go for days seeing each other only late at night when they're too tired to share much of themselves. The emerging crisis centers on their conflicting visions of their future. David wants children, and a wife who will create a home. Janis is ambivalent about children and committed to her career. Before coming for help, they had begun a pattern of bitter arguments that led only to each feeling let down and abused by the other. The marriage is in trouble.

The first question for any couple faced with a major crisis is the degree of their commitment to resolve it in a way that will let them stay together. Without this basic commitment to stick it out, you can't compromise or empathize with the other person's point of view. Compromise and empathy are absolutely critical if an angry conflict is to be resolved in a way that nurtures the love in the relationship and the growth of each person.

First off, you can't empathize and compromise if you can't listen. Most people who argue are so concerned with making their points that they're deaf to what the other person has to say, especially in marriages. When David was explaining why he wants Janis to stay home, Janis wasn't listening because she felt threatened and was preparing counterarguments in her mind. It was the same with David each time Janis spoke. They wound up yelling at one another but accomplishing little. It was like yelling at a stone wall. Later they started resorting to below-the-belt personal attacks because neither felt the other was willing to listen. This is particularly destructive because love arms you with enough knowledge that you can use unfairly to hurt your lover very deeply (fights that deteriorate into insult brawls spell real trouble, bad trouble).

Despite the hostility and bitterness festering in the relationship, David and Janis said they loved each other deeply and agreed they wanted to make the relationship work. The very fact that they came for help together was a sign of commitment. What they needed more than anything else was help in learning how to have a fair fight that could help them negotiate their needs. Here is the basic technique.

David and Janis sat across from one another, their knees touching. This proximity is important; it's a constant reminder of their commitment to work things out and to listen to one another. They made an agreement about how the fight would work. Three rules are critical:

1. One person speaks at a time and is never interrupted except for an occasional and encouraging "Tell me more."

2. After each person speaks, the listener must restate what was said to make sure the point is understood (this also encourages empathy). When you know that you must rephrase what someone is telling you, you listen without trying to "add on" your own thoughts.

3. The argument gets as much time as necessary to reach a resolution. No interruptions are allowed. No appeals to responsibilities at work or in the home are permitted as excuses for leaving. A fair fight requires that both people set aside ample time without interference.

The fight began with each side explaining his or her hurt and desire for the relationship to change. David told Janis that he very deeply wanted children, that they agreed to have children when they got married, that he is very disappointed. Janis restated David's position until she got what he was saying. She then explained her fears of getting locked into the role of wife and mother while David had an interesting life. Once forced to listen to Janis and to restate her feeling in his own words, David began for the first time to empathize with her. At this point, before any movement in the argument took place, David and Janis had already made a major step. The bitterness lessened as soon as each believed the other understood their feelings. They stopped trying to make each other wrong and began appreciating how they both were right from their own points of view.

This session eventually ended with David and Janis hugging each other and affirming their love. They decided that their needs could both be met within the relationship. Janis agreed to have children and David agreed that Janis ought to have her career. It became clear to both that they had to carefully plan their careers and face their need for assistance with child care. Once this conflict was moved from the arena of antagonism and misunderstanding to love and empathy, it stopped being a source of conflict and became an opportunity for David and Janis to grow. Getting the anger out. That's what empowered David and Janis to solve the problem that had seemed so insoluble.

Getting Angry at Work

Most of us spend a third of our lives in an environment where emotional honesty isn't a priority—the workplace. You hear talk now about humanizing the workplace, but most work environments allow one-way anger only, usually the authoritarian boss upbraiding a subordinate. The competition and complexity of human relationships at work make it inevitable that individuals at all levels are at times likely to feel frustrated and hurt. The resulting anger must be dealt with if it isn't going to create bitterness and reduced performance.

Remember, anger can't be suppressed without self-damage. If your boss fails to make good on a promise, you're going to be hurt and angry. No way around it. Many people take work-inspired anger home, let it out on their families, and create additional hurt and conflict at home. Others try to ignore the boss and wind up feeling resentment that impedes performance. ("Well, I sure won't put myself out for him/her next time.") That's destructive because poor performance doesn't just hurt the boss. It hurts your own reputation, self-esteem, and chances of promotion. A third course is to deny the anger by making excuses for the boss. ("He/she just forgot.") This often leads to ulcers or other self-chastisement for not standing up for yourself.

If you're mistreated by a superior at work, the first thing you have to do is appraise the openness of the relationship. Some boss-worker relationships are strong enough to sustain a major emotional confrontation somewhat like those we've discussed. That makes for a new mutual respect and a better work relationship. Some very rare bosses may even reward the subordinate who isn't afraid to stand up for what he/she believes. The far more likely outcome of a major expression of anger toward your boss is getting fired. Given that reality, you need additional skills to channel your anger.

Expressing and feeling your anger in a safe environment is the first step. You don't have to explode at your boss to feel a release. And instead of letting off steam at your family, you can go into a bedroom, take an old pillow, imagine it to be your boss's head, and beat it furiously with a bat or tennis racket. Sure you'll feel silly at first! Give it a chance. You'll get your anger going and feel better for it. Once your anger is discharged, you'll find it easier to go back to your boss and seek redress for the injury.

Most bosses will hear a brief, calm, positive statement if it's clearly intended to improve performance. If your boss is making excessive demands and putting too much pressure on you, you can say, "I work better and faster when the work comes at a more orderly pace and I have a clearer idea about the flow. We'll get more done if I can consult you on the schedules we're trying to meet."

If your boss fails to live up to a promise, you can say, "I get highly motivated when I know I can count on a fair reward for my best performance. I'd like to set down clear objectives that you want me to meet, and the rewards I can expect for meeting them."

You can make almost any request to change a hurtful situation if you do it in a positive way. Your boss will be hard pressed to turn you down when you ask for support in improving your ability to help him or her.

Perhaps *you're* the boss and have problems with subordinates constantly letting you down. What then? While a small minority of people can inspire performance with fear, this is usually the least effective way. Many bosses find that exploding at a secretary for not finishing a report on time doesn't get the next one finished any faster. Most often an angry explosion makes your subordinates feel resentful, so they slow down. Maybe you, the boss, expect your subordinates to function at your pace and fail to recognize that they're different people with their own levels of ability and can't necessarily keep up with the pressure just because you can.

Nevertheless, when an employee lets you down you'll be hurt and inevitably angry. Again, if you don't explode on the spot, you can take the anger home; you can suppress it until it begins to eat you from the inside; or you can learn to let it out safely and then hone your skills at communicating your expectations firmly but supportively.

Generally the more responsibility you have, the greater is your need for a daily physical outlet for frustration and hostility. The emotional and psychological benefits of regular running, tennis, squash, racquetball, or any other vigorous sport are equal to (or even exceed) the physical benefits. If you make any of these sports a regular part of your routine, your ability to handle anger and frustration will increase markedly.

Next, you can cultivate your ability to set clear goals that you and your subordinates know can be achieved. When you enlist cooperation, you increase motivation. The more freedom you give your subordinates to express their feelings, the more open they'll be to criticism if they let you down. When you criticize, focus on the *behavior, not the person.* Don't say "You're always late!" Try "This report is late! You agreed it could be done on time. I feel let down." That opens the door for the subordinate to offer whatever remedy may be possible.

Suppose a subordinate lets you down repeatedly. When you ask why a goal isn't being met, all you get is excuses. You'd do yourself a serious injustice to put up with the constant frustration. If the employee has been effective in the past, there may be extenuating circumstances. You can inquire about family or personal problems. Usually such a person just has not learned how to be responsible. I'd recommend a clear explanation of how you feel the person has not lived up to his or her promise, followed by a clear and direct dismissal. If you "can't" dismiss someone who is repeatedly letting you down, you're letting yourself down in a big way, and probably have difficulty expressing anger in all your relationships. As long as you feel uncomfortable with your anger, you weaken yourself and undermine the energy and power you bring to your work.

In general, any amount of time you spend getting comfortable with your anger will be worth the effort.

Dividends of Destructive Anger

Like all anhedonic behavior, destructive anger has its rewards. Whether you blow up at the drop of a hat or you can't let your anger out, you have to understand the emotional dividends you reap before you can change.

Here are the payoffs for a short fuse. A bad temper—

Helps you avoid facing the real causes of your frustration.

Instead of working on yourself and improving your ability to create your life the way you want it, you can fall back on a hostile attitude and blame everyone else for standing in your way. Some people get so much relief from this way of abandoning responsibility that they begin to think everyone is out to get them.

Can be a means of drawing attention from others.

If you let your friends know that you have a short fuse, they're likely to go out of their way to placate you. They may treat you as if your temper is a disability that's not your fault. ("Take it easy with Joe, he's got a bad temper.") That kind of care and sympathy is a powerful reward.

May make you feel important and powerful.

Some people have so little self-confidence that they only feel strong when the adrenaline of anger is rushing through their veins. You may also be proficient at making others feel guilty for pushing one of your buttons. If you can get someone else to ask "Where did I go wrong?" then you're one up and can relish the power.

Can be used as a means of avoiding genuine communication and compromise.

If someone points out a weakness in your reasoning, you can explode and end the interaction. Your temper is a safety ejection seat. You can bail out whenever the going gets rough.

May be used to cope with the fear of intimacy.

The less you think of yourself, the more fearful you're likely to be of getting close to others. If you slip into a relationship that gets too close, an angry explosion can spare you the explanations of why you can't go any further.

Can be used to manipulate others.

If you get the reputation of a hothead, people who work with you (certainly your subordinates) will develop a fear of touching off an emotional explosion. That allows you to make unreasonable demands while others remain silent. When they can't meet your demands, you have an additional reason for getting angry. It's a self-sustaining circle.

Can be a good smokescreen.

When you do a job poorly or make a mistake, you can explode in a rage to mask your failure. If you get angry enough, you may even convince yourself and others that the mistake was not your fault in the first place. Given enough outrage, no one will dare suggest otherwise.

Here are rewards for burying your anger and assuming a posture of compliance. You can—

Above all, avoid facing your real feelings.

Anger is a natural response to hurt. By suppressing it, you also suppress the underlying emotional injury. Avoidance of pain is the reward, even though the price of avoidance is anhedonia and a diminished sensitivity to all your feelings.

Laud yourself for your patience and understanding.

Perhaps you were told as a child that good boys and girls never get angry. When you follow this childhood rule, you can give yourself points for your strength and control. You commend yourself for being considerate of others, while you proceed to injure yourself.

Feel mistreated and abused.

When you keep a lid on your temper while everyone else pushes you around, you can sit back and complain about how thoughtless and cruel other people are. Some people find it is easier to complain than to take responsibility for their feelings and stand up for themselves.

Give yourself ulcers, headaches, or other physical symptoms that result from channeling your anger toward yourself.

These may not seem like rewards, but they become ways to appeal for sympathy and a ready excuse for avoiding something you find unpleasant. They may also seem preferable to facing the hurt underneath your repressed anger.

Win approval from others by making yourself into a doormat.

When you let other people think you're a "nice person" who "doesn't get angry," you give them an invitation to take advantage of you at every opportunity. It does no good to complain about how selfish and cruel people are. Denying your anger is equivalent to denying your power. You set yourself up to be a follower and never a leader. The reward is the security you achieve by always taking second place; the price is a diminished you.

Comfort yourself with a holier-than-thou attitude.

It's easier to deny your anger and take an accusatory stance toward people who express it destructively than risk expressing your anger and confronting your real feelings. Learning how to express anger constructively takes effort; playing the holier-than-thou role doesn't. You can make yourself feel superior while avoiding the hard work of honest self-expression.

You can avoid responsibility for taking control of your life.

If you never express your anger, you're likely to feel helpless. People take advantage of you and you feel you can't do anything about it. This feeling may escalate into a general belief that an individual can't really affect the world. Avoiding the work involved in taking responsibility for yourself is again the reward.

More Strategies for Making Anger Work

First you need to buy the idea once and for all that it's OK for you to get angry under the right circumstances and in the right way. It's more than OK! Anger can be a positive, even satisfying, experience when you use it constructively to improve your relationships and stand up for yourself. The key, of course, is the word *constructive.*

Once you recognize that anger can be positive, you're free to give your emotions more latitude and to experiment with your natural responses. Getting angry doesn't have to mean losing control or making yourself miserable. It can bring a complete release that prepares the ground for a frank discussion of your hurt and how you want a relationship to change. When you learn that anger can be positive, you become comfortable expressing it, and can discover its role in supporting inner joy. Here are the most important principles and techniques for making anger positive.

Your anger has four goals:

1. To communicate your direct feeling of hurt. (You want to let the other person know how you feel. Be specific —stick to the situation at hand. Don't draw from your slush fund.)

2. You want to change the hurtful situation. (Whatever may be wrong must be made right to whatever extent possible.)

3. You want to prevent recurrence of the same hurt. (By expressing your hurt and anger now, you can avoid a major emotional explosion in the future.)

4. You want to improve the relationship and increase communication. (Out of the anger can come a new level of mutual respect, understanding, and love.)

These points give your anger a direction while strong words fly along the way. When you're hurt and feeling angry, stop a moment for a brief self-inventory before you confront whoever hurt you. Ask yourself:

- "Why am I angry?"
- "What do I want to change?"
- "What do I need to let go of my hurt and anger?"

These practical questions help you clarify your goal when you confront the other party. General statements ("You make me furious") aren't very helpful. When you express anger, you should state *very specifically* what hurts you. One client said to her husband, "You keep promising to come home for dinner on time, but you've been late every night for the past two weeks and not once have you called to let me know. You make me feel you don't care, and that hurts! I'm angry about it!" She was then able to suggest a specific change.

It does no good to say "I want you to love me more." It's much too vague. A wife can say instead, "I want you to try harder to be home for dinner, and if you're going to be late, to call me by five o'clock." Husband and wife can both accept such a request. It then becomes possible to let go of the anger when specific conditions are met. This client learned to say "I'll feel better if you say you're sorry and agree to try to be home earlier." This is a condition the husband can meet, and the angry outburst can end with both the wife and the husband feeling stronger.

When someone is getting angry with you, try to listen to the message of hurt and restrain your own tendency to be defensive.

This takes great strength, but once you understand your own anger, you can accept anger from others and help them make it constructive even if *they* don't know how. You can ask what you did to cause the hurt, what you can do to change, and what is necessary for the anger to blow over.

If you feel too filled with rage to express yourself coherently, find some way to let it out physically.

Punch a pillow, yell in a closed room, take a long run, anything that allows you to vent your rage safely. Once you've cooled down, you can then ask yourself the three questions above and run the confrontation that will allow you to move to understanding and forgiveness.

When you're explaining your hurt, don't expect an immediate response.

The typical response to anger is denial or defensive counterstatements.

YOU: I feel hurt that you didn't show up last night.
FRIEND: I tried to call you, but your phone was busy.

If you know you were off the phone all night, you're likely to be further outraged. You can accuse your friend. ("That's a lie!") That'll assure further denials and more anger. Or you can stick to the issue of your hurt: "You hurt me last night and you're hurting me now! I know my phone wasn't busy because I didn't use it all night!" Sticking to your feelings is very difficult in the face of a denial, but that's what you have to do to get through. Persevere and you'll learn that by avoiding general accusations and repeating specific statements of feeling, you'll surmount the other person's defenses and your anger will work to open up the relationship.

Beware of trying to make the other person "wrong."

If someone hurt you, there's no value in trying to make them feel terrible about it. Usually the hurt is unintentional. If you try to make the other person say "I'm rotten for hurting you!" or "I'm stupid for making that mistake!" you're using your anger destructively. Making the other person wrong doesn't focus the anger toward change in the future. If anything, it keeps everyone caught in the unhappy past. Rather than seek to make the other person wrong or stupid, ask for an acknowledgment of your hurt and a commitment to avoid the same mistakes in the future.

If you say something you don't mean or back down from a statement you really believe, don't feel you've made an irreparable mistake and can't go back to your previous position.

Getting angry isn't like playing chess. You're trying to express feelings about an emotional injury. It's perfectly natural to get confused and have difficulty sorting out what you really feel. The person you're angry with may say something that gives you a new perspective and you may change your mind for a while. After you think about it, you see that you were right in the first place. Give yourself permission to change your mind. Explore your feelings until you get them all out just as they are.

Don't be afraid to say exactly what you want to change.

This is absolutely critical if your anger is to remain constructive. You'll get nowhere if you stop just when the other person shows some appreciation of your hurt. Yes, that would be enough to make you feel better. If someone stands you up, and he or she finally tells you that they are sorry and feel terrible about it, enjoy the relief, but remember to go further. Get a commitment that they won't stand you up again! It's the only way to really stand up for yourself and use the power that your anger gives you.

Take special care in your close love relationships to allow anger healthy expression.

All love relationships are ambivalent. Occasional anger is inevitable if love is to remain vital and passionate. When two people are close and growing, they're bound to develop conflicting needs and step on each other's toes. It is exceedingly helpful if you can agree to a ritual for negotiating your needs and having fair fights. One model of a fair-fight formula was discussed earlier in this chapter.

If you have difficulty getting angry, practice with a friend until you start feeling comfortable with it.

Of course, you can pay a therapist a lot of money for the same help, but most often people can do it for themselves. You and your friend can benefit by studying this chapter and then taking turns acting out your anger. Recall a situation: You were hurt and felt angry but couldn't express it. Have your friend play the role of the person who hurt you; you play yourself. Now experiment with alternative ways of getting angry. You may feel foolish at first. If you're feeling inhibited, do something physical (pounding your fist when you speak or shaking your finger) so you begin to feel the old anger. If you never fully let it go, it's still there and will come up. Remember your goal is to let the other person feel your hurt, hear your proposal for change, and agree to avoid the same behavior in the future. The key to making the exercise work is letting yourself feel genuinely angry. Don't hold back! Feel the blood rushing and the adrenaline flowing. You need to learn from direct experience that you can feel angry and yet remain under control enough to shape your anger positively.

What about anger in response to minor mistreatment by strangers?

A cabdriver gets lost and makes you miss your appointment; a surly waiter corrects your pronunciation of *escargots*. Twice! A salesperson ignores you at the counter because your purchase is small. You're likely to feel angry but there's little chance to express your anger so it'll reach a fully satisfying conclusion. You can follow an old proverb: "Wisdom is learning what to ignore." If your personality allows you to overlook these minor offenses without suppressing anger, you're fortunate. If you find your anger too strong to be ignored, frame the simplest possible statement to express it. Tell the cabdriver you're not giving him a tip because he doesn't know his job. Tell the waiter you want him to take the order silently. Tell the salesperson you find her behavior offensive. Once you've made your point, let it go. The more comfortable you become with anger, the more easily will you release it following these minor annoyances.

If you have a heavy backlog of old hurts and unexpressed rage, you'll do well to work on relieving this emotional slush.

Take them one at a time: write a letter to a person who hurt you. But then don't send the letter! Starting an old argument after months or years won't help; getting your feelings out will. You can also use imagery and imagine talking to the person who hurt you. Variations of this technique were discussed earlier in the chapter, with examples.

Finally, when your anger is spent, acknowledge that you feel better.

Don't apologize for getting angry; no apology is necessary. If anything, you should expect an apology from the person who hurt or mistreated you. Don't be premature in acknowledging that you feel better. Listen to your inner voice. It will tell you when your anger is fully released and your hurt can be forgiven. Forgiving does not mean forgetting; it does mean letting the other person know you're willing to let the past be and that you're willing to help make your relationship better and more open in the future.

Anger is a source of power. It needn't be feared and shouldn't be repressed. The happy paradox of anger is that when you become comfortable with it, you transform it into a power to sustain inner joy.

IX

Loss, Disappointment, and Growth

I walked a mile with Sorrow
    And ne'er a word she said
But, oh, the things I learned from her
    When Sorrow walked with me.
          —ROBERT BROWNING

Grief may be joy misunderstood.
          —ELIZABETH BARRETT BROWNING

A YOUNG BOY is rushed by ambulance to the emergency room where his family doctor waits. It's 5:00 P.M., usually a quiet time, but this boy, barely eleven years old, has taken a full bottle of Valium he found in the medicine cabinet.

The psychiatrist is called in to see the boy and his panic-stricken parents. Why did John try to kill himself? He has no history of emotional disturbance, nor do his parents. They are an all-American family. The father is an aerospace executive, the mother a real estate salesperson.

John plays center field in Little League, and his team played a local championship that day. In the eighth inning John's team had a one-run lead, until John missed an easy fly ball that allowed two runs to score. All the parents and all the players saw John make the error that cost his team the game and the local championship. Many of his team-mates and their parents were furious.

On the way home John's father said something like "How could you miss? It was an easy ball! We practiced it so many times." His mother recalls saying something to the effect that Bill Robinson's mother relished their embarrassment. When they finally got home, John ran up to his room. His parents stayed downstairs and poured themselves two stiff drinks each. At dinnertime they discovered John and the Valium bottle in his bedroom. When John recovered, he explained his attempted suicide. "I didn't want to grow up to be a loser," he said.

This frightening and telling case says a lot about what's happening. Winning has always been important, but once upon a time you didn't have to feel ashamed if you lost; nor did you have to feel devastated if you were disappointed. Knowing how to lose gracefully (and growing through your disappointments) was valued almost as much as winning. No longer. The old-fashioned desire to do your best has been transformed into a new cult of the winner. Everyone is supposed to win 100 percent of the time—at love, business, investments, on the freeway, even in the supermarket. To lose at anything has become a cause for self-punishment.

The new winner's gospel comes from professional football: "Winning isn't everything, it's the only thing." Though effective for psyching up professional football players for a Sunday afternoon, this attitude is catastrophic as a philosophy for life, for one simple reason: to have a winner, there must also be a loser. Loss and disappointment are as inevitable as death and disease. No one, not even the best teams, wins all the time. Knowing how to accept loss and disappointment—and growing from them—is just as important to your inner joy as winning.

Loss and disappointment are painful—no way around it. In this era of instant gratification, no one wants to talk about painful feelings. So we're surrounded by a wholesale denial of loss. Many people believe that to admit loss (and the pain that goes with it) is a sign of weakness, immaturity, or uptightness. In fact it's the denial of loss, the refusal to experience the pain and grow from it, that's the real weakness, the real anhedonic trap.

You can't get rid of pain by denying it. This was one of Freud's greatest early contributions. When you suffer any kind of loss, you're going to suffer some degree of pain. Unless you give yourself a chance to heal, the pain will persist underneath the layers of self-denial you heap over it. You may succeed in blocking the pain out of consciousness, but only at the expense of diminishing your total emotional sensitivity, especially your capacity for joy. The purpose of this chapter is to discuss the natural responses to loss and to explain how you can transform pain into compassion and ultimately into understanding and growth.

First Instincts

Following a major loss, the first response is helplessness. It seems nothing can be done. Out of frustration, it is very easy to fall into a cycle of self-punishment. Some people punish themselves by going over and over the event in their minds, constantly telling themselves, "If only I had done something different." An irrational longing persists that with enough self-punishment, the past can be changed. Of course, it can't.

Another response is cynicism and bitterness:

· "The world is cruel."
· "You can't trust anyone."
· "I'll never take a chance again."
· "People are no good."

The logic is "If I'm hurting, then I don't want to have anything to do with the world anymore." Self-protection becomes self-suffocation.

Loss, Disappointment, and Growth

A third response is self-pity:

- "Nothing ever works out for me."
- "I never get a break."
- "Everybody is against me."

After a major disappointment, no amount of sympathy can ease the initial pain. Self-pity represents an effort to provide the needed consolation from within. The problem is that once you begin feeling sorry for yourself, it can be hard to stop.

A fourth initial response (it often occurs side by side with the first three) is depression. A major loss literally rips away your energy and enthusiasm, leaving behind dreadful feelings such as:

- "Life isn't worth the effort."
- "Why bother?"
- "I'll never get over it."
- "I'm miserable and nothing will help."

Immediately following a loss, depression is perfectly natural —even valuable, as long as you don't get yourself stuck in it.

What few people seem to realize is that a loss or major disappointment inflicts an emotional wound that requires just as much care and attention to heal properly as a serious physical injury. Even after a minor cut, you wash it and put on a band-aid. A broken leg requires weeks in the hospital and months before full function is restored. A major loss requires just as much care and even more time to heal properly. Unfortunately, most people don't know how to treat the emotional wounds that result from loss and disappointment. The sad result is slow healing and unnecessary emotional scarring. It doesn't have to be that way.

You can transform the pain and suffering of loss into the energy and joy of growth. No one says it's easy, but with knowledge you can do it. Take a look at nature. Everywhere loss is a prerequisite to growth. When a flower blooms the bud is lost; when morning dawns night is lost; when the butterfly is born the caterpillar disappears. So too in human life. When the toddler walks the infant is lost. When the teen begins to drive the child is no more. When you grow old youth is left behind.

When you're hurting from the loss of a love or from a major disappointment at work, it is indeed hard to see that your circumstance contains any opportunities for growth. Nevertheless, they are there. Kahlil Gibran puts it beautifully: "The deeper that sorrow carves into your being, the more joy it can contain." This is not to say that you can't have joy without paying your dues in grief. The point is to learn that grief too can become an opportunity for growth when you accept it, experience your pain fully, and then learn from it. Tragedy need not make life ugly; it can increase its beauty.

Recognizing Loss

You'd think the emotional wounds from loss and disappointment would be easy to recognize. Yet people often come into my office who suffer symptoms of loss but don't associate the symptoms with a loss or disappointment at all. Our culture has made many people so ashamed to admit loss or disappointment that it is necessary to discuss how to recognize the disabling effects.

Of course, some losses are too painful to deny: death of a loved one, breakup of a relationship, a friend moving away, separation, divorce. But what about the less obvious losses? They may not cause such intense pain, but even minor losses can add up to a major case of anhedonia. Here are a few not-so-obvious losses:

- getting laid off from your job
- learning that an investment is going sour
- moving to a new town or state
- changing job or school
- coming down with a serious illness

- getting mugged, robbed, or raped
- losing a friend who moves away or gets married and changes
- being let down by someone you trust
- abandoning a long-term goal that you discover is unreachable
- discovering that a cherished ideal no longer makes sense in your life
- aging, losing physical abilities that you may have counted on
- diminished sexual drive or impaired ability
- unfulfilled expectations, learning that you don't get the promotion, sale, role, or contract you were counting on
- retiring
- a traffic accident
- getting stood up or left out

The emotional effects of loss vary widely from person to person, though of course there is always a degree of pain and sadness. Many people feel numb after a major loss. When the numbness wears off after a few hours or days, the initial pain is often transformed into one or more other symptoms. Some people feel helpless, fearful, or just empty. Others may become pessimistic, irritable, angry, restless. Guilt is common. So are reduced energy, sexual desire, appetite, and motivation. Nausea, indigestion, and headaches may occur. There may be a loss of concentration or manual dexterity. Disturbances of normal sleep patterns (either inability to get to sleep, early morning awakening, or sleeping more than usual) are also common.

While all these symptoms may arise from other causes, loss is frequently overlooked. There is a strong human tendency to forget losses and disappointments as quickly as possible. This is a mixed blessing. It helps us continue to function; it prolongs the suffering. When a loss is buried but not healed, the less obvious symptoms may persist for months, years, or in some cases for a lifetime. The greatest tragedy of loss and disappointment is often not the painful event itself, but the prolonged suffering when the natural healing process is not allowed to happen.

Stages of Recovery

Just as the body goes through distinct stages in healing a physical wound, so the mind must pass through three recognizable stages in the recovery from loss or disappointment. First come shock and denial. Unable to cope with a sudden emotional blow, the mind blocks it out temporarily. We say things to ourselves such as "I can't believe it!" "He couldn't have done such a thing!" "This isn't happening!" or we feel numb. After a major loss there may be complete emotional paralysis lasting from a few moments to a few months.

When the shock begins to wear off, the second stage gradually unfolds. This is the period of anger and depression. Whenever you're hurt by someone you love or trust, anger is an automatic and completely natural response, as is depression, with all the feelings of despair, fatigue, and sadness. Frequent crying may occur at this stage. (After a major loss this may last up to a year or more.) The key to moving on from this stage is fully experiencing the pain and allowing expression of the anger without guilt. This is where the healing often gets stuck.

The final stages of recovery are understanding and acceptance. This is the point where the pain of loss begins its transformation into a new opportunity for growth, and ultimately inner joy.

Once the pain is fully felt and the anger vented, the loss becomes a fact that can be accepted and understood. With time, it ceases to be so devastating that it must be blocked out. It becomes a painful event, but you have survived. Now it's an opportunity for you to learn something about yourself and the world. Energy and strength return, often in greater measure than before. Albert Camus summed up the crowning insight that marks the completion of this stage when he wrote: "In the midst of winter, I finally learned that there was in me an invincible summer."

Mending a Broken Heart

Late one afternoon Barbara was preparing dinner while her two sons were playing in the family room. She had expected her husband home from a business trip but by now she presumed he had missed his plane. She wasn't worried; he'd been late many times before. He'd call soon. Abruptly the music stopped. A news bulletin. A plane crashed moments ago near the local airport. When she heard the flight number, Barbara froze. No breath, no sound, no pain, no feeling. The music returned. "He's not on that plane," she told herself. "He's late, he'll be calling soon." She continued preparing dinner and ignored the trembling and nausea. "There's no need to call anyone," she kept telling herself. "Ron will call me." Later that evening, a call came; it was from the airline.

That was over three years ago. Today, sitting in my office, Barbara looks worn. Petite, with dark hair and blue eyes, she shows the signs of struggling with her grief for the past three years. She looks pale and drawn. There are dark circles under her eyes. She is reluctant to maintain eye contact. She wrings her hands unconsciously and is agitated. When she speaks about her husband and their relationship she becomes visibly more animated, but soon finds herself struggling against tears.

"There *is* no one like him," she says of him. "Strong he was, very determined, always knew how to take charge, but he was also sweet. He was always tender with me, always understanding, and he was a terrific father. The boys idolized him.

"He had a problem early in our marriage that I thought was going to destroy us. The boys were very young, Ron was just beginning to take on heavier responsibilities in the company. The pressure was getting to him and he started drinking. There was a crisis, but we solved it together. We didn't go to a counselor. Our love was strong enough to carry us through. . . . He was my source of strength, and he always told me how important I was to his success. . . .

It was as close to a perfect marriage as I could ever describe. No one can ever replace Ron. It will never be the same." The tears began to flow. Soon they became deep, wrenching sobs.

No loss is more difficult to overcome than the loss of someone you love; no loss is as painful. The death of a spouse is perhaps the most painful emotional experience a human being can undergo. Almost as heartrending is the pain of separation and divorce. Even if a relationship lasts for only a few months, separation results in deep emotional hurt. The greater the love and the closer the relationship, the deeper the hurt on parting.

The emotional devastation following the death of a spouse (or a divorce) often persists for one to two years. Depression, reduced interest in other people, crying spells, and reduced vitality are natural parts of the healing process during recovery from such a loss. Three-and-a-half years later, however, the healing process should be about complete. Normally, the person has moved to the third stage, understanding and acceptance. At this point, energy returns and a new vitality emerges with the desire to create a new life.

Looking at Barbara you can see that the healing process has been interrupted. She is stuck at the second stage; depression predominates. She thinks of Ron constantly. She has no interest in other men. She feels miserable. She has little energy. Sleep is a problem. She often cries for no apparent reason.

When these symptoms are allowed to persist for so long, there is a real risk that the loss will never heal and the person will be battling depression for the rest of his or her life. Barbara was fortunate enough to have a close friend who insisted that she get help.

When Barbara described her husband and their relationship, the reason why she was unable to recover from his death gradually became clear. Looking back, she could see their marriage only in terms of ideals. They had a perfect marriage. Ron was a man without equal. He not only loved her, he was understanding, compassionate, strong, sexually exciting, handsome. They fought, but always made up. She insisted that Ron never hurt her.

Of course, no one and no marriage is ever so perfect. Barbara's inability to recall Ron or their marriage in anything less than ideal terms was the tip-off. Behind Barbara's ideal memories was a torrent of anger she couldn't accept. The ideal memories kept the unacceptable anger at bay, but at the cost of keeping her tied to the past and buried by depression.

Anger is a normal response to loss. When you lose someone you love, it is completely natural and healthy to feel anger at them for leaving you. It doesn't matter whether they walked out on their own or were the victim of a tragic accident. The reason for the loss makes little difference to the underlying emotional chemistry. Loss results in hurt, which triggers anger. This is a law of the functioning of the human psyche. To heal from a loss, the anger must be accepted and expressed so the pain of the hurt can be fully felt and let go. When the anger is denied, the price is incomplete healing and persistent depression.

Barbara, like most people, could not admit her anger toward Ron, because her anger made her feel guilty. She loved him; he was such a good husband; he was taken away by a freak accident. How could she dare feel, much less express, anger toward him? That was Barbara's reasoning. She failed to recognize that anger following a loss, especially of someone you love deeply, isn't rational. It simply is. It must be resolved if healing is to set in.

During her first few sessions Barbara learned about the natural stages of recovery from loss. When she understood better that she was struggling to recover from the most painful and difficult of human experiences, she was able to stop punishing herself for her depression. She agreed that Ron would not have wanted her to go on feeling so unhappy, and would have wanted her to create a new life for herself and her children. Gradually she grew able to talk about Ron as he was, not as the ideal she had created. She was finally willing to risk exploring all her feelings about Ron.

Difficult issues began to come up. How did she feel about being left alone with two children? What about her sexual needs? Did she feel she was left economically secure? How did she feel about the change in life-style and her reduced income? What about all the men making passes at her? Perhaps Ron wasn't the ideal person she remembered. Perhaps she was angry with him for leaving her in this mess.

A simple exercise finally broke the dam of her feelings. I asked Barbara to close her eyes and picture Ron sitting next to her. This was to be her opportunity to tell him how she was feeling now that he was gone. "Oh, God, I loved you so much," she said. "How could you leave me? Can't you see how much I miss you now? I am miserable. It hurts so much that I don't know what to do. . . . I'm also feeling upset about a lot of things. I'm left here to raise your sons all alone; our finances are a mess. Why did you leave? Why didn't you let me die instead? The children ask why daddy left. What am I to say? You didn't spend enough time with them and now it's too late. What am I supposed to do? I'm afraid! Afraid about our future, afraid to begin dating again, afraid to live!"

Once the anger began to surface, it kept coming. When Barbara felt waves of anger at home, she was encouraged to act it out safely by pounding a pillow with her fists and giving vent to her angry thoughts. The critical point was to accept the anger without feeling guilty about it. When you lose someone you love and you are hurt, you have a right to be angry.

With the gradual release of her pent-up anger, Barbara began to come out of her depression. No longer did she feel the need to hold on to an idealized memory of Ron and their marriage. She could begin to appreciate her past as it was: wonderful but not perfect. Accepting the past as it was became the stepping-stone to accepting Ron's death and his wish that she would create a new life of her own. She began to see that remaining distraught was no proof of how much she had loved him. The greatest testimony to Ron's love and their marriage was her courage to pick up the pieces and finally choose happiness for herself and their family even in the face of the tragedy. This is the stage of understanding and acceptance.

Several months later Barbara was ready to begin inviting new people into her life. She could look back and see that a new woman had emerged from the tragedy and long-sought recovery. Having set her depression aside and taken back her personal power, she decided to go back to school and finish a degree in urban planning. She's dating again but in no hurry to marry. The paradox of working through the pain and anger of her loss is that she now has a greater love for Ron than ever before. It is a love that strengthens and comforts even though Ron is dead. She realizes that finding that kind of love again is not easy. She has to give herself time. With a whole life ahead, she is willing to give herself all the time she needs.

Coping with Loss as a Couple

When Tom and Rebecca came into my office, they were convinced their marriage couldn't be saved. Tom agreed to come only as a "last resort, so I don't feel I'm copping out." Rebecca said she wanted to save the marriage, but wasn't very hopeful. Each had numerous complaints about the other. According to Rebecca, Tom had become impossible to live with. He was irritable, picky, and wasn't giving her the love and affection she needed. Tom complained that Rebecca only made demands on his time and "refuses to give me the support I need." Their one point of agreement was that their sex lives had "gone to pot." "If it weren't for the children," Rebecca said, "we wouldn't be here."

Married for twelve years, Tom and Rebecca had three children, all in grade school. Their pride in their children was evident when either spoke about them. A primary concern was saving the children any further distress. This mutual pride and shared concern was evidence that the marriage might not be as shaky as it seemed. Clearly, it was once very strong or the children would not be doing so well, nor would Tom and Rebecca feel so comfortable talking about them together. When had the marriage begun to go sour? What happened to put a stress on their relationship?

There is an old saying that love is blind, meaning that lovers can't see each other's weaknesses. Love is blind in another way. Couples have a peculiar tendency to minimize or ignore the emotional and psychological impact of pressures from outside the relationship. When the relationship begins to show signs of stress, couples tend to start blaming each other for not living up to expectations instead of blaming the external source of pressure.

Tom and Rebecca fell full force into this trap. For eleven years their lives had worked out almost exactly as they had planned. Tom progressed at work; they had their children; and their standard of living steadily improved. Then one morning a year ago, Tom came to work only to find that the company was laying people off. Tom's boss told him not to worry about the shake-up because he had been with the company for so long. Two days later Tom found a pink slip on his desk. "All I got," says Tom, "was a month's pay and an 'I'm sorry.'

"On the way home that night, all I wanted to do was crawl into a hole," says Tom. "I couldn't face Rebecca. For God's sake, I'd been a good provider from the first day of our marriage. What was I going to say to our friends? To my in-laws? How could I tell anyone? I remember having this fantasy of taking off to hide out until I found a new job. All the way home I kept up my nerve by telling myself I'd get a new job tomorrow." Years ago, taking away someone's means of earning a living could be equivalent to a mortal wound. Today unemployment doesn't mean starvation, but the emotional effects are no less devastating.

Three months later Tom was still out of work. The marriage was beginning to suffer. "Ever since he lost his job," explained Rebecca, "Tom has been compulsive about maintaining his routine. Every morning he gets up at six thirty, just as he always did when he was working. After breakfast he heads for the family room where he set up his desk. I have no idea what he can be doing there all day, but he insists on quiet. It's hard having Tom around the house all the time. He sticks his nose into everything and I can't keep the house in order."

"I believe that routine is important," responds Tom. "Finding a new job is work, so I've put my nose to the grindstone and started turning up every opportunity. Hundreds of résumés have gone out. I've had a few interviews but no offers. Meanwhile Rebecca just piles on the crap. She's always telling me what she thinks I ought to do or how she thinks I'm wasting time. Not once does she say 'I understand what you're going through.' Meanwhile, I can't sleep. I wake up at 4:00 A.M. in a cold sweat. All I think about is, what are we going to do when the unemployment runs out?"

Like most couples who suffer a financial loss, Tom and Rebecca did not stop to consider what the loss was doing to their relationship. They expected each other to be strong and offer plenty of support, but neither was willing to recognize that the loss itself was a major wound that required first aid before untapped resources of strength could be mustered. The first thing Tom and Rebecca had to recognize was that their loss was an opportunity for a breakdown in their marriage—or a breakthrough. The choice was up to them and how they handled the crisis.

Neither Tom nor Rebecca had dealt with their feelings about Tom losing his job. Tom was angry and ashamed, Rebecca angry and disappointed. When we got these feelings out in the open, it was already clear that they had something important in common, their unexpressed anger toward Tom's old employer. To get this anger out so they could begin using the energy behind it, I asked them to try two exercises. First, since they are both tennis players, I asked them to go out on the tennis court and imagine that the tennis ball was Tom's former boss's head. Despite their misgivings, they agreed to try it. "Within ten minutes of beginning to smash the ball and curse with each stroke," Rebecca says, "we were laughing in each other's arms." I also asked them to write a letter to the company explaining how they both felt mistreated and how poorly the situation had been handled.

To compose a letter together they had to listen to each other and understand their mutual feelings of hurt and disappointment. Once they listened to each other they were able to appreciate how hard each was trying to cope. Getting the anger out in the open and reestablishing communication was a breakthrough. Tom's depression began to lift. Rebecca felt they were "onto something very good." They stopped blaming each other and started combining their resources to face their crisis.

The next step was finding Tom a new job. While embroiled in his marital crisis, Tom spent a lot of energy but accomplished very little. He pursued every opportunity halfheartedly instead of focusing on three or four openings that seemed most promising. With their new energy, Tom and Rebecca sat down together to discuss and then choose the three or four best options. No longer were they taking the attitude that they would accept whatever came along. They began to value the contribution and skills Tom would bring to whatever company might be lucky enough to land him. "For the first time since I lost my job," said Tom at this point, "I feel Rebecca is supporting me." Rebecca said, "Tom is finally recognizing that I can be a real help to him." Once the best options were chosen, Tom wrote strong personal letters to request interviews. He got four interviews and two job offers. The one he finally chose required that they move, but it was a position with a higher salary and a greater opportunity for advancement than his old job. Needless to say, Tom and Rebecca were pleased.

On the verge of a marital breakdown, Tom and Rebecca managed to transform their economic loss into a mutual breakthrough. They know more about themselves and each other, and are much closer for having faced a crisis and survived. With Tom's new job, they both feel they've been very fortunate. "It's a fairy-tale ending," says Rebecca. True, they were fortunate, but to a large degree they created their own good luck. By pulling together to face their loss, Tom and Rebecca were able to draw on hidden strengths. This renewed confidence visibly transformed Tom, who had become anxious, agitated, and doubtful about his abilities. He had important skills and valuable experience, but his assets were overshadowed by personal feelings of weakness that doomed his job-hunting efforts before he began. Only after both he and Rebecca had emotionally recovered from the loss could Tom's strength become apparent to his potential employers.

"I never was a Pollyanna," says Rebecca. "I never thought something like this could actually turn out for the best. The most incredible thing has been what's happened between us. It's like we've fallen in love again. We've never been so good together. We've both really grown."

Transforming Loss into Opportunity

It's ironic about many disappointments, especially those related to work and success: What you tell yourself about them is frequently more damaging than the disappointment itself.

When your plans don't work out as expected, you have two choices. Feel sorry for yourself, doubt your ability, and bemoan your bad luck. Or accept the loss, hold on to your self-confidence, and look for the opportunity hidden in your disappointment. If you sit there and tell yourself how stupid you are or how helpless you feel, you'll never find the opportunity. If you can find the courage to accept your loss and learn from it, you may discover that your disappointment really was the best thing that could have happened to you.

For five years Karen was a lead dancer with an important American dance company. She had dreamed of becoming a lead dancer ever since she saw *The Nutcracker* at age six. In college she discovered that she was more interested in modern dance than classical ballet; she finally joined one of the best modern companies. She wasn't an instant star by any means. For years she danced in the chorus, but at age twenty-eight, late for a dancer, emerged into leading roles. Then, after four short years at the top, she was on the verge of a major crisis. The physical stress and strain of dance had become too much. She ached continually. At thirty-two, Karen realized that her dance career was all but over.

With her love-hate relationship with dance coming to an end, Karen began suffering from severe insomnia. She had always had problems sleeping; now her insomnia became debilitating. To get any sleep at all she had to go through an elaborate ritual with earplugs, a black mask, aspirins, and a separate bed. She and her husband assumed that the crisis would pass, but with the approaching end of the dancing season, it got worse. Karen came for help.

Following any major disappointment, self-confidence usually takes a nose dive while old insecurities reappear. Ever since she was a child, Karen remembers struggling with feelings that she was not good enough to become a lead dancer. Now this old fear came back under the new guise of feeling "unattractive and unable to do anything but dance."

First Karen had to understand that the reemergence of old fears is not only natural but important to transforming her loss into growth. By accepting and then challenging these old insecurities, Karen could achieve a personal transformation to release new creative energies and new sources of personal power. A Hollywood producer met Karen at a party one evening and suggested she get into television advertising and eventually, the movies. When she began to audition and take acting classes, Karen was suddenly paralyzed by her old fears that she would never be good enough. The competition in television advertising is intense. Up to seven hundred people may audition for one thirty-second commercial. From friends Karen knew about the enormous rejection rate, and she had an intense fear of rejection. Her insomnia and headaches persisted, partly because of anxiety, partly to avoid her fears.

Just as you can't eliminate the pain of a major loss by denying it, you can't overcome insecurities by trying to force them out of your mind. To confront her fears Karen needed to expand her understanding of her loss. Yes, changing careers is stressful and difficult, but it can also be a challenge that offers new excitement. Yes, the loss of her old career is cause for anxiety and insecurity, but it can also be an opportunity for eliminating old fears and growing to a higher level of self-confidence and inner joy.

With this new perspective on her fears, Karen discovered confidence and enthusiasm about acting. She didn't get parts right away, just as she didn't become a lead dancer the first time she auditioned with her dance company. For the first six months, she made more progress against her fears than she did in getting parts.

To eliminate her old fears of rejection, Karen used the "what if" technique. Every time she started ruminating about a possible rejection or felt paralyzed with anxiety about failure, she asked herself what would be the worst thing that could happen if she failed. She would still have her loving husband, she would still be herself, she would still be able to enjoy the sunrises and sunsets. Gradually she learned to respond to a fear not with a "what if" but with a "so what if." This is not merely a verbal trick. To say "so what if" and mean it, you have to settle back into yourself and appreciate your strengths independently of what you are trying to achieve. The more you use this technique, the more automatic it becomes. Old fears and self-doubts wither as new self-confidence grows.

Karen also used "thought stopping." She was prone to self-defeating thoughts just prior to her auditions. "I'm going to forget my lines" and "I'm going to make a fool of myself" were her two most common self-putdowns. A controlled expression of will is the best antidote. Whenever these thoughts came up, she closed her eyes for a moment and aggressively told them "Stop" or "Go away." With practice, thought stopping becomes an automatic way to quickly eliminate troubling intruders and generate a surge of self-confidence.

Loss can become an opportunity for growth if you have the courage to face the psychological obstacles that the disappointment throws at you. Karen was an attractive person when I first met her; now she is radiant. Her new career is still in its early stages, but she is doing commercials. More important, she and her husband have discovered a new vitality, and have both substantially increased their daily measure of inner joy.

Forgiving Your Parents

You are a rare person indeed if you harbor no regrets or disappointments about your relationship with your parents. Even the best of parents make mistakes, and children suffer hurts that they sometimes carry for the rest of their lives, often without the parents even knowing when or how the wounds were inflicted. Here is a list of regrets expressed by one group of clients:

- "My father was a tyrant; he was always right, I was always wrong."
- "My parents never showed that they loved me. Our home was very cold."
- "The only time my parents showed that they cared was when I was sick. I got sick a lot."
- "My mother told me all men are no good and sex is dirty."
- "They fought all the time; I was always afraid they would get a divorce. Maybe they should have."
- "My mother was too domineering. She tried to make me a mama's boy."
- "My father never listened. I couldn't tell him how I was really feeling."
- "They made me feel unattractive."

Part of maturing is coming to terms with these old disappointments and appreciating that parents did their best. This coming to terms rarely heals old hurts completely. They just grow less significant, compared to the joys and sorrows of adult life. To whatever extent you hold on to old unresolved disappointments about your parents, you inhibit your capacity for inner joy. For many people the complete healing of those old wounds is possible, and without years of psycho-analysis. Commitment to your own growth, willingness to let intense feelings come to the surface, and patience with yourself are the principal requirements.

Daryl is sixty-two. For all his adult life he has been crippled by unresolved rage he feels toward his father. Daryl's complexion is red, his shoulders are raised and held back, he speaks staccato and tends to grind his teeth. When he first walked into my office, his anger was written all over his face. His principal reason for seeking help was his recent inability to hold a job or control his angry outbursts. "I took a woman out last week," he said, "went to a nice place, dinner was sixty bucks, but when I took her home she didn't even say thank you. It really pissed me off! I started screaming at her and was ready to slam her. I didn't, but on the way home I couldn't cool down."

Daryl has been a salesman most of his life. His job history is a self-destructive pattern of high achievement followed by disappointing performance and finally quitting to go somewhere else. He has typically begun each new job with a great desire to prove his ability, within a few months earning the praises of his superiors. "I wanted to prove I could do it," he says. "I usually get an offer of a big salary increase in the first two years. When I get it I really feel terrific, on top of the world, really fantastic." But the joy of his accomplishment never persisted. Within a year or two he would lose interest and his performance would decline. This pattern suggests that his primary motivation was winning approval from his superiors. Once he got it, his motivation slipped to zero.

Behind Daryl's rage and his desperate need for approval are bitter memories about his father, who died when Daryl was forty-two. Daryl's earliest childhood memory is huddling in a corner of the kitchen while his father yelled at him. He recalls being provoked into a fight with another child in the neighborhood. Daryl feels to this day that he had to defend himself, but he recalls bitterly his father running out of the house, taking off his belt, and whipping him for starting fights. "He never even asked," Daryl says between clenched teeth. "He just assumed it was my fault."

During World War II Daryl wanted to finish college before enlisting, but his father wouldn't have it. "He made me feel I had to get killed to save his pride," Daryl says. The sum total of Daryl's memory of his father is a bitter disappointment laced with anger and regret. At sixty-two Daryl has finally found the courage to challenge this crippling burden and take back the power he had lost.

To transform poisonous feelings about your childhood or your parents you need to admit those feelings exist. Make a list of your regrets and resentments connected with your parents. Beware of generalities. Daryl began by writing: "I hate my father"; "He never listened to me"; "He didn't ever show any love." These statements are not helpful; they're vague and don't bring to mind a particular relationship with a parent. They are generalities that could be written about anyone. To be useful, the list has to be as specific as possible, to recall the living human relationship. Daryl's list became useful when he began writing about "regret":

> I regret not telling him to go to hell when he slapped me on my thirteenth birthday because I forgot to take out the garbage.

and about "resentments":

> I'll never forgive him for pounding me when I was nine because he thought I started a fight when I hadn't. He wouldn't listen and beat me till I had a bloody lip.

Use time, place, what happened, how you felt; put as many specifics as possible into each entry.

Once the regrets and resentments are laid out, it's time to move to acceptance and forgiveness. Daryl's lists were emotional explosives. All Daryl had to do was read several of the entries out loud and he'd alternately seethe with rage and shed bitter tears. The more honest and specific the entries, the more powerful the emotional response to them. By defusing the pain and rage connected with unhappy childhood memories, you can recover the lost energy and discover new enthusiasm, freedom, and joy.

At first Daryl resisted the idea of forgiveness. "Why should I forgive the bastard?" he said. "He doesn't deserve it." But the forgiving is not for your parents; it's for you. Your regrets and resentments cripple you, not your parents. Moving to the level of acceptance and forgiveness will transform you, not your parents, and finally end their control over your life.

You can think of your regrets and resentments as clots of pain logged in your heart. To achieve the freedom and relief of forgiveness, these clots must be dissolved and brought to the surface where they can be felt and expressed. Because these painful memories have been kept out of sight for so long, they may be hard to uncover. The human personality resists change, so you're likely to encounter resistance to accepting your old hurts and forgiving your parents for causing them. Try this technique to help surmount resistance:

Begin by sitting comfortably and closing your eyes. Relax by using any one of the relaxation techniques described in chapter III. Now picture an old dusty filing cabinet in the back of your mind. It is sitting in a dark room cluttered with cobwebs. No one has been there for ages. Turn on the light. Look at the locks and bolts. The cabinets are obviously constructed to keep you out. It doesn't matter. You have the power to break the locks. Use your will to snap each lock and blow away the dust. The labels of each drawer come into view. One says "dad," another "mom," a third "grandmother," and so on. These are the records of the repressed hurts arising from your most significant childhood relationships.

Choose a drawer and open it. You'll find a set of folders, each containing details of a painful incident. Take out the first folder and read it carefully. You're going back to the event in your mind. When it first happened, you fought the hurt. This time, let the feelings come out. Whatever you feel—anger, rage, sadness—let it happen. If tears come, that's OK. Now go on to another folder. Recall that incident. Let those feelings surface. Keep looking at folders until you begin to imagine the person who hurt you walking into the room of your mind. Picture the person in detail—facial lines, body posture, gestures, voice, expression. When you can see the person clearly, you are ready to tell him or her what you are feeling. Don't hold anything back. Describe how much you were hurt by each incident you recall. Don't fight your feelings. Just express them to the person who hurt you.

When you can say to the person how much you hurt, the tears, shame, or anger may come. The pain will reach an intense peak and then begin *dissolving* throughout your body. Whatever feeling comes, let it happen. When you're done feeling all your pain, you'll begin to feel relief. The pain will subside. The relief will grow. You may feel as if the pain is washing out of your body. It is. The relief you feel is acceptance. No longer must you struggle to keep your old hurt locked up. It can come out where you can see that it is something that happened in the past and can't be changed. After repeating this exercise many times, it becomes possible to forgive.

This doesn't mean to forget. That would be losing part of your past and yourself. It means to recognize that you gain nothing by investing your energies in resentment and closing your heart. Forgiveness means opening that part of your heart that had been closed with pain. It means letting yourself love again.

This is an extremely powerful technique. You need to allow plenty of time. An hour would be the minimum each time you use it. The critical step is admitting how much you hurt and telling the person who hurt you how badly you are suffering. You may have to practice a few times, but when you've mastered the technique, its effects will be profound.

Note: This technique is not meant for people with severe emotional disturbances, except under psychotherapeutic supervision. Always finish with five minutes of ease and relaxation to regain your composure.

Another technique, less emotionally wrenching than the first, is to write a letter. The goal is the same. Bring all the pain of your loss to your awareness and tell the person who hurt you how much you hurt. Again, expect to resist the process at first. You may sit down and be so flooded with feeling that you draw a blank. That's OK. Stick with it. Soon the memories will come back, along with the pain. My experience is that clients who use this technique typically begin with a page or two and several days later wind up with ten-, twenty- or thirty-page letters to their parents. (You may want to share this letter out loud with someone whom you are very close to, and who you know will understand.)

Next, when you are ready, write a second letter telling your parents you're ready to forgive. Again, this doesn't mean to forget. The core of forgiveness is accepting the past and recognizing the futility of investing your energy in holding on to resentments. Daryl's first step toward forgiveness was the simple statement: "I hate you for what you have done to me, but I forgive you." That may not sound like forgiveness, but it is a crucial first step. The past doesn't go away, and the pain may take time to dissolve completely, but eventually you will be free from it.

These techniques are not to be taken lightly. They unlock intense feelings that you may hardly have realized were there. It's important to follow them through the emotional tidal wave that erupts until you feel the release and relief. Each time you let out some repressed hurt, you will change; you will feel different, better. An inner shift is taking place. The change may be dramatic or incremental. You may feel a great sense of freedom and energy. Or it may be subtle—a feeling of calm or thankfulness. Whatever the initial effect, the new emotional freedom will grow. One client who never had a good relationship with her mother compared the change to achieving a state of grace.

Forty Things to Do When There's Nothing to Be Done

Loss leaves you feeling helpless. You can't change the past, but the next best thing is to learn what you *can* change and make your disappointments serve your growth. Here is a brief first-aid manual for coping with loss. The strategies are divided into three groups, corresponding to the three stages of recovery from loss.

Shock and Denial

You can't believe it happened.

OK, that's a natural, sensible response. You feel numb, disoriented, helpless. All these feelings are OK too. Don't fight the present. The struggle to believe and at the same time disbelieve your loss is natural. Give it time. The loss is real. You are strong enough to admit it. Let yourself accept the reality that the worst has happened.

You hurt.

Don't try to deny it. Even small losses and disappointments (like losing a quarter in a pay phone) hurt a little. Big losses hurt a lot. The fact that you can be disappointed and hurting is proof that you're human. It's natural to be frightened of pain at first. Sometimes it can get so bad that it threatens to swallow you up. Don't panic or start fighting it. Lean gently into your pain. You won't find it bottomless. Let yourself be with the pain. When it is at its worst and you feel it all, you're already starting to heal.

Remember you are not alone.

"Misery loves company." You have plenty of company. You can't be human without suffering loss. Many great people have suffered terrible losses and survived. Jacqueline Kennedy lost her husband. Franklin D. Roosevelt lost his ability to walk. Think of all the people you know who suffered terrible losses. Like them, you will recover. The pain will pass and you will be stronger for having loved, lost, and survived.

Disappointment is a blow to your self-esteem.

No doubt about it. No one suffers a major setback without beginning to doubt themselves for a while. Your guilt, worry, self-condemnation, and self-deprecation are symptoms of your loss. Nothing more. They have only temporary reality. Don't give them prime-time status by paying them much attention. Better to tell yourself that you are strong enough to go on and transform your loss into something better.

Beware of the "if only"s.

Every time you punish yourself with what you might have done, you fall for the trap of trying to make believe that the past can be changed. It can't. "If only"s don't count, so don't use them.

Remember that a loss is just as much a wound as a cut or a broken bone.

It hurts, and you have to give it time to heal. More than anything else, you need plenty of time. You can be confident that you will heal. The same powerful healing forces that can mend a broken bone also mend the emotional trauma of a loss. Take heart, nature is on your side.

The greater the loss, the more time you'll take to heal.

In this era of instant gratification, many people are unwilling to give themselves the time they need. The cost of this hurry sickness is anhedonia. Don't make the same mistake. Time may be a luxury, but you deserve it. Be careful not to rush the healing. The result will be chronic strain. Real healing results in a new feeling of ease and appreciation for life.

The healing process is not smooth.

You're going to have ups and downs. One day you may feel the pain is almost gone; the next day you seem to hurt as much as ever. Don't worry about ups and downs. They're a sign that healing is underway.

Get more rest.

The number one prescription for all injury, physical or

emotional, is rest. You rest when you have a high fever; you need to rest now that you have suffered a major loss. Extra sleep will help, especially if you find yourself waking up exhausted. Set aside time in the morning and afternoon for relaxation and meditation. Beware of the rebound and another intense emotional involvement. It's best to postpone getting heavily involved for a while.

Establish a regular routine and stick to it.

Healing is most rapid when rest is alternated with dynamic activity. Too much rest will encourage self-pity and may make you lethargic. Activity is the best antidote. Plan for some regular exercise every day (this is good advice any time) and keep to a regular schedule at work. Balance is the key.

Recognize that your judgment is likely to be clouded for a while.

You'd be wise to postpone important decisions until you're well along recovering from your loss. Now is not the time to be thinking about changing your job or your residence. Nor is it the time to be looking for a new love relationship. If you have to make a major decision, you would be wise to consider it very carefully. Advice from friends may be helpful.

Let yourself accept comforting from friends and family.

You don't have to be ashamed that you hurt or that you suffered a loss. In a society that makes losing a disgrace, it takes courage to accept emotional support from others. If you need help you're supposed to go to a therapist. The odds are you don't need one and can get support from those close to you. Go ahead and ask for it. If you still feel terribly alone, professional help might be helpful. Feel free to seek it out.

Consult religious or philosophical teachings in which you have faith or from which you have benefited in the past.

All great teachings offer help in handling loss and growing from it. You may want to consult the Bible or the Torah, the Bhagavad Gita, or any book of great religious or philosophical wisdom.

Suicidal thoughts?

Yes, they may come if you have suffered a major loss. Almost everyone is unhappy enough to contemplate suicide at one time or another. These feelings of intense despair are natural symptoms of your pain. You can accept them as that without thinking you're losing your mind. A thought is just a thought; it doesn't require action. If you feel suicidal thoughts are getting out of hand, you should get help right away. You can always call the telephone operator (right now, if necessary) and ask her to connect you with the local suicide prevention agency. She may ask you if this is an emergency. Say yes.

Suicidal thoughts mean in part that you are beginning to feel the anger about being hurt. Instead of accepting the anger and getting it out, you are beginning to turn it against yourself. This is a mistake. The anger is OK, and needs to be expressed safely. You should be angry now; that is the next step in the healing process. You are making progress, so let's go on.

Depression and Anger

Feel depressed? OK. Join the crowd.

At any time millions of people feel depressed because they have suffered a major loss. There's nothing shameful about depression. When you suffer an emotional blow, the hurt isn't all in your mind. Biochemical changes occur in your brain that produce the feelings you call depression. The energy is literally drained out of you. Now is the time to let yourself be with your depression. Everything else can wait. Do your mourning now. If you postpone the healing process by pushing your depression aside, you may find yourself plagued by the blues for the rest of your life.

Don't try to pretend to feel better than you feel.

If you're low on energy, you'll only cause strain by trying to seem otherwise. Healing will be interrupted.

Cry.

Nothing is more natural after a loss or disappointment.

Don't believe that old sexist stuff about men not crying. If you hurt and the tears are coming, let them come. It is cleansing and serves the healing process by letting you feel your pain fully. Crying is an important and natural form of release. It has its own beauty.

Treat yourself gently.

You are more fragile now, there is no shame in that, so take it easy. Don't hurry, don't try to force yourself to do things like going to parties or to the movies when you don't want to. Ask a friend over for a quiet evening of music and talk. Avoid stressful situations that might force you to over-react. Now is not the time to take on new and difficult responsibilities. Tread slowly for a while. You deserve the special care.

Thinking of him/her?

If you have lost a love through divorce or separation, it's natural to dream about rekindling the relationship. But a forceful hand is best. Imagining that you can renew a relationship once it's over is another form of "if only." It's self-punishment, like pouring salt on an open wound. The only result is more pain. Don't indulge in self-punishment. Nothing is more painful than accepting the fact that a love relationship is over. Accept it now, face the realities, let yourself hurt. That's the way to healing, growth, and a greater capacity for love in the future.

It's about time you began dealing with your anger.

Everyone who suffers a loss or disappointment gets angry. Some may have trouble showing it, others difficulty in controlling it. But the anger is inevitable. To recover from your loss, you have to get the anger out. That is clear in the cases we have already discussed. The biggest obstacle to healing is bottled-up anger.

Beware of the rebound.

Following the loss of a love, everyone feels empty. Just as nature abhors a vacuum, so does the human psyche. You're likely to feel an intense desire to seize the very next opportunity to ignite a new fiery romance. Falling madly in love after a traumatic loss feels terrific for a while, but these rebound romances are almost inevitably doomed to disaster.

The result of a rebound romance is usually a second loss to mourn. Ugh.

Indulge in positive rather than negative addictions.

Now is a good time to start running, swimming, or playing tennis. It's also a good time to start meditating or taking walks in the woods. These are intrinsically healing activities and naturally pleasurable—"positive addictions." Beware of the tendency to seek solace in society's traditional escape activities. Alcohol may numb the pain, but in the long run will only prolong your suffering. So too will marijuana, ups, downs, and all the other recreational drugs. Momentary highs mask the pain. What you need to do is be with it. If you're a calorie junkie, you'll need to take special care to avoid putting on unwanted inches. The temporary solace you may get from food will be offset by the drop in your self-image as your waistline expands. The only drugs you should be taking during this period of healing are those prescribed by your doctor.

By all means, pamper yourself.

Were you to suffer a broken leg, you'd find friends and relatives bringing you fruit and candy to cheer you up. Though you've suffered an emotional wound that's just as serious, you're expected to show up for work every day as if nothing happened. You live in a world that doesn't acknowledge that emotional wounds hurt badly. The only way to fight back is to pamper yourself. Here are some suggestions: Take a hot bath, get a massage, buy yourself something you would really enjoy, get a manicure/pedicure (or any other cure), take a trip, go to a fine restaurant, buy yourself a cashmere anything, take a day off and go hiking, sailing, skiing, follow a whim and enjoy. You don't have to feel guilty about over-indulging. You deserve it.

Be willing to let go of your pain.

Paradoxically, pain can become a friend. You may be tempted to hold on to it longer than necessary. The unconscious thinking goes something like: "I've lost something really important to me, but at least I have my pain." The pain itself becomes a source of stability, albeit unhappy. At some point your pain will gradually slip away. Let it go. Only then can you go on to the next step where surviving your loss begins to pay off. You discover the new you, more powerful, more loving, and wiser than before.

Take your time to heal at your own pace.

Friends or relatives may tell you "It's about time you got over it" or "That's enough crying, now you'd better get on with your life." This advice is well intentioned, but remember you have the right to experience your pain fully, and to live through each stage of the healing process fully. Telling yourself "It doesn't matter" or "I'm all right now" when you don't feel that way is a phony attempt to move on prematurely to the stage of acceptance and understanding. If you've suffered a major loss, it may take a year or more before you have really reached the stage of acceptance. Not that your life has stopped in the interim. It does mean you have the right to take it a little easier during that time, to pamper yourself, to do your mourning at your own pace.

Acceptance and Understanding

Now is the time to begin transforming your loss into personal growth. As the pain lessens, your thinking becomes sharper, your judgment grows clearer, your concentration improves, you begin to be less self-preoccupied. Your feelings are more alive. You are stronger. There's no reason to settle for just putting the past behind you. You can learn from it and discover new inner strengths.

Forgive.

Whether your lover left you, your friends betrayed you, your boss fired you, or the fates dealt you a bad break, you gain strength by forgiving the person or the fates as soon as you can. Remember, you don't forgive for the other person's benefit, but for your own. Also, forgiving does not mean forgetting. To forgive originally meant "to return good treatment for ill usage." You have been ill used. When you can return good feeling toward the person who injured you, you are finally free.

Forgive yourself.

OK, you made a mistake, maybe it was a stupid mistake. Perhaps you lost something very important, a lot of money, a big business deal, whatever. Things would be different now if you had done something else. But there is no point in punishing yourself any further. You were who you were at the time you made your mistake. There was nothing else you could do, because of your level of consciousness at that time. All other speculations are imaginary. Forgiving yourself is acceptance, and a step toward freedom and wisdom.

Try to begin seeing the positive in your loss.

Yes, there *is* something positive! You've learned something about the world and yourself. Perhaps you were naive; or didn't understand how complicated love relationships can become; or how people change; or how ruthless the business world can be. The point is: Your loss is an extraordinary opportunity for rapid growth. Take advantage of it by examining why you lost and what you need to do to avoid making the same mistake in the future.

Accept that you're a better person for having loved and lost, rather than having never loved at all.

You became involved in life, you took a risk, you exercised your abilities. You aren't a coward. All that speaks well of you. Now you are stronger for having lived through your disappointment and learned from it.

Let yourself change.

The lesson you're learning may not be easily expressed yet. Learning may be going on at a nonverbal level. Perhaps you're more cautious, examining risks as well as potential rewards. One client said she felt her sensitivity had grown. "I can feel more," she said. No need to articulate the changes. Just let them happen. Your personality is shifting as new power becomes available. You may feel different, even a little strange. That's OK. You're on the right track.

Invite new people into your life.

At long last, you're ready to begin pursuing your life at full swing. Make new friends. Have the neighbors over for a drink. Join a health club or social group where you will meet new people. Don't be afraid to be friendly.

Feel like trying something new?

That's perfectly natural at this stage; go ahead and follow your inclination. One client always wanted to play the piano. Another had long planned to start running and finally joined a local running club. Gardening, sewing, cooking, Great Books, tennis. Take classes. Stretch yourself. Get involved. Let yourself grow.

Rekindle old interests.

During your healing period you may have let some of your activities slide. Now is the time to get back to them. Enjoy!

Give of yourself.

The only way to begin using your new strength is to start flexing your muscles. You're not so fragile anymore; you can take risks, share your feelings, trust yourself to love again. Start by sharing yourself in small ways. Offer to help a friend with a project; volunteer to help at a hospital or nursing home; drive an elderly person to the grocery store. When someone asks you about yourself, you don't have to protect yourself. There's no need for a mask. You know what the world is about, and you can handle it. The greatest joys are in sharing your real feelings. Let yourself get involved.

Accept your memories.

Forgiving does not mean never looking back. On a quiet Sunday afternoon you may find memories of your loss drifting back. This is normal. It doesn't mean you're slipping back into a depression. Some sadness will be there. Life has its tragic dimension, but tragedy has its own beauty. Remember the magnificence of the great tragic dramas: *Antigone, Macbeth, Othello.* Without tragedy life would become flat. Sadness is important.

Set aside time to enjoy solitude.

Having loved, lost, and survived, you are more able to find pleasure in yourself. Solitude is the incubator of creativity. Take walks in the park alone. Set aside an evening to stay home with a good book. Don't fill up these periods with the idle chatter of TV or radio. Better to let yourself think. That's an activity we all do too rarely.

Take hold of your new freedom.

You know much more now about yourself and about others. No longer must you react to the world. You can create the world you want to live in. No longer are you so dependent on others; you can choose when, where, how, and with whom you want to spend time. No longer are you naive about the world. You can choose one of your dreams and take the careful steps to make it come true. No longer need you hold yourself back out of fear of failure or loss. You've been through it all and survived. You know how the world works, and you have the power to get what you want out of life. You have discovered the invincibility of your inner joy.

Congratulations for a job well done! You deserve applause for having suffered your loss, given yourself the time to heal, and come out stronger for it. It's time to celebrate!

X

Sharing Inner Joy

To make the world work for 100 percent of humanity in the shortest possible time through spontaneous cooperation without any ecological offense or the disadvantage of anyone.

—R. Buckminster Fuller

This is the true joy in life. To be used for a purpose recognized by yourself as a mighty one.

—George Bernard Shaw

INNER JOY brings deep personal satisfaction, but also leads to something more. It changes your perception of yourself and your relationship to your world. As you become more cognizant of your personal power, you develop a new appreciation of your interdependence with every other human being, and for that matter, the whole living, growing, evolving biosphere that we call earth. This transformation of outlook is almost paradoxical. The more you appreciate your inner dimension of being, the more committed you become to transforming your own world. A desire emerges to see all your relationships and your thinking reflect the same level of integrity and joy that you experience as a baseline state of personal existence.

Rebuking those who try to solve social problems without attending to their inner lives, Socrates once admonished: "Let him who would move the world first move himself." What he might have added is that once you do change yourself, changing the world becomes a biological and psychological imperative. This is particularly significant in view of the criticism of the human potential and personal growth movements as a narcissistic absorption with self at the expense of social commitment. While the pursuit of personal growth may require an intense period of self-involvement, the flowering of inner joy creates an impelling drive to help make the world work.

This book is intended to help you "move yourself," but to the degree it succeeds, it becomes something more. The techniques and strategies we describe have been painstakingly developed and refined over many years of work emerging out of a long commitment to the belief that human beings are indeed capable of enormous personal transformation. To whatever extent you put these suggestions to use, you are likely to derive significant personal benefit. You will break through old barriers and past resistances to new levels of strength and satisfaction. You will overcome anhedonic behavior and experience more pleasure in almost everything that you do. You will become attuned to your inner voice and discover your power to create the life you want. But with the expansion of inner joy, you will come face to face with your own desire to make the world a better place.

Of all the benefits, this is perhaps the most significant. This is not a matter of speculation; it reflects our observation of thousands of clients and the most recent research on personal growth. People who experience more satisfaction in their own lives are no longer obsessed with trying to find happiness outside themselves, and become naturally concerned with the happiness and well-being of others. The growth of inner joy increases sensitivity to the suffering of others plagued by poverty, hunger, and disease. Heightened appreciation of living leads to an expanded awareness of biological interdependence, the fragile ecological balance that sustains life, and the terrible risks humanity is taking by continuing to spoil the earth.

The more conscious you become of your own strength, the less able you are in the face of human problems and suffering to deny the inner query: "What can I do?" When you begin experiencing your power to change your own life, it becomes difficult to justify inaction with the old myth, "One person can't make a difference." It becomes difficult to justify indifference with stock phrases such as "It's someone else's problem" or "I don't have time; I'm too busy." Once you make inner joy a part of your existence, it becomes impossible to turn your back on other people and world problems.

With the growth of inner joy, writes psychiatrist and teacher Robert Assagioli, "there wells up a realization that life is one, and an outpouring of love flows through that awakening individual towards his fellow man and the whole creation." There you have it, the most significant dimension of inner joy: its intimate connection with love. Inner joy may be just another way of looking at the experience of universal love. If so, then the prospect of large numbers of people discovering their power to nurture inner joy may herald a new era of human relationships and understanding. An idealistic speculation? Yes, but one that may be worth pursuing.

Spiritual Crisis and Growth

At some point in your life you are almost certain to undergo a spiritual crisis. You may suffer a deep doubt about the life direction you have chosen and the value of following it. None of the beliefs or principles that have ordered your world and established your place in it will be immune from question. Your faith in the value of success, money, marriage, and work will be severely shaken. You may even fear an imminent nervous breakdown. At the core of this crisis will be an emerging desire to do something that will make a tangible contribution to human betterment and give your life indisputable meaning. The more aware of inner life you grow, the more likely a spiritual crisis becomes.

Only in the last ten years have psychologists begun to understand the symptoms, dynamics, and significance of spiritual crises. When Jung boldly introduced the issue of spiritual growth fifty years ago, he was rebuked by his colleagues. Later Erikson discussed the issue in his outline of the eight stages of the life cycle. Today it is becoming apparent that the spiritual dimension of the personality is vital to health and that denial of spiritual issues can lead to physical and emotional illness. A spiritual crisis can disrupt work, family life, and self-esteem, and lead to many symptoms including headaches, anxiety, gastrointestinal distress, and depression.

The current dislocation of social values is contributing to the frequency of spiritual crises and making it more difficult to resolve them. Many people are struggling with the baffling fact that old roles and values that are supposed to make human relationships work, no longer serve. Women brought up to function as care-givers in the family are finding themselves thrust by their own inner needs, economic pressures, and new social expectations into new roles that they must struggle to define. Parents face the unsettling fact that they cannot use their own upbringing as a model for raising children because social values and expectations have changed so radically. Marriage vows are no longer regarded as religious sacraments; they've become more like business partnerships, sustained or dissolved according to the profit and loss of each person. Words like *fidelity* and *responsibility*, once clear in meaning, are subject to interpretation. The net effect of these changes is increased pressure to create meaning and direction from within. Trying to deny the complex issues that emerge during a spiritual crisis only prolongs the turmoil and makes matters worse. The only way out is to go forward.

"When Pia and I first began having our doubts," said Jerry, "we didn't know what was happening to us. Here we were with everything we wanted, two homes, three fine children, a new car every year or so, vacations when and where we wished, but there was something missing. Despite all that we had, our level of happiness had begun to decline and we started turning on one another. It wasn't an obvious thing at first, but the stress was there and it grew until we thought we were on the verge of divorce."

"It started with picking at one another," explained Pia. "Jerry would come home from the bank irritable and there was nothing I could do to get him out of his mood. We'd gotten so involved with owning things that I found myself spending all my time taking care of everything. There was always something to be done on the house or a repairperson to call, or something I needed to buy. Our whole lives had become buying, buying, buying. With the children grown, there wasn't anything deeply important to both of us that we shared and put our whole selves into together. Everything had become so ephemeral."

Jerry and Pia had been married for twenty-two years when they went through this spiritual crisis together. He was a bank executive with an excellent income, and until recently she was spending all her time in the home. They came for help because they felt they were bored, "falling out of love" and in danger of having their marriage fall apart. Both felt the excitement had gone out of their sex lives. Only when it became apparent that the marriage was basically sound despite their complaints did I begin to see that the underlying problem might be spiritual.

Jerry and Pia were well-integrated individuals who had learned to fulfill their personal needs. Even during the worst period of their crisis, you would have to say that they both reflected inner joy. The source of their distress was not an inability to take control of their lives, but the failure to appreciate the need for a deeper meaning. Neither Jerry nor Pia was able to go on playing the game of measuring achievement by how much was owned. They had played that game well. Now they faced the gnawing question, "Isn't there something more?"

At first, Jerry and Pia were uncomfortable with the idea that their problem might be spiritual—a word they associated with religion. They felt they already got all they needed out of church. "We go to church almost every

Sunday," said Pia. Only when we began to discuss how they put their Sunday principles into Monday action did they begin to recognize that their spiritual needs might require something more than church attendance. There comes a time when values can't just be believed; they must be lived.

An incident at a cocktail party finally precipitated a breakthrough in their self-understanding. "I was standing there listening to one of Jerry's friends talk about his son. The boy is fifteen and plays football. Early in the season he was apparently hurt, an eye injury of some sort. His father was saying the boy could lose sight in one eye if he gets hurt like that again. So this father was standing there boasting about how tough his boy is, and the way he insisted on playing. The father said, 'The kid is no loser, that's for sure.'

"I was stunned. This man was boasting about his son's courage in risking losing his sight in order to be a winner at football. For some reason it hit me all of a sudden that these were the values I was accepting. Jerry and I were completely caught up in being 'winners,' playing the game of money and status without giving thought to what's really important in life. All of a sudden, this question hit me: 'Is this the way I want to spend the rest of my life?' "

"After the party, we stayed up talking almost all night," explains Jerry. "For the first time in years and years we started asking ourselves what we really believed and what we really wanted out of life. We'd talked before, but not about the basic assumptions. It was always about what we wanted to add to our lives, and never about what we needed so we'd feel our lives were worthwhile, or what we wanted to be able to look back on ten years from now. That conversation was an awakening. We realized we needed to do something more important. I hadn't felt so much excitement since way back in college."

Jerry and Pia discovered that, having achieved the material success they had been striving for, they had a deep spiritual need to do something to make the world a better place. They wanted to do something more than give to charity, which takes no more effort than writing a check, or attend a lecture, which is even less demanding. They wanted to join their energies in a project that they could influence directly and see clearly in their community.

They went to their minister to discuss their feelings, and to find out if there might be something they could do through their church. "The more we talked with our minister," says Jerry, "the more excited we got about doing something local and important. When the minister mentioned the idea of a new church school building, it struck me that here was something that required my skills. We decided to take it on."

"I knew it was right," adds Pia. "It's a big project, big enough so it'll take the two of us and a lot of help from many others to make it happen."

Now in the middle of fund raising and architectural planning, Jerry and Pia will tell you that they are happier than they have ever been before. Gone are the feelings that something is missing, the pointless bickering, the dull conversations, the boring sex. Both are buzzing with energy and excitement. They've always got something important to discuss and when they argue, it's about an issue they both really care about. A secondary benefit and a sign of their new spiritual health is the renewed fire in their sex lives.

What will happen when the church school is built? Yes, if they fall back into the old patterns of thoughtless self-gratification, they'll feel stifled once again and their marriage will suffer. Having discovered the joy of making a contribution together, anything less will seem disappointing. But Jerry and Pia now understand their spiritual needs. They know now that the only avenue left for them to experience deep fulfillment lies in making the world a better place. After the church school, they will find another project; finding the right project will be part of the joy.

At fifty-six, Jerry has nine more years before he plans to retire. Prior to his spiritual crisis, he dreaded his sixty-fifth birthday; he couldn't see living out the rest of his days on the golf course or by the swimming pool. Now the fear is gone. He knows there is more than enough work, much of it more challenging than managing investments at the bank, and that there are many important projects in need of people with his background. Today Jerry and Pia look forward to the rest of their lives with greater enthusiasm and a greater sense of hope and purpose than ever.

You Can Make the World Work

There is a conspiracy in the world today. Its core is one simple and destructive belief—"The world doesn't work." Many of the world's leading scientists are part of the conspiracy. So are many of its leading politicians, social planners, and economists. Hordes of engineers harbor this belief and there is no lack of labor leaders to expound this view. At all levels of society the problems are so complex and of such scope that it seems almost foolish to believe they can be solved.

Take a quick inventory and it's easy to get depressed. Above all, there is the rapidly diminishing supply and soaring cost of critical raw materials, especially the enormous problem of oil, and the prospect of chronic energy shortages and skyrocketing energy costs for decades to come. There is the growing loss of faith in political leaders and government, in the ability of people to rule themselves. Closely related is the apparent inability of the huge bureaucracies to function effectively. The world political situation is loaded with tension. Nuclear proliferation appears inevitable. The global balance of power seems inherently unstable. Terrorism has become a way of life for any group that feels disenfranchised. The industrial nations seem increasingly vulnerable. Within the industrialized nations—and between the industrial nations and the developing ones—the gap between rich and poor grows. More people go hungry today than a decade ago; famine and disease plague almost half the world population.

So the belief that the world doesn't work appears to have substantial evidence to support it. If you sit down and take an inventory of only the major problems you can quickly convince yourself that there is nothing you can do. In the face of such an enormous list, any individual, no matter how much power he or she may have, seems powerless. But put the list aside. Pick out a local, human-sized problem, set specific objectives, and put your energies to the test. The picture changes.

You have enormous power to make a part of the world work.

Elaine is a teacher. For fifteen years she worked in a city school system where she tried to nurture, motivate, counsel, and inspire her students to appreciate the magnificence of their minds and discover how exciting learning can be. "I tried very hard," she says, looking back on those years of struggle. "I was so determined to break through to those children and make my classes exciting places to be. But the longer I stayed and the harder I tried, the more clearly I saw that it wouldn't work. There were too many obstacles. Too many students with problems at home. I didn't have the freedom I needed. I didn't have enough contact with parents. Drugs were always around, even among the young children. It was a constant battle to control the classroom. All you need is one or two disruptive students and learning comes to a halt. Given the rules of the system, there is a limit to what you can do."

Elaine finally admitted to herself that the school system where she taught wasn't working. A personal crisis followed.

"It struck me right in the face one morning: 'You're wasting your time!' It was like a slap. Here I was getting dressed to go to work, and I suddenly saw that the whole day was going to be futile. I wasn't going to get through my lesson plan; you never do in that school. At best, I might get through to three or four of my best students. Is that justification for all the work? Suddenly, teaching looked like just another job. Putting in time, picking up a paycheck. I began to feel very sick."

At this point, Elaine had every reason to give up and leave

teaching. "I wanted to quit," she recalls, "but when I told my husband, he insisted we take off for the weekend. We went to the mountains. It was quiet; we took long walks. We talked and I tried to understand my feelings and what I wanted to do. I played with the idea of going back to school or getting another job, but my husband wouldn't let me off the hook so easily. He kept posing the question: 'Would you really be any happier?' By the end of the weekend I was clear about my feelings. I wanted to teach, and I'd have to find some way of continuing."

Elaine did not renew her contract with the board of education. Instead, she began pouring her energies into creating a school of her own. She worked with two basic ideas that she thought would make her school work. First, she wanted to return to basic education, primarily English and math. Second, she wanted maximum parental involvement. Neither of these ideas are revolutionary, but they proved to be enough to get support from a local foundation and from a dozen parents who were dissatisfied with their children's education. Elaine began with twelve students.

"The first year was the toughest," she says. "We were back to the one-room-schoolhouse model of education. The students varied in age, ability, and achievement, so it took time to learn how to give each student individual attention while moving the whole class forward. It also took some adjustment for the students. School begins at eight thirty sharp and goes until four. There are no recesses, no gym, no art or music classes. We're not equipped for these frills. We can't afford them, and the children can't afford the time. That's our philosophy. I felt that if we challenged the children and got them to see what they can achieve, the whole thing would take off on its own."

Visit the school today and you'll see that indeed it has. There are now fifty students and two assistants. Eleven- and twelve-year-olds talk excitedly about Mark Twain and Emily Brontë. When the teacher is speaking, the whole classroom is silent in rapt attention. There are no discipline problems. Many students eagerly stay after school to work on extra projects or to do homework in a quiet environment. The underlying feeling at the school is one of excitement about learning. Among exceptional children this might seem ordinary, but these students are from the inner city; few of their parents own any hardcover books except the Bible.

What does the future hold? The school is still strapped for money. The tuition is based on the parents' ability to pay, so some students pay only a fraction of what their education costs. The difference is made up by private funding that Elaine's husband helps procure. "Each year it's touch and go," he says, "but we'll make it. This school is too good to close. I'm never quite sure how we'll manage, but I know we will. This school is going to grow. What goes on inside these three classrooms is too important to stop." This faith that the school can work and will not only survive but flourish is fundamental to its survival. The seed of doubt and the fear of failure have no place to grow in the minds or hearts of the school's staff or supporters. That is the essential precondition to assure its continued success.

It's easy to level criticisms, to question Elaine's achievement. You can assert that she has taken the brightest students out of the impersonal atmosphere of a large inner-city school and placed them in a small learning environment conducive to maximum growth. Or you can argue that the parents are exceptionally motivated because they enrolled their children in this school. The more committed you are to the belief that the world doesn't work and the individual can't make a difference, the more you might want these criticisms to stick. But they don't. Many of the students were troublemakers in the city system. Yes, many are bright, but as many are less so. Her students reflect a typical mix that you'd find in any city classroom. Only a handful of these students come from homes where both parents finished high school. Elaine has learned to inspire the parents. "Every parent wants the best education for their children," she believes. "You have to show them in clear language how they can help."

The only valid criticism, if you can call it that, is that the school only works because Elaine is an exceptional person. No doubt that's true. She is an energetic and committed woman who radiates inner joy. When she is in front of her classroom, her enthusiasm for what she is teaching lights up the classroom. If a student is even partly willing to give the school a chance, he or she is bound to become caught up in Elaine's excitement about learning. Her confidence in herself and her students reassures parents and encourages them to believe that they can help their children finish high school and in all likelihood go on to college. Elaine's persuasiveness inspires supporters to provide the financial assistance that keeps the school alive. Elaine is indeed exceptional.

From one perspective, her experience is proof that the world doesn't work. She struggled for fifteen years only to meet year after year of frustration. But that conclusion is based on what she left, not on what she created. An alternative conclusion might be that, given a hundred teachers with Elaine's energy and commitment, even a large city school might become a fantastic learning environment. Perhaps Elaine had to leave the school system to appreciate her real ability and assert her full power. Clearly her success is not a matter of luck, nor is it so unique that it can't be duplicated. Elaine's success illustrates the power of the individual to make a small part of the world work even in the face of what appear to be insurmountable odds.

Making your part of the world work is not easy. It takes the patience to listen to your inner voice and the courage to act on the quiet messages you hear. It also takes standing up for what you believe. Once you admit that the old roles and models no longer work, you free your own creative power. You face the stark truth that you are the one responsible for creating the new roles and models that do work. This is a challenging discovery, but also a source of great inner joy.

From Me to We

In times of economic scarcity people tend to become less concerned with others and more protective of their own self-interest. Generosity is superseded by selfishness. This basic economic and psychological principle explains much of what is going on in our society. All across the country, people want to cut taxes because they're fed up with paying for social programs that provide no direct benefits to themselves. There is a great cry from the business sector to roll back environmental legislation to reduce costs. On college campuses students focus on getting the grades that will provide entry into postgraduate education leading to lucrative careers. The ideal of a liberal arts education is all but dead. Some of the most popular books are manuals telling you how to cultivate power in the office and look out for your own economic interests, no matter what. The dominant ethic has become "As long as I get mine" and "To hell with everybody else."

In the face of this trend, we're running into economic realities that may be forcing an ethical shift back toward a balanced concern for social (as well as individual) interests. The energy shortage is a prime example. This enormous problem is affecting the life of every person on the planet. There is no way to solve it without cooperation at many levels of our society and between the nations of the world community. Should the ethic of exclusive self-interest prevail, the likely outcome is a continuing crisis and ultimately war over the last drop of oil. When R. Buckminster Fuller first coined the phrase "spaceship earth," it seemed a wonderful metaphor to match the new pictures of earth taken from the moon. Today this concept seems to sum up the human condition. Despite all the differences within nations and between them, we're all dependent on the resources of this small biosphere and we had better put more effort into learning how to use those resources for everyone's benefit, or we risk destroying the ship that sustains us.

In our society of relative plenty, it's possible to ignore pressing world problems until one of them touches your life directly and deeply. David is a lawyer, a partner in a prestigious law firm. Ever since graduating from college he has had one goal in mind. "I want to become financially independent as fast as I can." He comes from a modest background (his father was a carpenter and his mother a secretary), but for as long as he can remember, there was strong emphasis on education and the opportunity that this country provides for anyone to make it.

Shortly after graduating from law school, David married Amy. They had been living together through his senior year, despite protests from both parents. "We got married to make everyone happy," explains David. "The piece of paper didn't mean anything to us, but the parents wanted a big ceremony. Two hundred guests, a band, the works." David is happy now that he went through with the wedding. "The pictures still mean a lot to me," he says.

On the fast track, David whizzed through his bar exams and was flooded with job offers. Near the top of his class, he was a highly prized catch for any of the major firms. He went to work with a salary that allowed them to skip the romance of struggling for the first few years and start living very well. They bought a house, a car, beautiful furniture. What with all their wedding presents, they stepped into a very comfortable life-style. "We both thought we had it made," David recalls.

David's career goal was to become a top tax attorney. "At the time," he says, "all I wanted was to get to the top. There's an enormous amount of money to be made helping corporations and wealthy individuals find loopholes in the tax laws. The clients have a lot of money or else they wouldn't need help reducing their taxes. Ethical questions didn't bother me. The law was the law, as far as I was concerned. I was getting paid to show people how they could work legally and still save money. It was a big game with big bucks for winning."

Money and "making it" were all David thought about until Amy came home one afternoon after visiting the doctor. She felt weak and nauseous and so went for a routine examination. She wanted to know whether she was all right. Her doctor found large, hard lymph nodes. A biopsy later showed Amy had lymphoma, cancer of the lymph glands, and surgery was performed. Despite chemotherapy and the best treatment available, Amy died eighteen months later.

David first came for help a year after Amy's death, because he still hadn't gotten over the loss. He was depressed. He rarely went out and wasn't making many new friends. He reported sitting home listening to music or watching TV and suddenly bursting into tears. His work was suffering and he had become worried about his ability to maintain his job. Only at a friend's urging did David come in for help.

From the first meeting it was obvious that David would have to make significant internal changes if he was to recover from his loss. He was a totally externally oriented person who measured all his success by what he owned and what others thought of him. He was hardly in touch with what he felt or believed and had few internal resources to help him cope with so much pain. David started a three-month program aimed at helping him cope with the loss and, in the process, to discover his own power of inner joy. His progress was slow. It took considerably longer for him to work through his loss than we had expected. Nevertheless, the healing began, and with it came a major shift in his ethics and attitudes.

When David was well into his recovery from his loss, I suggested that he become more involved with other people. His social life had been so narrowly defined by his friends at work and Amy's friends that he was at a loss where to begin meeting new people. Of the many suggestions I made, the one that appealed to him most was the Sierra Club. He explained his choice by a longtime interest in backpacking, which he had never pursued. This choice ultimately precipitated a radical change in his outlook and his future:

"I got a brochure in the mail announcing a speaker. The lecture was on environmental pollution and its relationship to cancer. I'd tried to stay out of all the social action stuff because I was too busy, but this time the topic hit me right in the stomach. I had to go."

"That lecture changed my life. I'd been aware of reports about environmental causes of cancer, but I'd never paid much attention because I thought the issue was highly debatable. Then I started listening to the facts. The incredibly potent carcinogen dioxin is now found in the Arctic Ocean. PCBs show up regularly in mothers' milk. The food dye Red #2 has been used for years and years after it was proved to be a potent carcinogen. There are already enough radioactive wastes to make the whole United States uninhabitable for hundreds of years and there is still no absolutely safe way of storing them. Millions of men and women and their families exposed to asbestos fibers are almost certain to develop a deadly cancer. Ninety percent of all cancers have at least some partial environmental cause. The lecture left me stunned and angry. I went home that night wondering whether Amy would be alive today if someone had done something ten or twenty years ago."

The shift that had been going on within David made him receptive to the speaker's call for help. "What happened to me over the next few months after the lecture was an awakening. I started reading about the ecosystem and what we're doing to it: lead accumulating even in the snows of Greenland, acid rains, ozone being stripped from the ionosphere, mercury appearing in fish, pesticides concentrating in the food chain, all getting worse every year. For the first time I saw this incredible threat—and so few people committed to doing much about it. Finally I had enough. I knew that I had to do something."

David's awakening to social commitment changed his outlook and his life. No longer is financial independence his number one goal. He wants to "do something important to make the world a better place." He is still a partner in his law firm, but he has cut back his work to four days per week so he can spend at least twenty hours a week as a legal consultant to environmental action groups. "The way I see it," he says, "my four days doing tax work pay for me to spend two days on what I feel is really important."

When he talks about his beliefs you discern a new ethic that respects individual freedom while emphasizing the importance of social responsibility. This ethic is rooted in biology and the appreciation of the earth as a fragile ecosystem with limited resources to sustain life. Some of his beliefs may seem contradictory and most are still gestating, but the basic shift is clear. David no longer frames problems in terms of "you *or* me" and instead thinks of "you *and* me."

You can argue that he is still working out his loss and

using environmental action as an outlet for his anger. To a degree that may be so, but it isn't all. In working through his loss David discovered that the final source of joy lies within himself. That discovery prompted him to question the wisdom of spending his whole life in the quest for accumulation of wealth. He opened up to other concerns, principally his desire to leave the world a better place. The environmental movement provides a perfect opportunity for him to use his skills to express his commitment, but the desire to make the world a better place emerges from deep within.

Solving a World Problem

Most of the problems that you read about in the news seem so vast that they dwarf individual capacity for comprehension. In our technological society this feeling of individual limitation is compounded by the belief that problems can only be solved by the "experts." They're supposed to have the answers. When the experts fail repeatedly, you think, "If they can't solve it, I sure can't hope to do very much."

Partly this attitude flows from the great achievements of the last decades. Polio was epidemic until Jonas Salk discovered a vaccine. Suddenly the brilliant expert delivered the solution to a government that then had only to distribute it widely. After President Kennedy announced the space program, a relatively small number of people proceeded to design the technology that ten years later allowed the world to watch men walking on the moon.

Today public confidence in the experts is waning because the major problems seem to defy solution. Efforts to end poverty through social programs in this country proved a failure. Now the energy shortage grows while solutions are hotly debated. World hunger remains a chronic problem. It is very easy to conclude that no experts exist for these problems, only many people with conflicting proposals and opposing views.

Perhaps the situation isn't as bleak as it appears. Perhaps these problems remain unsolved not for lack of workable proposals but because there is too little public will to act on them. Perhaps the problems seem insurmountable not because they're so large but because *too few people have decided that the problems can be solved.*

Susan is a mother and housewife who is discovering that she can play an important role in solving what appear to be intractable world problems. She first came to our center because she was overweight, depressed, and thought her life was "going downhill." Susan does not have deep psychological problems, nor is there a serious problem in her marriage. The root of her symptoms is a feeling of powerlessness. She is classically anhedonic, feeling unable to create satisfaction in her own life and blaming her depression on a world that she feels is "all messed up."

The first step in Susan's transformation was helping her change specific anhedonic behaviors and discover her power of inner joy. The second step was encouraging her to act on her desire to "get involved." A breakthrough in her life came when she learned about the Hunger Project, a nonprofit organization launched by est founder Werner Erhard, and the efforts of hundreds of thousands of people all over the world to end hunger in the next two decades.

The Hunger Project baffled me at first [Susan says]. I couldn't understand it because it was different from any other organized effort I was familiar with. The basic message is that by becoming aware of the problem of world hunger and committing yourself to end it, you'll help create a context for solutions to work and for you to find your own way to participate. In time, that message began to make sense to me. Now I see that the Hunger Project is so revolutionary it might just succeed.

I had always known that hunger is a perennial world problem, but like most people I treated hunger and starvation as abstract events out there somewhere, very distant from me and my family. Like everyone else, I assumed it was inevitable, that there isn't enough food to feed everyone, that you can't control population effectively, and that producing enough food is not a realistic possibility. Whenever I saw pictures of starving children or read about the famines, I felt helpless. It was another proof that the world is a mess, so I tried not to let it sink in.

My perception of the problem and my relationship to it changed radically when I started reading some of the literature of the Hunger Project. I didn't realize that fifteen to twenty million people die every year from hunger and that the problem is getting worse! I never thought it was improving, but at least I thought it wasn't getting worse. I was also shocked to learn that world experts on food, population, and nutrition believe that there actually *is* enough food at this very moment to feed everyone! That really shook me. It means that millions of people starve to death each year because there is no collective will to end hunger. In the United States, millions of tons of food are thrown away every year while millions of people starve all over the world

When I finally let the reality of world hunger sink in, I had an incredible experience of new self-awareness. It was like rediscovering myself, because as a child I had always wanted to accomplish something important. I realized for the first time that I had become so involved in my own personal concerns that I had become apathetic about the world. In a way, I had given up, resigned myself to accept world events without trying to influence them. Then I realized that I am bigger than world hunger. The problem exists only because people create the context for starvation. I have the power to do something to change that context, and create the belief that hunger need not exist, and that the world community collectively has the power to feed all its people.

Once I understood the basic message, I discovered all kinds of things I could do right in my own community. First of all, I started reading everything I could find. I was surprised to discover that the newspapers report hunger-related stories almost every day. There is always something about population, agricultural production, weather, or famine. The stories were always there, but with my changed attitude I started noticing them. I also arranged with my minister to have three Sundays devoted to discussions of world hunger and what we can do. I helped arrange a PTA program on hunger and I began volunteering for a local hunger organization in their food collection drive. These are just a few of the things

I found I could do. The real point is that once you understand that hunger can be ended and that you have the power to help, you find all kinds of opportunities to do something.

Since she became involved in the Hunger Project Susan is a dramatically changed human being. Her efforts to alter some of her anhedonic attitudes were important, but the most significant change for her came with the discovery of her power to participate in solving a huge world problem. She no longer feels trapped in her role as wife and mother because she knows that she is doing something in addition to raising her family. Her energy level is way up and her optimism is contagious. "There's no doubt about it," she says. "I'm getting as much from the Hunger Project as I'm giving. That's part of the joy." Susan's husband is so impressed with her transformation that he too has enrolled in the Hunger Project. The two of them now set aside time to work on the project together. "Even my kids want to help," she says. "When I was putting a decal END WORLD HUNGER on my car, I explained to my five-year-old daughter that we were doing this because fifteen million people are starving. Her reply was 'What are we going to do, mommy?' "

Is Susan fooling herself? Is she really making a contribution to solving the enormous problem of world hunger? Or is she just creating a flurry of activity to meet her own need to feel she *is* doing something? If you're a firm believer in the powerlessness of the individual, you'll see Susan's story as an exercise in self-deception. Critics of the Hunger Project assert that all the money being collected is only used to talk about ending hunger and not buying any food. These criticisms are based on the old model of social change: A paternalistic leadership prepares a plan to attack a problem, enlists people to fulfill the various roles, and tells them what to do. The failure of this approach is nowhere more evident than in the area of world hunger, where the experts agree that the means for solving hunger already exists, but famine persists.

With the discovery of inner joy, a new model of social action becomes possible. No longer do individuals require leaders to spell out exactly what they are to do like cogs in a machine. The best alternative is a leadership which assumes that informed and committed individuals will find their own best ways, given their localities and resources, to contribute to solving the problem. That is the basic assumption underlying the Hunger Project, and it seems to be fostering success.

In less than two years, nearly one million people have enrolled in the project and pledged their personal commitment to ending starvation on earth by the end of this century. More than one hundred thousand people are enrolling each month. They fast one day per month and donate the money saved to end hunger. They support local food relief organizations, sponsor public discussions of hunger, write representatives in government to support public action to relieve hunger, speak to local clubs and organizations, organize fundraising events to provide support for the Hunger Project and food relief.

It's basic with the Hunger Project that each person who enrolls is the whole project. This makes explicit that the project depends on the power of each individual to draw from within herself or himself to create an effective form of participation. This new thinking often produces dramatic results. A man in New Rochelle, New York, enrolled his mayor, school superintendent, city manager, governor, and lieutenant governor. A Hawaiian woman signed up her entire state legislature and congressional delegation. A Massachusetts couple signed up fifty thousand members of their community. A team of forty runners in the Boston Marathon generated pledges for over $600,000 while 2300 spectators were enrolled along the way.

The Hunger Project and Susan's story are evidence that the individual *can* have a significant impact on world problems and the course of world events. Once you understand that the means exist to solve hunger, the energy crisis, and illiteracy, these huge problems are reduced to a human scale. The real problem is not the lack of available solutions, but the lack of awareness and commitment to make the solutions work. This discovery can lead to a remarkable inner transformation. The act of commitment to solve a major problem can in itself be terrifically empowering. The more inner joy you commit yourself to share, the more you have to give. The discovery of your ability to influence your world positively becomes a discovery of the limitless flow of inner joy.

A Social Awakening

We are living through an intense period of individual and social transformation. Wrenching changes are discernible at every level of the society and neither the outcome nor the significance of these changes is yet clear. Through the confusion and the pessimism, however, a new vision of the individual may be taking shape and a new demand for social institutions that nurture individual growth may be gathering momentum. No longer are people willing to put up with needlessly circumscribed lives defined by stifling jobs, joyless consumption, personal anxieties, and unhappy relationships. All at once in the past decade, millions of people have become aware that their lives can be made so much richer, deeper, fuller, more pleasurable and satisfying.

During the very early stages of this collective awakening, the interest in the inner self appeared to be an exercise in withdrawal from social involvement. Tom Wolfe coined the phrase "the Me decade" to describe the sudden explosion of interest in the inner self and personal growth techniques. Later Christopher Lasch used the phrase "the culture of narcissism" to describe the phenomenon. Both phrases are pejorative. The pursuit of inner growth, say the critics, is a naive attempt to achieve inner peace while all around the society is crumbling. The picture is something like Nero playing his flute while Rome burns.

Now it is becoming apparent that the critics are wrong. People are beginning to achieve the inner shift of consciousness described in this book. With the growth of inner joy, they are not turning away from others, but toward them.

They are not shunning social problems but becoming involved in the search for new solutions. The growing momentum of this resurgent social commitment suggests that the recent implosion of the spirit may herald a new social vitality. The historian Arnold Toynbee observed that in times of social crisis some of the most forward-looking members of great civilizations turn to introspective and spiritual pursuits. Whether the civilization weathers the crisis or declines into social chaos depends on the success of its members in forging a new view of themselves, their society, and their collective future.

With the pursuit of inner joy yielding concrete results in people's lives, individual and social effects are becoming observable. Bridging the gap between developing individuals and a troubled society is a new sense of integrity. People empowered by inner joy find that they can't sit back and disclaim responsibility for social problems. They can't put up with roles, relationships, and institutions that do not reflect their inner values. The barrier between the inner self and social commitment is breaking down. Changes within individuals are leading to parallel changes within institutions, notably health care, some local governments, and a few forward-looking corporations. There is a growing sense of community among those committed to this process of parallel individual and social change. While the hour is still early in this collective awakening, the signs of change are no longer mere shadows.

Inner joy is the basis for a new sense of individual autonomy. People are learning to trust themselves and their power to create joyous lives. Self-trust breeds self-assertiveness and a new demand among evolving people for a voice in the major and minor decisions affecting their lives. Gone is the blind faith in technology, science, and the "government program." Gone is the power of Madison Avenue to dictate tastes to these self-fulfilling individuals. Instead, this growing body of self-aware people is discovering that the dictates of the inner self deserve primary attention. This means taking full responsibility for the world we all live in and for the world we are all creating. It also means upholding the belief that the individual can make a difference and that major social problems will yield to solutions based on a new vision of human capacities.

Inner joy is also the basis for an end to individual alienation and the birth of a new sense of community. Thirty years ago, in *The Lonely Crowd*, David Riesman documented how technological, suburban society fragments community and isolates individuals in nuclear families. Lacking the social supports of the past, the alienated individual begins to view the world as a hostile, competitive rat race. To replace the lost security, conformity in dress, attitude, and behavior becomes the norm. In the end, the alienated individual erects barriers to hide real feelings and protect himself from others. The result is a gradual inner suffocation. It is that inner loss of self that spawned the search for personal growth and inner joy. Now that the old internal barriers are crumbling, self-fulfilling people are openly accepting their desires for caring, intimacy, and close friendships. They are celebrating their desire to share themselves and they are learning that this desire for human sharing requires a friendly and nurturing community in order to grow.

To find the new communities mushrooming amid our fast-paced, high-technology society, you have to know where to look. In schools, hospitals, health centers, universities, scientific laboratories, large and small corporations, and government agencies, evolving individuals are working to put their new visions into practice. These individuals, unified by a commitment to unfolding human potential and creating institutions that nurture individual growth, are connecting with one another to form the new communities. Some of the new communities are dispersed throughout the country, while others function in a localized area. Leaders tend to function as coordinators and facilitators rather than policymakers. At the heart of each community is the network, a loosely organized channel for communication about the community's common interests. A list of the new, crisscrossing communities and networks is too long to enumerate, but it includes groups interested in nutrition, health, medicine, appropriate technology, scientific research on consciousness, simple living, sports, entrepreneurship and small business, human development in large corporations, education, psychic research, meditation, women's rights, sexual freedom, rights of the elderly, humanizing birth and death, new politics, environmental protection, and world hunger. These communities, still very young, promise to be potent forces for change in the years ahead.

Inner joy is also becoming the basis for a return to an old ethic about work and consumption. For the past several decades our society has functioned on the premise that more is always better, and that the way to happiness is through the accumulation of things. The rediscovery of the inner self shakes the foundation of this mass production—mass consumption ethic. If joy stems from within, then the accumulation of things for their own sake no longer makes sense. In fact, needless consumption and the waste that goes with it appear to be violations of the ecological balance. In reaction, evolving individuals are finding that inner joy is a stepping-stone to simplifying their lives. This doesn't mean a rejection of modern comforts but it does involve a commitment to stop wasting energy, food, and natural resources. Inner joy breeds an ethic of frugality, conservation, quality, and craftsmanship. Evolving individuals take pride in their own work and seek out handmade, durable quality goods. They look for this quality and durability in manufactured goods, even if they must pay a premium. Sensitive to the importance of creative and meaningful work, these self-fulfilling individuals demand work that provides an opportunity for personal satisfaction. The rebirth of crafts is the most striking illustration of this deep change in attitudes. Yet even in the large corporations there is a new concern for quality of work and product.

Perhaps more than anything else, inner joy nurtures an appreciation for life and a commitment to make the world work. Personal transformation reveals the enormous power of nature and restores an awe and respect for the magnificent processes of growth and transformation at work throughout nature and human societies. Self-fulfilling individuals are enthusiastic about life; they want to get everything out of it they can. Committed to their own growth, they have no time for complaints, gloomy forecasts, and pessimism. While they don't deny the serious problems that plague the world, they don't feel overwhelmed either. Through an array of personal growth techniques they have learned that their own lives need not remain limited by the past. So too, they reason, the mistakes and problems of society need not limit our collective future. Seeing your own life change is the best proof that you have the power to change the world.

History records the dream of an ideal society—creative, peaceful, productive, just—in every generation. On what basis can such a society ever become a reality? A remarkable agreement has existed among philosophers and scientists throughout the ages: If an ideal society is possible, it will arise only from the minds and hearts of fully developed human beings. Bertrand Russell expressed this consensus when he wrote:

> When I allow myself to hope that the world will emerge from its present troubles, I see before me a shining vision: a world where work is pleasant and not excessive, where kindly feelings are common, where minds released from fear create delight for eye, ear, and heart. Do not say this is impossible. It is not impossible if men would bend their minds to the achievement of the kind of happiness that should be distinctive of man.

Never before in history have so many people been so committed to their own internal transformation. Never before has the process of personal transformation been so well understood. In this century science has begun the exploration of outer space, but even greater achievements have occurred through the exploration of inner space. The tools for personal transformation are now available. People are discovering inner joy. Though the social effects of this great transformation are just beginning to be seen, the significance of this collective commitment to personal growth is likely to be far greater than anyone currently imagines. Of course there will be setbacks, but there will also be great leaps.

Neither individual nor social transformation is ever smooth, but once begun, it continues until it is complete. The astounding fact today is that inner joy is within the reach of anyone who wishes to take advantage of the available knowledge and tools for transformation. Anyone with the desire and commitment can raise life to its highest value.

ACKNOWLEDGMENTS

MANY PEOPLE have contributed to our experience and understanding of inner joy. We thank all from whom we have drawn ideas and inspiration, especially Maharishi Mahesh Yogi, Abraham Maslow, Roberto Assagioli, Werner Erhard, George Leonard, Arnold Lazarus, William Schutz, and other leaders in the human potential field. The staff and clients at the North County Holistic Health Center provided a wealth of material. For their excellent work, friendship, and support, we thank Dr. Barnie Meltzer, Deborah Andrews, Lani Blissard, Cathy Bufkin, Sally Cote, and Sharon Smith. We thank Dr. Rosalie Chapman, Deborah Gullang, and Robin Kory for editorial suggestions. Others who have helped in numerous ways are Cherylyn Davis, Lindsey Doria, Jason Doty, Warren Farrell, Mike and Donna Fletcher, Phylene Garbasz, Alta MacKay, Ali and Sibyl Rubottom, and Nora Stern. Finally, we thank Peter Wyden, Peri Winkler, and William Fitelson for their support in making this book happen. To all who have helped in ways large and small, we thank you.

Harold would like to express his love and deep sense of shared celebration to Sirah Vettese for her devotion, high energy, and inner joy. Also, Harold would like to acknowledge his father for his indomitable inner joy throughout his conquest of a serious disease.

ABOUT THE AUTHORS

Harold H. Bloomfield, M.D., is a practicing psychiatrist and Director of Psychiatry, Psychotherapy, and Family Counseling at the North County Holistic Health Center in Del Mar, California. Born and raised in New York City, he received his psychiatric training at Yale University School of Medicine. He is a member of the American Psychiatric Association and the San Diego Psychiatric Society. Dr. Bloomfield is widely published in popular magazines and professional journals. He and Robert Kory are co-authors of the best-selling *TM: Discovering Inner Energy and Overcoming Stress* and *The Holistic Way to Health and Happiness*.

Robert B. Kory is past vice-president of the American Foundation for the Science of Creative Intelligence, and has taught management seminars on human development and optimum health.